Adobe
Photoshop™

Library of Congress Catalog No.: 94-76910

ISBN: 1-56830-118-9

10 9 8 7 6 5 4 3 2

The information in this book is furnished for informational use only, is subject to change without notice, and should not be construed as a commitment by Adobe Systems Incorporated. Adobe Systems Incorporated assumes no responsibility for any errors or inaccuracies that may appear in this book. The software and typefaces mentioned in this book are furnished under license and may only be used or copied in accordance with the terms of such license.

PANTONE® Computer video simulations used in this product may not match PANTONE-identified solid color standards. Use current PANTONE Color Reference Manuals for accurate color. *Pantone, Inc.'s check-standard trademark for color. PANTONE color computer Graphics" © Pantone, Inc. 1986, 1993.

Pantone, Inc. is the copyright owner of PANTONE Color Computer Graphics and Software which are licensed to Adobe to distribute for use only in combinations with Adobe Photoshop. PANTONE Color Computer Graphics and Software shall not be copied onto another diskette or into memory unless as part of the execution of Adobe Photoshop.

PostScript™ is a trademark of Adobe Systems Incorporated ("Adobe"), registered in the United States and elsewhere. PostScript can refer both to the PostScript language as specified by Adobe and to Adobe's implementation of its PostScript language interpreter.

Any references to "PostScript printers," "PostScript files," or "PostScript drivers" refer, respectively, to printers, files and driver programs written in or supporting the PostScript language. References in this book to the "PostScript language" are intended to emphasize Adobe's standard definition of that language.

Adobe, the Adobe Press logo, Adobe Illustrator, Adobe Photoshop, Adobe Dimensions, Adobe Type Manager, ATM, Adobe Garamond, Classroom in a Book, CLASSROOM IN A BOX, and PostScript are trademarks of Adobe Systems Incorporated which may be registered in certain jurisdictions. ImageWriter, Apple and Macintosh are registered trademarks of Apple Computer, Inc. AppleColor and QuickTime are trademarks of Apple Computer, Inc. Amiga is a registered trademark of Commodore Computer. PixelPaint, and Supermatch are trademarks of SuperMac Technology, Inc. Kodak is a registered trademark and PhotoCD is a trademark of Eastman Kodak Company. *Helvetica and *Times are trademarks of Linotype/Hell AG and/or its subsidiaries. QMS ColorScript is a registered trademark of QMS, Inc. Trinitron is a registered trademark of Sony Corporation. Radius is a trademark of Radius, Inc. CameraMan and MoviePlay are registered trademarks of Vision Software. Other brand or product names are the trademarks or registered trademarks of their respective holders.

Printed in the United States of America by Shepard Poorman Communications, Indianapolis, Indiana.

Published simultaneously in Canada.

Adobe Press books are published and distributed by Hayden Books, a division of Macmillan Computer Publishing, USA. For individual orders, or for educational, corporate, or retail sales accounts, call 1-800-428-5331. For information address Macmillan Computer Publishing, 201 West 103 Street, Indianapolis, IN 46290.

CONTENTS

INTRODUCTION

Adobe Photoshop™ software is an image-editing program that lets you create and produce high-quality digital images, without the expense of high-end workstations. As an electronic darkroom, Adobe Photoshop lets you manipulate scanned photolithographs, slides, and original artwork in a variety of ways. The program combines a full range of selection tools, painting and editing tools, color-correction tools, and special effect capabilities (such as rotation and filtering) that allow you to edit images in one of several color modes, including RGB and CMYK. The ability to work in multiple layers gives you the flexibility to experiment and make corrections easily. As a production tool, Adobe Photoshop produces high-quality color separations and halftones that you can print using the numerous printing options.

PREREQUISITES

Before beginning to use Adobe Photoshop, you should have a working knowledge of the Macintosh® and its operating conventions. You should know how to use the mouse and standard Macintosh menus and commands. You should also know how to open, save, and close files. If you need to review these techniques, see the documentation that comes with your Macintosh.

ABOUT *CLASSROOM IN A BOOK*™

This is the revised version of the Adobe Photoshop *Classroom in a Book*™ for Adobe Photoshop 3.0. Created by the Educational Services group at Adobe Systems, Inc., *Classroom in a Book (CIB)* is a project-based series of lessons that you can complete at your own pace. You can expect to spend between 30 and 40 hours with this product.

HOW DOES IT WORK?

Classroom in a Book consists of a series of design projects with complete information for creating them. You'll create projects for a fictitious international culinary corporation named Gourmet Visions. Within this context, you'll work on a cookbook cover illustration, a table-top promotional piece, a poster, a wine label and more. By the end of Lesson 5, you'll be able to create this brochure cover that includes a variety of images, text and special effects.

Classroom in a Book teaches you the basics (as well as some advanced techniques) for using the Adobe Photoshop program's features and capabilities. When you've completed this tutorial you will have a good working knowledge of the program and will be well on your way to becoming an experienced Adobe Photoshop user.

The tutorial includes 14 lessons. Each lesson contains step-by-step instructions for creating the projects, along with lots of explanation and tips and techniques. Lessons 3, 6, 9, and 13 are review lessons that give you a chance to practice the skills you've learned in the previous lessons.

Lesson 1 gives you an overview of the Adobe Photoshop program's latest features, including palettes and layers, and gets you started using painting and editing tools. In Lesson 2 you'll learn about working with selections. By the time you finish Lesson 2, you'll be ready to review everything you've learned up to that point by creating a table-top promotion in Lesson 3.

Lesson 4 introduces you to paths, masks and channels while you create a poster for a produce customer. In Lesson 5, you combine a variety of images create a striking brochure cover. By the end of Lesson 6, you will have combined a variety of techniques to create a wine label.

In Lesson 7, you learn color correction strategy and practice a variety of color correction techniques. Scanning, resolution and resizing issues are discussed in Lesson 8. Then in Lesson 9 you will put it all together to create the cover of an annual report.

Lesson 10 gives you information on converting images to different modes. In Lesson 11 you spend time learning about printing and producing color separations. In Lesson 12 you learn about working with different types of file formats, and importing and exporting files. In Lesson 13, you'll review the information you've learned so far to create a trade show poster.

In Lesson 14, the final lesson, you will learn some advanced layer masking and grouping techniques as you create a photo collage.

WHAT YOU'LL LEARN

In these lessons, you will learn how to do the following:

- use the painting and editing tools
- use, create, and edit layers
- make and manipulate selections
- create and use masks
- store saved selections in channels
- color-correct all or part of an image
- resize and change the resolution of an image
- convert from one image type to another
- prepare color separations
- print images
- use Adobe Photoshop with Adobe Illustrator™ artwork
- use layer masks and layer groups

WHO SHOULD USE IT?

Classroom in a Book is designed for users at many levels. If you're new to Adobe Photoshop, you'll get a good grounding in all the basic features. If you have been using Adobe Photoshop for a while, you'll find *Classroom in a Book* teaches many advanced features including tips and techniques that are included with the latest version of Adobe Photoshop.

SELF-PACED LEARNING

Using *Classroom in a Book* is similar to taking a 40-hour training course. In this case, you get to choose when and where you do the work. Final exam scheduling is also up to you.

OTHER RESOURCES

Classroom in a Book is not meant to replace documentation that comes with Adobe Photoshop. Only the commands and options used in the lessons are explained in this book. For comprehensive information about all of the program's features, refer to the *Adobe Photoshop User Guide*. You will find the *Quick Reference Card* packaged with Adobe Photoshop a useful companion as you work through the lessons in this book. For additional practice in using Adobe Photoshop, try doing the lessons in the *Adobe Photoshop Tutorial*. For instructions on advanced techniques, see *Beyond the Basics*. To learn advanced techniques in a self-paced tutorial format, look for the *Adobe Photoshop Advanced Classroom in a Book*.

Getting Started

Before you begin using Adobe Photoshop *Classroom in a Book,* you need to make sure that your system is set up correctly and that you have installed the necessary software.

WHAT YOU NEED TO DO

To get ready to use Classroom in a Book, you need to do the following things. (We'll give you more details later.)

• Check the system requirements.

• Install Adobe Photoshop, as described in the *Getting Started* booklet that came with the Adobe Photoshop application.

• Install the font that is included with the *Classroom in a Book* software. (This is optional.)

• Copy the *Classroom in a Book* files that come with this package to your hard drive.

CHECKING THE SYSTEM REQUIREMENTS

The system requirements are the same as those for the Adobe Photoshop 3.0 program, except that you need a CD-ROM drive to access the *Classroom in a Book* files.

System requirements

To use Adobe Photoshop 3.0, you need:

• An Apple Macintosh computer with a 68020 processor (or any later model) with a minimum of 6 megabytes (MB) of application random-access memory (RAM).

• Apple system software 7.0 or higher

• 32-bit QuickDraw™, version 1.2 or higher (included with the Adobe Photoshop software)

System Recommendations

In addition, Adobe Systems recommends the following hardware and software:

• A Macintosh computer with a 68030 or 68040 processor

• 16 MB (or more) of application RAM

• A color monitor with a 24-bit or 32-bit video display card

• A Macintosh-compatible scanner

• A PostScript™ printer

• Acceleration products bearing the *Adobe charged* logo

Special considerations

In addition, there are several more requirements that apply only to *Classroom in a Book.*

• To use the *Classroom in a Book* files, you need a double- or triple-speed CD-ROM drive.

• To watch the Adobe Teach™ movies included with this package, you need to have QuickTime™ and the Movie Play application installed in your system.

INSTALLING THE SOFTWARE

You need to install the Adobe Photoshop program, the special *Classroom in a Book* student font (optional), and the *Classroom in a Book* files.

Installing Adobe Photoshop

Install the Adobe Photoshop program. Adobe Photoshop *Classroom in a Book* does not include the Adobe Photoshop program software. You must purchase the software separately. The *Getting Started* guide that comes with Adobe Photoshop 3.0 includes complete instructions for installing Adobe Photoshop.

Installing the special font

The *Classroom in a Book* electronic files use one special Adobe™ Type 1 font—Adobe Garamond™ Semibold. This font is included in a folder named

Student Font. Using this font is optional—an Adobe Photoshop file containing the type image is also included on the CD-ROM disc. If you want to use the font instead of the image, you must first install the font in your system.

Copying the *Classroom In A Book* files

The *Classroom in a Book* CD-ROM disc includes folders containing all the electronic files for the *Classroom in a Book* lessons. Each lesson has its own folder. You will need to install these folders on your hard disk to access the files for the lessons. To save room, you can install the folders for each lesson as you need them.

These folders are included:

*Projects	Lesson07
Adobe Teach™	Lesson08
Extras	Lesson09
Lesson01	Lesson10
Lesson02	Lesson11
Lesson03	Lesson12
Lesson04	Lesson13
Lesson05	Lesson14
Lesson06	Student Fonts

The files are locked for your protection, so that you don't inadvertently write over the original files. When you open the files, you will see an alert box telling you that you cannot save changes. Click OK to open the file, then give the file a new name when you save it.

To install the *Classroom in a Book* folders:

1 Create a folder on your hard disk and name it *Adobe Photoshop CIB.*

2 Copy the folders from the CD-ROM disc into this folder.

Creating a Projects folder

While you're working through *Classroom in a Book*, you will create and save many Adobe Photoshop files.

We recommend that you make a Projects folder and put your work files there. In fact we've included one in the Adobe Photoshop CIB folder. The asterisk (*) at the beginning of the name keeps the folder at the top of the list for easy access. (If you ever want to keep a file or folder at the end of a list, you can put a ~ in front of the name.) As you work through the lessons in this book, you will store the files that you create in the Projects folder.

Throwing away your Preferences file

We recommend that you throw away your Preferences file before you begin each lesson. Instructions for doing this are included in each lesson.

IF YOU WANT TO PRINT

You will learn about preparing your documents for printing in Lesson 11. If you want to print any of the lesson files before you get to Lesson 11, you can follow these steps to prepare your computer for printing:

1 Make sure you are attached to your printer and that it is on.

2 Launch the Adobe Photoshop application and follow the steps in Lesson 1 to calibrate your monitor in order to get accurate color print-outs.

3 Choose Preferences from the File menu and Printing Inks Setup from the submenu.

4 Choose the ink type you will use from the Ink Colors pop-up menu. (If you don't know what to select leave the default of SWOP), then click OK.

5 Choose Page Setup from the File menu, then click the Screen button, click the Use Printer's Default Screens button, and click OK.

6 Choose Print from the File menu, then click the Print in CMYK option, and click Print.

Refer to these steps when you want to print any one of the lesson projects.

Lesson

1

LESSON 1: PAINTING AND EDITING

Adobe Photoshop is a powerful image-editing program that allows you to edit and colorize images, retouch proofs, create original or composite artwork, and produce prepress color separations. Whether you're an art director, an electronic publisher, a photographer, an animator, a multimedia producer, or a service bureau, Adobe Photoshop gives you the tools you need to get top-quality, professional results.

Classroom in a Book teaches you the basics (as well as many of the advanced techniques) that you need to start getting the most out of Adobe Photoshop, right now. The projects in this book focus on a fictional international culinary corporation named Gourmet Visions. This mythical company contains several divisions that import and export foods and beverages, publish cookbooks, and manage a chain of specialty food markets. The projects you'll create in these lessons are those that might be produced by the Gourmet Visions art department.

Unlike a real work environment, *Classroom in a Book* is designed to let you move at your own pace, and even make mistakes! Although the lessons are designed with specific projects in mind, and provide step-by-step instructions to help you achieve these results, there is built-in room for exploration and experimentation. The goal of *Classroom in a Book* is not only to teach you Adobe Photoshop but, more importantly, to allow you to realize the power of your own imagination.

This lesson introduces you to Adobe Photoshop, and acquaints you with the painting and editing tools in the toolbox. The painting and editing tools allow you to make changes in images, from subtle corrections to dramatic artistic effects. Even if you won't be using Adobe Photoshop as a painting program, you'll find that learning the painting and editing tools, techniques, and

options will give you a head start in finding your way around the program, working with tools and using other features.

It should take you about an hour to complete this lesson.

In this lesson, you'll learn how to do the following:

- calibrate your monitor
- open a file
- work with palettes
- view, select, and create layers
- choose and change the foreground color
- sample color with the eyedropper tool
- paint with the pencil, paintbrush, and airbrush tools
- edit with the eraser tool
- use the Brushes/Options palettes
- use the Picker/Swatches/Scratch palettes
- blend colors using the smudge tool
- change the painting and editing modes
- save a file

At the end of this lesson you'll have an impressionistic version of the beginning image. This final image will serve as the starting point for the project in Lesson 2.

Source file (01Begin)   *Ending image (01Work)*

THROWING AWAY THE PREFERENCES FILE

The Adobe Photoshop preferences file determines the command and palette option settings when you start Adobe Photoshop. Because there are so many settings that can be changed, it's a good idea to throw away your preferences file before beginning each *Classroom in a Book* lesson.

Adobe Photoshop 3.0 will automatically create a new *Photoshop 3.0 Prefs* file whenever you start the program and it cannot find an existing *Photoshop 3.0 Prefs* file. By resetting the defaults, you'll be sure to display the same values in dialog boxes as are shown in the CIB Book lessons.

Important: If you want to save the current settings, rename the Photoshop 3.0 Prefs *file rather than throw it away. You must then rename the file back to* Photoshop 3.0 Prefs *to use the saved settings with the program.*

To reset the program's defaults:

1 Locate the *Photoshop 3.0 Prefs* file in the Preferences folder in the System folder.

If you can't find the file, choose Find from the desktop File menu, enter **Photoshop 3.0 Prefs** in the text box, and click Find.

If you can't find the file, don't worry — you probably haven't started Adobe Photoshop for the first time yet.

2 Drag the *Photoshop 3.0 Prefs* file to the Trash.

3 Choose Empty Trash from the Special menu.

CALIBRATING YOUR SYSTEM

Before you begin working in Adobe Photoshop, you need to *calibrate* your monitor. Calibration is the process of adjusting your screen display and some Adobe Photoshop settings so that the colors you see when you display an Adobe Photoshop image match the colors you see in a final printed image.

All monitors display colors using a mixture of the primary *additive colors* of red, green, and blue (RGB). Combining these colors produces a large percentage of the visible spectrum. Your monitor can only display color using the RGB system.

When you print, the color you see is the result of color being absorbed or subtracted by the inks on the page. In theory, mixing the primary *subtractive colors* of cyan, magenta, and yellow (CMY) should produce black (K). In actuality, some extra black must be added to absorb all the color from a printed page.

You'll learn more about RGB and CMYK color in Lesson 7. For now, you just need to know that you calibrate your system to make the RGB colors you see on the screen match the CMYK colors used to print a final proof.

In this lesson, you'll calibrate your monitor and enter some values for printing inks and papers. Before you do your own work in Adobe Photoshop, you'll want to perform the entire calibration process as described in the *Adobe Photoshop User Guide*.

Standardizing your work environment

The first adjustment you'll make is to standardize your room lighting and monitor settings so that the calibration will be accurate for your work environment.

To adjust the lighting, brightness, and contrast:

1 Make sure your monitor has been on for about half an hour so that its display has stabilized.

2 Set the room lighting at the level you plan to maintain, then adjust the brightness and contrast controls on your monitor.

Because changes in lighting, brightness, and contrast can dramatically affect your display, try to keep the room free from external light sources. Tape down your brightness and contrast controls once you've set them.

3 Change the color of your screen to light gray to prevent background color from interfering with your color perception.

Adjust the screen gray by using the miniature desktop in the General Controls control panel. Click the white menu bar in the miniature desktop until a black-and-gray checkerboard pattern appears, then click the gray swatch below the miniature desktop to set the pattern.

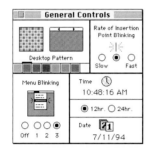

Calibrating your monitor

Calibrating your monitor consists of adjusting the monitor grays to make them as neutral as possible. This prevents your monitor from introducing a color cast in your images. You calibrate the monitor by first setting a target gamma, then adjusting the whites, the grays (gamma), the color balance, and finally the blacks.

***Important:** If you have a third-party monitor-calibration utility installed (such as Radius™ Calibrator or SuperMatch™ by SuperMac), use either that utility or the Adobe Photoshop Gamma Control Panel described below. Using both utilities will miscalibrate the monitor. If you use a third-party calibration utility, you'll need to enter the values suggested by the utility into the Monitor Setup dialog box.*

To calibrate your monitor:

1 Choose Control Panels from the Apple menu and open the Gamma Control Panel.

If you can't find this control panel, see *Adobe Photoshop Getting Started* for installation instructions.

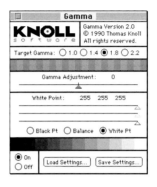

2 Make sure the Gamma software is on (the On/Off buttons are in the lower-left corner).

3 Click the button in front of 1.8 to set the target gamma.

This is the default setting for Macintosh displays. For information on the other target gamma settings, see the *Adobe Photoshop User Guide*.

4 Click the White Pt button.

5 Hold up a piece of paper similar to the stock you'll be printing on and drag the three slider triangles until the monitor white matches the paper as closely as possible.

This adjustment compensates for the bluish tint found in most 13-inch monitor displays and the reddish tint found in most larger displays.

6 Drag the Gamma Adjustment slider until the gray areas in the gamma strip above the slider match the patterned gray areas in the strip (that is, the strip appears to be continuous-tone gray).

7 Click the Balance button, then drag the three slider triangles until the gray areas in the strip below the sliders become a neutral gray (that is, they contain no color tints).

This adjustment controls the monitor's mixture of red, green, and blue components and compensates for color casts in the monitor.

8 Click the Black Pt button, then drag the three slider triangles until there is no color tint in the shadow tones in the lower strip.

You might need to make further adjustments to your gamma setting after setting the white and black points.

9 Close the Gamma Control Panel and the Control Panels window.

Entering the Monitor Setup information

After adjusting the monitor, you enter the monitor settings in the Monitor Setup dialog box.

To enter the monitor settings:

1 Start the Adobe Photoshop program by double-clicking the applicatino icon in the Adobe Photoshop folder.

Note: If you have questions regarding installing the software, see the Getting Starting guide that came with your Adobe Photoshop software.

2 Choose Preferences from the File menu and Monitor Setup from the submenu. The Monitor Setup dialog box appears.

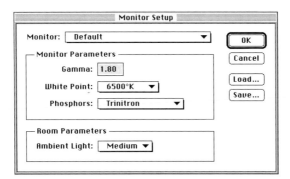

3 Choose your monitor from the Monitor pop-up menu.

4 Enter 1.80 in the Gamma text box (or the gamma value suggested by your calibration utility).

5 Make sure that 6500K from the White Point pop-up menu is selected for Macintosh monitors.

If you changed the monitor type, a different default White Point value might be displayed. Third-party calibration utilities sometimes require different temperature settings.

6 Make sure that Trinitron from the Phosphors pop-up menu is selected (or the type for your particular monitor).

7 Choose High, Low, or Medium from the Ambient Light pop-up menu.

A Medium setting indicates that the room lighting is about as bright as the image on the screen.

8 Click OK to close the dialog box.

Entering the Printing Inks Setup information

Another important component in correct calibration is compensating for the printing inks and paper used to print the final image. Since printing inks have a specific density, ink types use varying amounts of coverage to produce the same colors. Similarly, certain papers absorb more or less of the printing ink to produce identical colors. You can think of the information you enter in the Printing Inks Setup dialog box as telling Adobe Photoshop what printed cyan looks like, what printed magenta looks like, and so on, given a certain set of inks and paper stock.

By adjusting the settings in the Printing Inks Setup dialog box, you can anticipate these ink and paper inconsistencies and allow for them in the monitor display. If you set these parameters before you begin working, you'll avoid unexpected surprises when you print your images.

To enter the printing and paper characteristics:

1 Choose Preferences from the File menu and Printing Inks Setup from the submenu. The Printing Inks Setup dialog box appears.

```
┌─────────────── Printing Inks Setup ───────────────┐
│                                                    │
│  Ink Colors:  [ SWOP (Coated)          ▼ ]  ( OK ) │
│                                                    │
│  Dot Gain: [ 20 ] %                     (Cancel)   │
│  ┌─ Gray Balance ──────────────┐                   │
│  │  C: [1.00]   M: [1.00]       │        (Load...)  │
│  │                              │        (Save...)  │
│  │  Y: [1.00]   K: [1.00]       │                   │
│  └──────────────────────────────┘                  │
│  ☐ Use Dot Gain for Grayscale Images               │
└────────────────────────────────────────────────────┘
```

When you're doing your own work, you will change the values in this dialog box depending on the requirements of individual projects. For the lessons in *Classroom in a Book*, you will use the default settings.

2 Make sure that SWOP (Coated) from the Ink Colors pop-up menu is selected. Click the down arrow to examine the other selections.

Standard Web Offset Proofing (SWOP) inks printed on coated paper are the most commonly used inks in the United States. These inks differ slightly from those used in Europe.

Note: The other selections may be appropriate when you are printing to your local print shop for a proof.

3 Make sure that 20 is entered for the dot gain.

Printed colors consist of a series of dots. *Dot gain* is a printing characteristic that causes dots to print larger than they should, producing darker tones or colors than expected. Different printers and papers have different dot gains.

4 Click the Use Dot Gain for Grayscale Images checkbox, then click OK.

With your system calibrated, you're ready to begin working in Adobe Photoshop.

OPENING A FILE

Adobe Photoshop works with bitmapped, digitized images (that is, continuous-tone images that have been converted into a series of dots, or picture elements, called *pixels*). You can bring images into Adobe Photoshop by scanning a photograph, slide, or graphic; by capturing a video image; or by importing artwork created in drawing programs. You can also import previously digitized images—such as those produced by a digital camera or the Kodak® PhotoCD™ process. For more information about the kinds of files you can use with Adobe Photoshop, see Lesson 12 in this book, and Chapter 3 in the *Adobe Photoshop User Guide*.

Before you begin editing an image, you'll take a look at the artwork you'll finish in Lesson 2—the *Creole Classics* cookbook cover—and examine some of the Adobe Photoshop software's latest features.

To open a file:

1 Choose Open from the File menu (or press Command-O). A dialog box appears so you can choose a file.

The *Classroom in a Book* files are stored in individual lesson folders. The files you'll use in this lesson are in the Lesson 1 folder.

2 Open the Adobe Photoshop CIB folder, then open the Lesson 1 folder.

3 Select the *01Final* file.

A preview thumbnail of the selected file appears in the left part of the dialog box.

4 Click Open to open the file.

Adobe Photoshop *Classroom in a Book* files are all locked to protect them from being changed. When you open a class file, you will need to click OK or press Return before you can click the Open button.

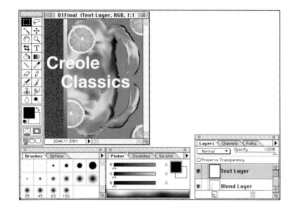

The *01Final* file is in Adobe Photoshop 3.0 format—the default format for saved images. The image appears in a document window. When you start Adobe Photoshop, the menu bar, toolbox, and three palette groups appear on the screen. The toolbox contains selection tools, painting and editing tools, foreground and background color selection boxes, and viewing mode controls. The palette groups contain a variety of options that you'll use when working with images.

WORKING WITH PALETTES

By default, the palettes appear in three groups that can be reorganized to suit your needs. The *Brushes/Options* group contains painting and editing settings. The *Picker/Swatches/Scratch* group contains options to choose, edit, and create colors. The *Layers/Channels/Paths* group contains options for adding and deleting these elements in an image.

Adobe Photoshop has two additional palettes, the Info palette and the Commands palette. To display these palettes or any other palette, you choose the Palettes command from the Window menu, then the appropriate Show command from the submenu.

You can also display palettes using the preassigned function keys. See the *Adobe Photoshop User Guide* for more information.

The Picker/Swatches/Scratch group of palettes appears in the middle of the group of palettes on your screen, with the Picker palette in front. To bring a palette to the front of a group, click its palette tab.

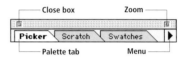

To display a palette:

1 Click the Swatches palette tab.

The Swatches palette pops to the front, and the Swatches palette tab turns white.

2 Click the Scratch palette tab.

The Scratch palette pops to the front, and the Scratch palette tab turns white.

Moving and using palettes

All the Adobe Photoshop palettes are *floating*. To move a palette anywhere on the screen, drag its gray title bar. Floating palettes always appear in front of any images you have on the screen. You may want to move a palette to the right side of your screen to see more of the image.

To move a palette:

1 Click the gray title bar at the top of the Picker/Swatches/Scratch palette group and drag the palette group to the right above the Layers/Channels/Paths palette.

Notice that the palette group snaps to an invisible alignment grid above the Layers palette group.

All the palettes have pop-up menus. To choose a command, click the triangle to the right of the name to display the menu.

2 Click the Scratch palette tab.

3 Click the black triangle to the right of the Picker/Swatches/Scratch palette tabs. The Scratch palette pop-up menu appears.

Each palette has its own unique menu.

4 Release the mouse button without selecting any menu commands.

Hiding and collapsing palettes

All of the palettes are *collapsible*. To increase your work space, and collapse a palette, click the zoom box in the top-right corner of the palette group. Click the zoom box again to display the entire palette. You can also double-click any palette tab to collapse or expand the palette.

To collapse and hide a palette:

1 Click the zoom box in the top-right corner of the Brushes/Options palette's title bar.

The palette collapses to the bottom of your screen so that all you see are the palette tabs and the menu triangle.

2 Click the zoom box again. The palette expands to full size.

3 Double-click the Brushes palette tab. The palette group collapses.

4 Double-click the Brushes palette tab again. The palette expands again.

Most of the palettes can be resized. (You can't resize the Picker, Scratch, or Options palettes.) To make a palette larger or smaller, drag the size box in the lower-right corner of the palette.

5 Click the Swatches palette tab.

6 Drag the size box in the lower-right corner of the palette down about one inch. The palette is resized, creating room to add more colors.

7 Click the zoom box in the upper-right corner of the palette to return to the original size.

(If you've resized a palette, you have to click twice in the zoom box to collapse it. The first click returns the palette to its default size, the second collapses it.)

To hide individual palettes, click the palette's close box in the top-left corner, or choose the appropriate Palettes/Hide command from the Window menu.

8 Click the close box in the top-left corner of the Picker/Swatches/Scratch group of palettes.

Press the Tab key to hide or display all the open palettes. Pressing Tab is the only way to hide and redisplay the toolbox.

9 Press the Tab key once to hide all the palettes, then press it again to display all the open palettes.

To open a closed palette, choose the Palettes command from the Window menu, then choose a Show command from the submenu.

10 Choose Palettes from the Window menu and Show Swatches from the submenu.

The Picker/Swatches/Scratch group appears on your screen with the Swatches palette in front.

Reorganizing palettes

Palette groups can be rearranged, separated, and reorganized. If you have a small screen, you can put all the palettes that you use into one group. If you have a larger screen, you might want to separate certain palettes from their groups.

To separate a palette from a group, click the palette's tab and drag the palette out of the original group. Dragging a palette over an existing group adds the palette to that group.

To reorganize palettes:

1 Click the Swatches palette tab, then drag the Swatches palette up and away from the Picker/Swatches/Scratch group of palettes.

The Swatches palette becomes its own group.

2 Click the Swatches palette tab (not the gray bar at the top of the palette) and drag the Swatches palette on top of the Brushes/Options group.

The Swatches palette is added to the Brushes and Options group.

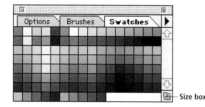

— Size box

3 Drag the Swatches palette tab back on top of the Picker/Scratch group.

4 Move the Picker/Swatches/Scratch group back down to the bottom the screen by dragging the title bar of the palette group to the new location.

In this lesson, you'll use many of the toolbox painting and editing tools and color selection boxes, plus the Brushes/Options group of palettes, the Picker/Swatches/Scratch group of palettes, and the Layers palette. Other palettes are discussed in later lessons.

USING THE LAYERS PALETTE

Every Adobe Photoshop image contains one or more *layers*. The bottom layer is called the *background*, and is created as part of every new document. When you scan an image and open it in Adobe Photoshop, that image becomes the background layer.

You can create additional layers that act like transparent acetate sheets stacked on top of the background. By drawing, editing, and pasting on separate layers, you can try out different combinations of text, graphics, and special effects.

To display layers:

1 Make sure the Layers palette is in front.

2 Click the zoom box in the top-right corner of the palette to expand to the full size of the palette.

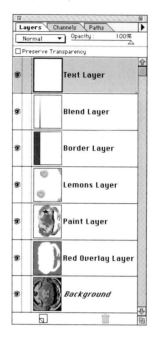

The Layers palette lists the layers in the active window from top to bottom. A thumbnail of the layer appears to the left of the layer name and is automatically updated as you edit the layer. The currently selected layer is highlighted.

The artist who designed the *Creole Classics* cookbook cover used the original scanned photograph as the Background layer, then created six additional layers: the Red Overlay layer, the Paint layer, the Lemons layer, the Border layer, the Blend layer, and the Text layer. Working in multiple layers allows you to make corrections more easily and gives you greater creative flexibility.

Layers will be covered in detail in later lessons. You'll start with a brief introduction to this exciting new feature.

Selecting layers

The Text layer is highlighted, indicating that it is the currently selected layer, or *target layer*. You can only select and edit one layer at a time. The document title bar reflects that the Text layer is the current target layer.

To select layers:

1 Click the layer named *Border Layer* in the Layers palette. The item is highlighted and the layer name appears in the title bar of the document window.

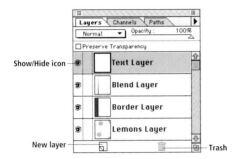

The Border layer is now the target layer. Any actions that you take only affect this layer.

2 Drag the Opacity slider triangle in the Layers palette to 75 percent.

The Border layer becomes 75 percent opaque and you can see the lemons underneath. The change only affects the border element in the image.

3 Drag the Opacity slider back to 100 percent.

Viewing layers

The eye icons indicate that a layer is visible. You can view any combination of layers by clicking in the far left column to show or hide layers. You'll practice this after viewing an Adobe Teach movie.

Time-out for an Adobe Teach movie

If your system is capable of running Adobe Teach movies, you can see a preview of the techniques taught in the next section.

Depending on the amount of memory you have, you may have to close the Adobe Photoshop program while you watch the movie.

To play the movie:

1 From the Finder, locate the Adobe Teach folder and open it.

2 Double-click the file named *Adobe Teach 1*.

3 When you see the splash screen, choose Start from the Movie menu.

4 You can use the Rewind command in the Movie menu to rewind the movie and start it again.

5 For more information on playing the Adobe Teach movies, see the "Getting Started" section of this book.

6 Choose Close from the File menu.

7 Return to the Adobe Photoshop program.

And now, back to the lesson

1 Click the eye icon for the Text layer to hide the text.

The eye icon and the text disappear.

2 Click again in the far-left column of the Text layer. The eye reappears and the text is visible again.

When you print a document, only the visible layers are printed.

3 Click the eye icons for the Background and Red Overlay layers to hide them.

A layer is transparent except where there is color applied. The checkerboard pattern indicates transparent areas.

If you accidentally click in the second column from the left, you will see the move icon. You'll be learning about that feature in later lessons. For now, if you click that icon, just click it again to turn it off.

4 Try showing and hiding different combinations of layers.

If you drag through the far-left column, you can show or hide a series of layers.

5 Drag through the far-left column.

All the eye icons disappear, and the layers are all hidden.

6 Drag through the far left column again.

All the eye icons and layers reappear.

To view a single layer, press the Option key on your keyboard while you click the eye icon in the left column. To view all layers, press the Option key and click the eye icon a second time.

7 Press Option and click the eye icon column for the Paint layer.

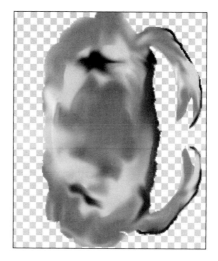

Just the Paint layer becomes visible. The checkerboard pattern indicates the transparent areas.

8 Press Option and click the eye icon for the Paint layer again to view all the layers in the file.

Rearranging layers

The stacking order of the layers can be rearranged, allowing you to experiment with different design effects.

To rearrange layers:

1 Click the Lemons Layer thumbnail to select it.

2 Drag the Lemons Layer thumbnail up in the Layers palette until it is between the Blend layer and the Text layer. When you see a black insertion point release the mouse button.

The Lemons layer thumbnail appears on top of the Border layer and the Blend layer. In the document window, the lemons appear on top of the border and blend elements.

3 Drag the Paint layer to the top of the Layers palette, then drag it back below the Border layer. Try rearranging the other layers by dragging them up and down in the Layers palette.

The background layer cannot be moved and is always at the bottom of the stack of layers. (To move the background, you need to make a copy of it, then move the copy.)

Tracking layer sizes

Adding layers to a document increases the size of the image file. In order to reduce file size and increase printing speed, you can *merge* several layers, or *flatten* all the layers in a document. It's a good idea to save a copy of the file with all the layers intact, in case you want to make more changes.

In the lower-left corner of your document window (*01Final*) is the file size indicator.

To move palettes to see document size information:

1 If necessary, move the Brushes palette to see the lower-left corner of the window.

The first number is the size of the file without any layers (a flattened file). The second number shows the size of the file with layers.

```
204K/1.14M    ▶
```

This file is about 1.14 megabytes with seven layers. After you have merged all the layers, the file will be 204K. Each layer adds to the file size by nearly 100 percent.

You'll learn how to merge and flatten layers in Lesson 2.

2 Move the Brushes palette back to the lower-left corner of your screen.

Working in layers

Working in layers allows you to experiment with separate elements and print different combinations of visible layers. As you work through the lessons in this book, you will learn to create and edit layers, use layer options, and prepare a file with layers for printing.

For now, you'll hide all the layers except the Paint layer and the Red Overlay layer. You'll use the painted crab as a reference while you're learning the painting tools. This lesson allows you some leeway in the settings and colors you'll use to paint. You will probably find it helpful to keep the final version open and use it to refer to as you paint your own interpretation of the crab.

To hide layers:

1 In the Layers palette, click in the eye column if necessary to hide all the layers except the Red Overlay layer and the Paint layer.

2 Make sure the Red Overlay layer and Paint layer are visible.

All you should see in the document window is the painted crab and the red background. Now you're ready to prepare your work area for the rest of the lesson.

PREPARING THE WORK AREA

Since you won't be working in this image, it doesn't need to take up as much room on your screen.

To reduce the *01Final* window:

1 Choose Zoom Out from the Window menu.

The image is now half its actual size.

2 Drag the window to the upper-right corner of your screen to view as a reference file.

Opening another file

Now you'll open the *01Begin* file, which you will use as a starting point for your painted crab.

To open the file:

1 Choose Open from the File menu (or press Command-O).

2 Make sure the Lesson 1 folder is open.

3 Double-click the *01Begin* file.

Setting up the palettes

Now you'll set up the palettes that you will use during the rest of the lesson.

1 Click the close box in the upper-left corner of the Picker/Swatches/Scratch group of palettes.

2 Reduce the size of the Layers palette by clicking the zoom box in the upper-right corner of the palette.

3 Double-click the Brushes palette tab to collapse the palette.

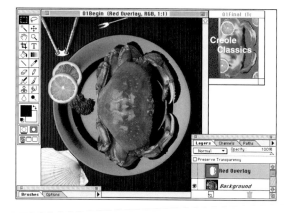

Displaying the rulers

Since you're going to be painting in a specific location in this window, you'll probably find it helpful to display the window rulers. When the rulers are visible, moving a pointer inside the window displays position markers on the rulers.

To display the rulers:

1 Click the *01Final* window to make it the active window.

2 Choose Show Rulers from the Window menu (or press Command-R).

The rulers appear along the left edge and at the top of the *01Final* window.

3 Click the *01Begin* window to make it active, then choose Show Rulers from the Window menu.

As you can see, each open window has its own ruler setting. Ruler settings apply to the current work session only; you must redisplay the rulers when you next open a file. When you want to turn off the rulers, choose Hide Rulers from the Window menu (or press Command-R).

CREATING A NEW LAYER

The *01Begin* image contains two layers: the original scanned image, which is the Background layer, and the Red Overlay layer that you will use later in this lesson. Only the Background layer is visible at this time. Before you apply paint to the image, you'll create a new layer that will act like a transparent acetate sheet on top of the other layers, protecting them from change. When adding elements to an image, it's a good idea to work in multiple layers.

To create a new layer, you can either use the New Layer icon at the bottom of the Layers palette or choose New Layer from the Layers palette pop-up menu.

To create a new layer:

1 Choose New Layer from the Layers palette pop-up menu. The New Layer dialog box appears.

2 Type **Painting** for the name of the new layer, leave the other settings at the defaults, and click OK.

The new layer is added to the top of the layer list and is now the target layer. You'll use the underlying crab as a guide while you paint, leaving the original image unchanged.

Now you're ready to use the painting and editing tools to transform the crab from dull to delightful.

USING THE PAINTING AND EDITING TOOLS

There are a variety of painting and editing tools in the toolbox. You use a combination of these tools when you're creating or editing an image.

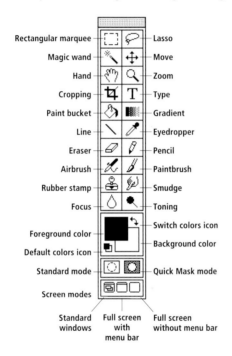

In general, the *pencil tool*, the *airbrush tool*, the *paintbrush tool*, the *line tool*, and the *rubber stamp tool* are referred to as the painting tools. Sometimes the *paint bucket tool* and the *gradient tool* are also included in this category.

The *eraser tool*, the *cropping tool*, the *eyedropper tool*, the *smudge tool*, the *focus tools*, and the *toning tools* are referred to as the editing tools. The *type tool* is in a category by itself. In this lesson, you'll use several of these tools to paint the crab.

PAINTING WITH THE PAINTBRUSH TOOL

The painting tools add or change pixels in the image as you drag them. Depending on the opacity or pressure you've chosen for the painting tool, you can completely obscure the underlying color or let part of the underlying color show through.

The number of colors you can work with depends on the system you're using. An 8-bit color system, for example, can display a maximum of 256 colors simultaneously; 24-bit or 32-bit systems can display more than 16 million colors.

To begin painting, you're going to use the *paintbrush tool*, which uses soft-edged strokes to paint with the default foreground color, which is currently black.

To paint with the paintbrush tool:

1 Make sure that the Caps Lock key is not turned on so that you will be able to see the tool icon.

2 Click the paintbrush tool in the toolbox and move the pointer into the image area. Notice that the pointer turns into a paintbrush.

3 Double-click the Brushes tab in the Brushes/Options palette group. You will see a palette with a variety of brush shapes.

Once you have chosen the paintbrush tool, a box appears around the third brush from the left in the middle row of the Brushes palette. This is the default brush for the paintbrush tool (each tool has its own default brush). The Brushes palette for the paintbrush tool contains soft-edged and hard-edged brushes of various sizes. The brushes in the third row are too big to show accurately; the number below the circle tells you the diameter of the brush.

4 Double-click the third brush from the left in the middle row. Notice the brush options for this particular brush, then click OK.

5 Make sure the Background layer is visible, the Red Overlay layer is hidden, and the Paint layer is the target layer.

6 Paint around the contours of the crab's body and legs, as shown in the illustration below.

9 Click the fifth brush from the left in the top row of the Brushes palette.

10 Still using the paintbrush tool, paint two lines inside the crab shell, as shown in the illustration below.

Don't worry about the precise location or width of the areas you paint. The exact appearance of the paint isn't important. The point of all the exercises in this lesson is to help you become familiar with the painting tools, not to create an exact replica of the final image.

While you're painting, you can use Undo to delete the last brush stroke.

7 Choose Undo Paintbrush from the Edit menu (or press Command-Z).

The Undo command always reverses your last action. In this case, the last paint stroke disappears. Because this command allows you to change your mind, feel free to experiment while you're learning Adobe Photoshop. Keep in mind, however, only your *last action* is undone by this command. (In Lesson 2, you'll learn how to use the Revert command, which reverses *all the actions* you've performed in the current work session.)

8 Choose Redo Paintbrush from the Edit menu to redo your last action.

You can toggle back and forth to compare the results of two actions.

The hard-edged brush gives a different texture to the paint.

11 Take a look at the Paint Layer thumbnail in the Layers palette. It reflects the changes that you have made so far.

USING THE ERASER TOOL

If you change your mind, use the eraser tool to delete pixels in the target layer. The eraser deletes pixels in a layer as you drag through them.

To use the eraser:

1 Click the eraser tool in the toolbox and move the pointer into the image area. Notice that the pointer turns into an eraser.

2 Drag over the black paint in the legs and on the left side of the crab. The eraser deletes the pixels in the painted layer, but not in the underlying Background layer.

You can also change the brush shape of the eraser for more precise control.

3 Click the fourth brush from the left in the top row of the Brushes palette and finish erasing the painted lines on the back and legs of the crab. Refer to the illustration below. Again, don't worry about precision, just get a feel for the eraser tool.

Now you'll use more painting tools to add color to your image.

USING THE FOREGROUND AND BACKGROUND COLORS

Adobe Photoshop uses the *foreground color* to paint, to fill selections, and as the beginning color for gradient fills. The *background color* is used when you delete pixels in an opaque area of color, and as the ending color for gradient fills.

The default foreground color is black and the default background color is white. The current foreground and background colors are shown in the *color selection boxes* in the toolbox. Clicking the *switch colors icon* reverses the colors. Clicking the *default colors icon* returns the foreground color to black and the background color to white.

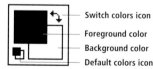

Switch colors icon
Foreground color
Background color
Default colors icon

You're going to change the foreground color using the *Color Picker*. The Color Picker lets you choose colors from a broad color spectrum.

To change the foreground color:

1 Click the foreground color selection box in the toolbox. The Color Picker appears.

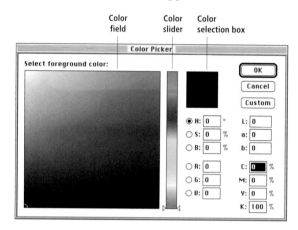

The current foreground color is indicated by a circle marker in the lower-left corner of the color field and is shown in the Color Picker's color selection box. In this case, black is the current foreground color. The Color Picker has a number of settings that let you choose colors from different color models (such as RGB and CMYK), or designate colors by numeric values. See the *Adobe Photoshop User Guide* for a complete explanation of the Color Picker.

2 Drag the white triangles up to the yellow color near the bottom of the color slider. (If yellow is not showing in your Color Picker, be sure the H button under the color selection box is selected.)

Notice that the circle marker remains in the same location.

3 Click near the upper-right corner of the color field to choose a bright yellow color.

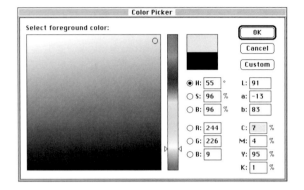

The new foreground color appears in the top of the Color Picker's color selection box (the old foreground color appears in the bottom half of the box).

If you see an exclamation point next to a color, it means that the color you have chosen is not within the CMYK gamut, or range of printable colors. Don't worry about it right now—you'll learn about color gamuts in Lesson 7.

4 Click OK to close the Color Picker.

The foreground color selection box in the toolbox displays the new foreground color.

You can use the standard Apple Color Picker instead of the Adobe Color Picker to designate new colors by changing the setting in the Adobe Photoshop General Preferences dialog box. See the *Adobe Photoshop User Guide* for more information.

PAINTING WITH THE PENCIL TOOL

Now you're going to use the *pencil tool* to paint with the yellow color. The pencil paints hard-edged strokes using the foreground color.

1 Click the pencil tool in the toolbox and move the pointer into the image area. Notice that the pointer turns into a pencil.

When the pencil tool is selected, the Brushes palette contains hard-edged brushes. The default brush for the pencil tool is much smaller than the default brush for the paintbrush tool.

2 Draw a large oval on the back of the crab.

The line is very thin and hard-edged like a colored pencil.

3 Click the fourth brush from the left in the second row of the Brushes palette.

4 Draw another oval slightly inside the first one. Don't worry about accuracy right now. The area that you're painting is the undercoat for the other colors you'll add to the crab.

In order to see your painting efforts more clearly, you're going to show the Red Overlay layer.

5 Click the far-left column of the Red Overlay layer in the Layers palette. The eye icon and the Red Overlay layer appear because this layer is above the Background layer.

The crab shape is now filled with white, so that you can more easily see what you're painting. The red serves as the background color of the cookbook cover. You'll learn how to select areas and paint them in Lesson 2.

USING THE TOOL POINTERS

When you move the pencil tool into an image, the pointer turns into a pencil icon. Sometimes, when you're using the pencil tool (and the other painting and editing tools), it's difficult to know exactly where the painting will begin or how big a brush you are using.

The Precision cursor

Each of the tool pointers has a "hot spot"—the spot where the action begins. When you want to edit or paint with real precision, you might want to turn the pointer into this "hot spot" cross hair. Using the intersection of the cross hair, you can focus on the area you want to paint or edit.

To paint using the cross hair:

1 Click the fourth brush from the left in the first row of the Brushes palette.

2 Move the pencil tool to the bottom claw and press the Caps Lock key.

The pencil turns into a cross hair.

3 Use the pencil to paint with precision along the claw edges (use the final file for reference).

4 Release the Caps Lock key to return to the pencil icon.

The Brush Size cursor

Another helpful option is the Brush Size cursor preference, which sets the cursor to reflect the size of the selected brush.

To set the brush size preference:

1 Choose Preferences from the File menu and General from the submenu.

2 Click Brush Size under Painting Tools, then click OK.

The cursor turns into the brush shape. When you change the size of the brush, the new size will be reflected in the cursor icon. You can still use the Caps Lock key to activate the cross hair cursor.

3 Click the fifth brush from the left in the second row of the Brushes palette and paint on the crab. Notice the larger brush-shaped icon.

4 Click the sixth brush from the left in the second row of the Brushes palette and paint on the crab.

5 Continue painting (turning the cross hair off and on and switching brushes) until your selection somewhat resembles the following illustration.

6 Choose Save As from the File menu.

7 Type **01Work** for the file name and open your Projects folder.

8 Click Save to save the file into your Projects folder.

SAMPLING A NEW FOREGROUND COLOR

When the color you want to use for the foreground color is in an open image, you can use the *eyedropper tool* to sample the color.

1 Click the eyedropper tool in the toolbox and move the pointer into the image area. Notice that the pointer turns into an eyedropper.

2 Position the eyedropper over the red in the image and click.

The foreground color selection box in the toolbox turns to red.

3 Click the paintbrush tool in the toolbox and click the fifth brush from the left in the top row of the Brushes palette.

4 Paint a small solid red oval on top of the yellow area on the crab's shell.

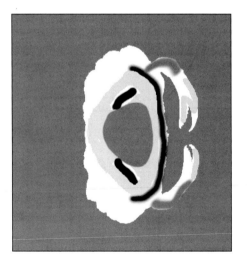

CREATING A NEW BRUSH

Adobe Photoshop doesn't limit you to using only the brushes available on the Brushes palette. You can easily create new brushes for use with any tool.

1 Click the triangle in the upper-right of the Brushes palette to display the pop-up menu, and choose New Brush.

The New Brush dialog box appears (the values in the box are the settings for the currently selected brush).

2 Enter 10 for the diameter, press Tab, and enter 5 for the hardness. You can either drag the slider or type in numbers to enter the new values.

The diameter controls the size of the brush. The hardness is a measurement of the hard center of the brush and is a percentage of the diameter of the brush.

3 Press Tab and leave the spacing at 25.

4 Press Tab and enter 45 for the angle, then press Tab and enter 50 for the roundness.

As you enter new settings, the preview box in the lower-right corner of the dialog box shows you the new brush.

5 Click OK to close the New Brush dialog box.

Look at the bottom row of the Brushes palette. The new brush appears in the next available space on the palette. If you add several brushes to a palette, you can resize the palette to see more than four rows of brushes. You can also use the Delete Brush command in the palette pop-up menu to get rid of brushes you no longer need. (At the end of this lesson you will learn how to save this new brush for later use.)

6 Use your new brush to paint on the front claws of the crab (using the final file as a reference).

CHANGING THE BRUSH OPACITY

So far, you've been using the Brushes palette to select brush shapes; now you'll try the Options palette. The Options palette contains options for each tool in the toolbox, including paint opacity, painting modes, and features unique to each tool.

To change the brush opacity:

1 Click the Options tab in the Brushes/Options group of palettes.

The Options palette comes to the front and reflects the name of the currently selected tool.

```
Bru| Paintbrush Options        ▶
  Normal        ▼  Opacity :    100%
                                   △
  ☐ Fade :       steps to  Transparent ▼
  Stylus Pressure : ☐ Size ☐ Color ☐ Opacity
  ☐ Wet Edges
```

The Opacity slider in the Options palette controls the transparency of the paint. For the paintbrush and pencil tools, the default opacity setting is 100 percent. Since you've been painting with 100 percent opaque paint, the yellow areas you've painted over with the red paint have been completely obscured. Lowering the opacity setting makes the paint you apply more transparent.

2 Drag the Opacity slider to 50 percent.

3 Paint over some more of the yellow areas with the red paint.

You can see that the paint now takes on an orange tone as the red and yellow pixels overlap.

4 Set the Opacity back to 100 percent.

The paintbrush has a special option called *Wet Edges*. This feature gives the paintbrush the texture of a watercolor brush, with a translucent center and solid outer edges.

5 Click the Wet Edges checkbox in the lower-left corner of the Paintbrush Options palette.

6 Click the Brushes palette tab, then click the third brush from the left in the second row.

7 Paint a little red on each claw.

Try various opacities with the wet edges option. Feel free to add your own interpretative touches.

USING THE PICKER/SWATCHES/SCRATCH PALETTES

To continue painting, you're going to choose a new foreground color. You've already learned two ways to change the foreground color; you can choose a new color from the Color Picker, or you can use the eyedropper to sample a color in the image. The Picker/Swatches/Scratch group of palettes provides several other ways of selecting foreground and background colors.

To choose a color from the Swatches palette:

1 Choose Palettes from the Window menu and Show Swatches from the submenu. (If the Picker/Swatches/Scratch palette is already open, click the Swatches palette tab.)

```
 Picker \ Swatches \ Scratch \    ▶
```

The Swatches palette appears at the front of the group of palettes. It contains 122 colors of the default Adobe Photoshop palette. Like the Brushes palette, you can customize the Swatches palette by adding and deleting colors.

As you move the pointer over the color swatches, it turns into an eyedropper. When you click, the new color appears in the foreground color selection box in the toolbox.

2 Click the dark green color swatch in the fifth row (seventh from the left).

3 Do some improvisational painting on your crab with the green color as you vary the opacity settings, brushes, and other colors.

4 As you continue to paint, switch back and forth between the pencil and paintbrush tools.

When you use multiple tools, Adobe Photoshop remembers the last brush and opacity used for each specific tool. The last brush you used is automatically reselected when you return to a tool.

5 To turn off the Wet Edges effect, click the paintbrush tool, then click the Options palette tab, then deselect the Wet Edges option and continue painting.

Stop painting when your image has enough green, yellow, red, and black (you can always come back later and add more color or replace colors with other colors).

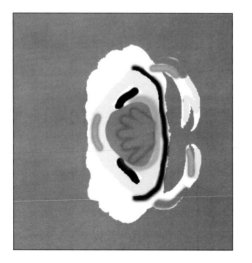

For the rest of the lesson you'll use standard tool cursors or access the precision cursor by pressing the Caps Lock key.

6 Choose Preferences from the File menu and General from the submenu.

7 Click Standard under Painting Tools, then click OK to turn off the brush shapes preference.

8 Choose Save from the File menu (or press Command-S).

Reorganizing the Picker/Swatches/Scratch palette.

You are going to use both the Swatches palette and the Scratch palette in the next section. To make it easier to work with both palettes, separate the Scratch palette from the Swatches palette.

To separate a palette:

1 Click on the Scratch palette tab.

2 Drag the palette up and to the right until it separates from the group.

3 You can now move this new palette independently from the other parts of the group. (To put this palette back into its group, you would drag the Scratch palette tab on top of the Swatches/Picker group. Leave the Scratch palette separate to continue.)

Mixing a new color

The Scratch palette lets you select colors or mix new colors. You can use any of the painting tools to paint on the scratch pad. To eliminate colors, use the eraser. You will mix colors in the Scratch palette now.

To select a color:

1 Click the paintbrush tool, then press the Option key to temporarily access the eyedropper.

When you have the paintbrush, pencil, airbrush, gradient, line, or type tool selected, holding down the Option key automatically displays the eyedropper so you can sample a color.

TIP: YOU CAN USE THE ZOOM TOOL TO MAGNIFY THE SCRATCH PAD AS YOU PAINT NEW COLORS. EVERY STROKE BUILDS UP THE OPACITY OR PRESSURE, DARKENING THE UNDERLYING COLOR.

This technique works in the image area, too. Using this shortcut, you can select a new foreground color without switching the tools in the toolbox.

2 While pressing the Option key, click anywhere in the Scratch palette to change the foreground color.

3 Try dragging through the colors in the scratch pad, and watch the foreground color selector change.

When you release the mouse button, the foreground color changes to the selected color.

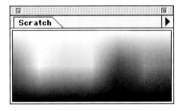

To mix a color:

1 Choose Clear from the Scratch palette pop-up menu.

The colors are cleared and a white scratch pad area appears.

2 Click the blue swatch in the middle of the fifth row in the Swatches palette (sixth from the right).

3 Click the Brushes palette tab.

4 Make sure that the paintbrush tool is selected, then click the fifth brush from the left in the second row of the Brushes palette.

5 Click the Options palette tab, make sure that the opacity is set to 100 percent, and make sure that Wet Edges is turned off.

6 Use the paintbrush to paint in the empty scratch pad.

7 In the Swatches palette, click a medium gray swatch in the second row, set the opacity to 36 percent in the Paintbrush Options palette, then paint over the blue in the scratch pad.

8 Click the red swatch in the top row of the Swatches palette, set the opacity to 14 percent in the Options palette, and paint in the scratch pad again. Overlapping colors builds layers of colors in the Scratch pad.

This red tint changes the color slightly but you should be able to detect the difference. If you can't, increase the opacity a little, and paint again.

9 Hold down the Option key and sample the newly created colors in the scratch pad. Select a purple-gray color and make it the foreground color.

TIP: IN MANY CASES YOU CAN SELECT A TOOL FROM THE TOOLBOX BY TYPING THE FIRST LETTER OF THE TOOL. TYPE 'P' FOR THE PENCIL, 'B' FOR THE PAINT-BRUSH, 'E' FOR THE ERASER, AND 'A' FOR THE AIRBRUSH.

Adding a color to the Swatches palette

Since you will use this color several times to finish painting the crab, you are going to add it to the Swatches palette now.

To add a color to the Swatches palette:

1 Be sure the new purple-gray color is the foreground color.

2 Move the pointer over the empty white space in the bottom row of the Swatches palette. Notice that the pointer turns into the paint bucket tool.

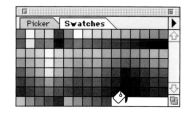

3 Click to add the color to the Swatches palette.

To delete a color, you can press the Command key and your cursor will turn into a scissors icon. If you click a color, you will delete it from the palette.

4 Collapse the Swatches palette by double-clicking the Swatches palette tab or clicking once on the zoom box in the upper-right corner of the palette.

5 Close the Scratch palette by clicking the close box in the upper-left corner.

PAINTING WITH THE AIRBRUSH TOOL

The *airbrush tool* lays down a diffused spray of the foreground color. If you press down in one location, the paint builds up in that area.

To paint using the airbrush:

1 Click the airbrush tool in the toolbox and move the pointer into the image area. Notice that the pointer turns into an airbrush.

2 Make sure the Options palette is displayed.

The opacity setting in the Airbrush Options palette is replaced by a pressure setting with a value of 50 percent. You specify a high pressure percentage for a strong effect and a low percentage for a more subtle effect.

3 Click the Brushes palette tab.

The Brushes palette changes to reflect the default settings for the airbrush. The brush size is large—35 pixels in diameter.

4 Begin painting with your new purple-gray color around the edges of the crab, over the white areas.

5 Select a smaller brush and click the Options palette tab, then change the pressure in the Airbrush Options palette to 100 percent to paint the purple-gray areas in the bottom claw and leg.

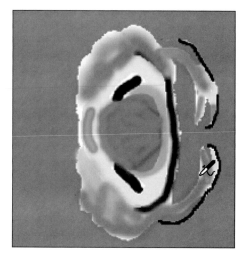

Changing the fade-out rate

Up to this point, all your paint strokes have been even along their entire length. To make the stroke look more like a real brush stroke, you're going to change the airbrush *fade-out rate*. The fade-out rate determines how many pixels are colored with each stroke before the paint fades out completely. The higher the fade rate, the longer the paint flows before it fades out. You can make the paint fade out from the foreground color to transparent, or from the foreground color to the background color.

To set the Fade-out rate:

1 Click the Fade checkbox in the Airbrush Options palette and enter 20 (the Transparent option is automatically selected).

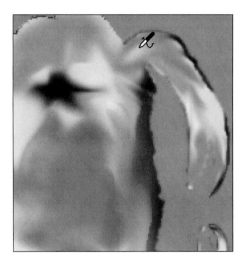

You'll try this out in the red area so that you can really see the effects of this setting.

2 Paint one vertical stroke about one-half-inch in length in the red background.

3 Change the Fade option to 40 and paint a second stroke of the same length next to the first one.

You can see that the first stroke, with the lower fade-out rate, becomes transparent first.

4 Change the Fade to 60, then select the Background option from the pop-up menu.

5 Try painting strokes in the red background and compare them to the previous airbrush strokes.

As you finish the stroke, the paint fades out to white, the current background color.

6 Double-click the Swatches palette tab, then press the Option key and click the bright pink swatch in the first row of the Swatches palette.

Using the Option key with the eyedropper samples a new *background* color. The background color selector box should be bright pink, and the foreground color selector box should still be blue.

7 Try painting more strokes in the red background and compare them to the previous airbrush strokes. The color fades out to pink.

8 Use the airbrush tool with the new fade setting and any brush shape you choose to paint in the claws of the crab.

9 Change the pressure and fade-out rates as you spray the purple-gray paint toward the green in the center of the crab shell. (In addition to the airbrush, the pencil and paintbrush tools also have options for fade-out in their dialog boxes.)

10 Use the pencil, paintbrush, and airbrush tools with different brushes to paint the rest of the crab.

11 Click the eraser tool and erase the practice airbrush strokes in the red background.

Try varying combinations of opacity, pressure, and fade-out rates. Don't forget to hold down the Caps Lock key when you want to paint with pin-point accuracy. You can use the final image as a guide, or you can let your imagination run wild.

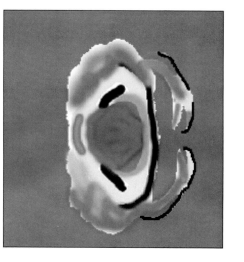

12 When you've finished painting, deselect the Fade checkbox for the airbrush tool by clicking the tool in the toolbox, clicking the Options palette tab, then clicking off the Fade check box.

Note: Repeat step twelve if you used the Paintbrush or Pencil tool with the Fade setting.

13 Choose Save from the File menu (or press Command-S).

SMUDGING A SELECTION

As a final step in painting the crab, you're going to use the *smudge tool*. The smudge tool simulates the action of dragging a finger through wet paint. The tool picks up color from the starting point of the stroke and pushes it in the direction you drag. By varying the pressure in the Options palette, you can change the force of the smudge.

To use the smudge tool:

1 Choose Zoom In from the Window menu to magnify the image so you can see the effect of the smudging more easily.

2 Click the smudge tool in the toolbox and move into the image area. Notice that the pointer turns into a finger (*smudging* is smearing the color with your fingers).

3 Start in the green area of the back, then press the mouse button and drag into the other colors.

By default, the pressure setting for the smudge tool is 50 percent, so the two colors are about equally blended.

4 Vary the pressure and the brush size as you continue to smudge.

Smudging allows you to create some very interesting effects. Stroke sharp lines with a fine brush to create streaks of color, or use a circular motion to create a swirl effect as you smudge. Your crab should be beginning to take on a softer, more blurred quality.

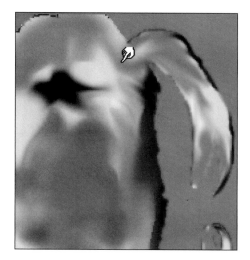

5 Try to smudge the left edge of the crab in the white and red areas. You won't see a difference because the red and white edge of the crab is on a different layer and the smudge tool works on one layer at a time. You'll see how to smudge through multiple layers in just a minute.

6 Choose Save from the File menu (or press Command-S).

Using the painting and editing modes

The Options palette contains another setting that you use with the painting and editing tools. To the left of the opacity/pressure slider is a pop-up menu that currently reads *Normal*. This is the Mode pop-up menu. The *painting and editing modes* control which pixels are affected as you paint.

When the default Normal mode is active (as it has been up to now), each pixel you paint or edit changes. The amount of change depends on the tool's opacity, pressure, or fade-out settings. Changing the painting mode determines whether or not a pixel is affected *in any way* when paint is applied over it. See the *Adobe Photoshop User Guide* for information on all the painting and editing modes.

To use a different painting mode:

1 Scroll to the right edge of the crab back (or any place where you have a dark color and a lighter color near each other).

You may need to move palettes to see the area you want to paint.

2 Make sure the Smudge Tool Options palette is visible and choose Darken from the Mode pop-up menu.

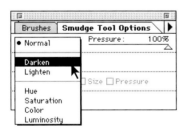

3 Set the pressure to 100 percent. Then, starting from the light-colored area, use short strokes to smudge back and forth into the darker area.

The Darken mode affects only pixels that are lighter than the beginning color. The smudge is apparent in the lighter areas, but does not affect the darker pixels since they are darker than the pixels you started the smudge with.

4 Choose Lighten from the Mode pop-up menu.

The Lighten mode affects only pixels that are darker than the beginning color.

5 Smudge back and forth again, from the light area to the dark area.

Only the darker pixels are changed.

CHANGING YOUR MIND

Since smudging using the painting modes can produce some unusual and unique effects, you may not be happy with your first attempts at using the Lighten and Darken modes. As you already know, you can undo your last action using the Undo command. Adobe Photoshop provides another way to correct your mistakes or change your mind. You can use an eraser option to erase portions of a layer and revert to the last-saved version of the file.

To erase part of the layer:

1 Click the eraser tool in the toolbox.

2 Click the Erase to Saved checkbox in the lower-right corner of the Eraser Options palette.

The eraser icon turns into an eraser and page icon.

3 Drag through the area of the image that you just smudged.

The eraser deletes the changes you just made by reverting to the last-saved version of the file. (If you want to erase the entire Painting Layer, you can click the Erase Layer button.)

4 Try using the smudge tool with the painting modes again.

Sample Merged

To get the softened effects around the claws and legs, choose Sample Merged from the Smudge Tool Options palette, then smudge the edges of the crab.

To smudge multiple layers:

1 Click the smudge tool.

2 Click the Sample Merged checkbox in the lower-left corner of the Smudge Tool Options palette.

3 Change the mode to Normal.

The smudge tool normally works on one layer at a time (as do most of the tools). However, if you check the Sample Merged option from the Smudge Tool Options palette, you can smudge the colors of the underlying visible layers with the colors of the target layer.

4 Click the Brushes tab and select the first brush in the second row.

5 Smudge the edges of the crab shape.

6 Continue experimenting with the smudge tool (and any of the other tools) until you're satisfied with your image. It should look something like the following illustration.

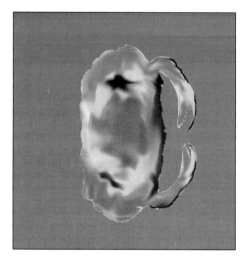

7 Choose Zoom Out from the Window menu.

8 Choose Save from the File menu (or press Command-S).

You now have a layer that just consists of the colors you have been using to paint the crab. If you want to start over or try painting the crab again, create a new layer by choosing New Layer from the Layers palette pop-up menu, naming the layer **Paint 2** and clicking OK, then clicking the eye icon to hide the original painted layer, and paint as you like.

And there you are! In just a short time you've transformed this crab into a dramatically different image that bears only a slight resemblance to the original image.

SAVING THE PALETTES

As you were learning to work with painting tools and palettes, you customized both the Brushes palette and the Swatches palette. These same palettes, with the new colors and brushes, will appear the next time you open Adobe Photoshop, unless you delete the preferences file.

As you become more familiar with Adobe Photoshop, you will probably find yourself using customized palettes more and more. As you add colors and brushes, you may want to save individual palettes to use with specific projects. (For example, Adobe Photoshop provides some swatch palettes to use with specific custom inks.)

To save your palettes:

1 Click the Brushes tab, then choose Save Brushes from the Brushes palette pop-up menu.

2 Open the Projects folder, type **New Brushes** to name the palette, and click Save.

When you're doing your own work, you might want to save this palette in the Adobe Photoshop Brushes and Palettes folder along with the other palettes.

3 Make sure the Swatches palette is selected, then choose Save Swatches from the Swatches palette pop-up menu.

4 Type **New Swatches** to name the palette and save the file in your Projects folder.

You can also save the Scratch palette using the same steps. You don't need to do that now.

To change the contents of a palette or add to a palette, you use the Load Brushes, Load Swatches, and Load Scratch commands in the palette pop-up menus. To return to the default palettes, choose the Reset command from the appropriate palette pop-up menu.

SAVING PREVIEW ICONS

Your files are automatically saved with individual preview icons. If you're working with several versions of an image, these icons can be real timesavers. You can use them to locate specific files quickly and visually.

You can also create thumbnail previews for previewing documents when you are opening files using the File/Open command.

To check preview preferences:

1 Choose Preferences from the File menu and General from the submenu (or press Command-K). The General Preferences dialog box appears.

2 Click the More button.

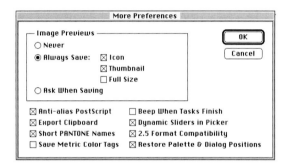

You can choose to save your documents with preview icons, thumbnail previews, or full-size previews. The preview icon is the icon you see in the Finder. The thumbnail preview is the preview image that appears in the Open dialog box. The full-size previews are the 72-dpi images intended for use in page layout applications. You can choose to save previews always or on a file-by-file basis.

If you import your Adobe Photoshop files into page layout programs, the full-size preview option is especially handy. It allows you to see a clear, 72-dpi preview instead of a blurry representation.

3 Make sure the Icon and Thumbnail options are checked, then click OK in the More Preferences dialog box, then click OK again.

Note: *If you do not have QuickTime installed on your computer, you will not see any previews. See your* Adobe Photoshop User Guide *for more information.*

4 Choose Save from the File menu (or press Command-S).

When you open Adobe Photoshop and see this file in the Finder, you'll be able to pick it out by its bright red background and colorful crab.

5 Choose Close from the File menu (or press Command-W).

Viewing thumbnails and preview icons

To finish up, you will now view the preview icons in the Projects folder to see your saved files from Lesson 1.

To view preview icons:

1 Choose Open from the File menu.

2 Make sure the Projects folder is open.

Notice the preview thumbnail of the *01Work* file in the dialog box.

3 Click Cancel.

Now you'll view the file icons in the Finder.

4 Choose Quit from the File menu to quit the Adobe Photoshop application. Don't save changes.

5 Locate the Projects folder and double-click.

6 Make sure to choose By Icon from the View menu in the Finder.

Notice the *01Work* file icon and the two saved palette icons.

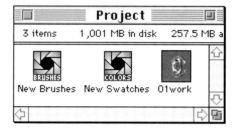

Keeping program icons on makes searching for files fast and easy. However, turning off preview icons can make saving faster and requires less file storage space on your disk.

Congratulations! You have explored palettes, layers, and the painting and editing tools and options. You're well on your way to understanding the excitement and adventure of image editing with Adobe Photoshop.

Lesson

2

LESSON 2: WORKING WITH SELECTIONS

I n this lesson, you'll learn how to make and work with selections in an Adobe Photoshop image. You'll start the lesson by making selections in a scanned image, and creating an edited version of the beginning image. Then you'll open the painted crab file that you saved in Lesson 1 and add other painted selections and type.

It should take you about two hours to complete this lesson.

In this lesson, you'll learn how to do the following:

- load a selection

- use the marquee and magic wand selection tools

- magnify and move around in an image

- add to and subtract from a selection

- zoom in and zoom out in an image

- save a selection

- copy and paste a selection

- clone areas using the rubber stamp tool

- fill a selection with a color and a pattern

- crop an image

- fill a selection with a gradient

- add type with the type tool

At the end of this lesson you'll have a compelling, impressionistic cookbook cover, sure to entice any seafood lover.

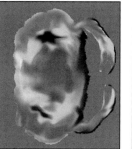 

Beginning image (02Begin) *Ending image (02Final)*

BEGINNING THIS LESSON

At the beginning of each of the remaining *Classroom in a Book* lessons, you'll find a section just like this that reminds you to reset your program's defaults and tells you how to set up your windows and palettes before you begin working.

To reset the program's defaults:

1 Make sure that you have Quit Adobe Photoshop.

2 Locate and drag the *Adobe Photoshop 3.0 Prefs* file to the Trash.

If you can't find the file, choose Find from the desktop File menu, enter **Adobe Photoshop 3.0 Prefs** in the text box, and click Find.

3 Choose Empty Trash from the Special menu.

4 Launch the Adobe Photoshop application.

Once you have launched the program, notice that the palettes and colors have been reset to the defaults. At the beginning of every lesson you will reset the defaults by throwing away the preferences file. This will make the steps in this book easy to follow.

TIP: PRESS THE RETURN KEY TWICE WHEN OPENING A CLASSROOM IN A BOOK FILE. YOU'LL QUICKLY BYPASS THE LOCKED FILE ALERT BOX.

Opening your working file

To start this lesson, you need to open the *02Crab* file.

To open the file:

1 Choose Open from the File menu, then open the Adobe Photoshop CIB folder and the Lesson 2 folder.

2 Double-click the *02Crab* file.

3 Click OK in the locked file warning box.

Note: Remember, all the CIB files on the CD are locked so you do not accidentally save over the original file. Every time you open a Adobe Photoshop CIB file, the same locked file dialog box appears; just click OK or press the Return key to open the file.

This image has only one layer—the Background layer. When you scan a photograph, the scanned image becomes the Background layer.

Organizing palettes

Before you start the lesson you will collapse the Picker/Swatches/Scratch palettes and the Brushes/Options palettes.

To collapse the palettes:

1 Click the zoom box in the upper-right corner of the Brushes/Options palette (or double-click any palette tab).

2 Click the zoom box in the upper-right corner of the Picker/Swatches/Scratch palette (or double-click any palette tab).

WORKING WITH SELECTIONS

Making a *selection* is one of the first steps for much of the work you'll do in Adobe Photoshop. You didn't work with selections in Lesson 1 because you were painting on a layer. In this lesson, you'll use the *selection tools* to isolate the part of the image you want to work on, then use the painting and editing tools or the menu commands to complete the action.

For example, to change the color in part of an image, you select the area and then use the Fill command. To create photomontages, you select part of one image and paste the selection into another image. To create special effects, you select an area and apply one or more filters. If you don't make a selection, the tools and commands affect the entire layer. When you're color-correcting an image, for example, you often work without a selection.

To see how this works, you're going to experiment with a saved selection in the *02Crab* file.

To display the selection:

1 Choose Load Selection from the Select menu.

The Load Selection dialog box appears. Selections are stored in a special part of the file called a *channel*. (You'll learn how to display and use channels in Lesson 4.)

2 Leave the default settings and click OK.

Look at the shell in the lower-left corner of the image.

You see a series of "marching ants" around the edge of the shell. This is the *selection marquee* or *selection border*. Any action you take now affects only this selected area.

3 Choose Stylize from the Filter menu and Find Edges from the submenu.

Adobe Photoshop comes with many different filters that let you dramatically change the appearance of an image. You'll learn more about these filters in later lessons.

Applying the Stylize filter changes the selection, emphasizing the color contours in the shell. Notice that only the area within the selection changes.

Each image can have only one active selection at a time (although you can save several selections within one image). A single selection doesn't have to be contiguous; you can have several areas included in one selection.

Making a selection

Now that you understand how a selection works, you're going to make your own selection in the *02Crab* image. There are four selection tools in the toolbox.

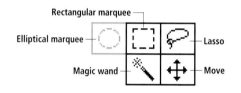

The *marquee tool* allows you to select rectangular or elliptical areas by dragging a selection marquee in the image. The *lasso tool* allows you to draw a freehand outline around an area. If you've used other drawing or painting programs, you're probably already familiar with these types of selection tools.

The *magic wand tool* allows you to select parts of an image based on the color similarities of adjacent pixels. This tool is useful for selecting odd-shaped areas (such as the crab), without having to trace a complex outline using the lasso. The *move tool* allows you to move selected pixels in an image or to move an entire layer.

Adobe Photoshop also includes a fifth selection tool—the *pen tool* located in the Paths palette. The pen tool lets you draw precise *paths* of straight and

curved lines, which you can then convert into selections. You'll learn how to use the pen tool in Lesson 4.

Using tool options

For your first selection, you're going to use one of the marquee options to make an elliptical selection. As you learned in Lesson 1, each tool in the toolbox has its own Options palette. To access the Options palette for any tool, double-click the tool in the toolbox. The Options palette for the specific tool pops to the front of the Brushes/Options group.

To access the selection marquee options:

1 Double-click the rectangular marquee tool in the toolbox.

The Marquee Options palette appears. There are several marquee options available.

2 Click the Shape pop-up menu. There are four shape options: Rectangular, Elliptical, Single Row, and Single Column. Select the Elliptical option.

The marquee tool icon in the toolbar changes to an ellipse.

Making an area-based selection

You're ready to make an elliptical selection of a lemon slice.

To select the lemon:

1 Move the Brushes palette slightly to the right so you can see most of the shell in the lower-left corner of the window.

2 Move the pointer into the image area. Notice that the pointer turns into a cross hair.

3 With the crosshair icon, click the upper-left corner of the bottom lemon slice and drag down and to the right.

The marquee around the previous selection of the shell disappears (remember, you can have only one active selection at a time). A new marquee begins drawing the selection border from the corner where you clicked. However, this doesn't produce exactly the selection you want.

Click point   *Resulting selection*

4 Choose Undo Marquee from the Edit menu (or press Command-Z).

The Undo command always reverses your last action. In this case, the selection border disappears around the lemon and reappears around the shell.

5 Hold down the Option key, position the cross hair in the white center of the lemon, and drag to select the lemon.

Holding down the Option key starts the marquee from the center. This makes it easier to select the lemon shape.

Click point with Option   *Resulting selection*

Duplicating a selection

Now that you've got the lemon selected, you're going to add a third lemon slice to the image.

Your first inclination is probably to drag the selection to the new location. Go ahead and try this now.

To duplicate a selection:

1 Drag the lemon slice down and to the right.

You probably expected the original lemon slice to stay in its location, and a new lemon slice to appear as you dragged. But, instead, you're left with an empty white space! What you see is the *background color* of the image. In Adobe Photoshop, dragging a selection moves the actual pixels. This image has only one layer—the Background layer. While other layers are usually partially transparent, the Background layer is like a canvas with paint applied to it. If you delete or move pixels, you'll see the color of the canvas. The background can be white or it can be the current background color.

2 Choose Undo Move from the Edit menu to return the selection to its original place.

The lemon slice is still selected. To duplicate a selection and move it to a new location, you copy the selection, paste the copy into the image, then drag the copy.

3 Choose Copy from the Edit menu (or press Command-C). The lemon slice is copied to the Clipboard.

4 Choose Paste from the Edit menu (or press Command-V).

Although it appears that nothing has changed in the image, a copy of the lemon slice has been pasted directly over the original selection.

5 Drag the copy down and to the right.

Don't worry about the exact location or if there is some extra space around the lemon slice. The important thing is that you've just had a taste of how easy it is to manipulate images in Adobe Photoshop.

Pasting a selection makes it the current selection. You can see that the selection border is now around the lemon slice that you dragged.

6 Choose Save As from the File menu.

7 Type **02Work1** for the file name.

8 Open your Projects folder and click Save.

Making a color-based selection

When you used the elliptical marquee tool, you selected the pixels in a specific area. The magic wand tool works in a slightly different way—it selects adjacent pixels based on their color. For your next selection, you're going to use the magic wand tool to select the crab.

To select the crab:

1 Click the magic wand tool in the toolbox and move the pointer into the image area. Notice that the pointer changes into a wand.

2 Position the magic wand in the right half of the crab's shell, in the reddish area between the eyes, and click.

About half of the crab shell is selected (the lighter areas in the shell, the legs, and the claws are not selected). Your selection might be slightly different, depending on exactly where you placed the magic wand.

Notice that the selection border around the lemon slice disappears. This is because each Adobe Photoshop image can have only one active selection at a time. Usually when you begin a new selection border, the previous selection disappears. There are several ways, however, to *add* to a selection.

Growing a selection

One way to increase a color-based selection is to use the Grow, Similar, and Modify commands from the Select menu. The Grow command selects *adjacent* pixels of the same color. The Similar command selects the same color pixels wherever they appear in the image. The Modify command provides ways to expand, contract, or smooth a selection.

To increase a selection based on color:

1 Choose Grow from the Select menu (or press Command-G).

The selection increases so that most of the shell and parts of the legs and claws are selected. The lighter-yellow sections of the crab (and the red areas that are not adjacent to the current selection) are still unselected.

Both the magic wand tool and the Grow and Similar commands select pixels that are alike in color. How similar the color must be is determined by the *tolerance* setting in the Magic Wand Options palette. A higher tolerance selects pixels with a wider color range; a lower tolerance limits the selection to pixels that are very close in color.

2 Make sure the Magic Wand Options palette is displayed, then increase the tolerance setting to 45.

Increasing the tolerance will add the lighter red and yellow pixels to the selection when you next use the command.

3 Choose Grow from the Select menu.

Now you've selected almost all of the crab. There are still some small sections in the middle of the shell and the tips of the claws that need to be included.

Adding to and subtracting from a selection

Using the Grow command is a convenient way to add incrementally to a selection when there are clear color distinctions. To make more precise adjustments to a selection border, you use the lasso tool.

Remember, each click of a selection tool normally starts a new selection. When you want to add to or subtract from a selection, you hold down the Shift key (to add) or the Command key (to subtract) as you enclose areas using the lasso.

To add to a selection:

1 Click the lasso tool in the toolbox and move the cursor into the image area. If you're outside the selected area, the cursor turns into a lasso; if you're inside the selected area, the cursor turns into an arrow.

2 Hold down the Shift key and draw a lasso around most of the areas on the crab's back that aren't selected. Leave a few unselected areas.

Start drawing from within the current selection and be sure to start and end the lasso at the same point. If you don't, Adobe Photoshop will draw a connecting selection marquee between the point at which you began drawing and the last point.

If you start moving your selection, you probably forgot to hold down the Shift key. Choose Undo from the Edit menu to return the selection to the previous position, and try again. Your selection should now include most of the crab's back.

Just to experiment, try subtracting part of the shell from the selection.

To subtract from a selection:

1 With the lasso tool selected, hold down the Command key and draw a lasso around the center of the shell.

You can see that the area you enclosed is no longer part of the selection; it is deselected.

2 Choose Undo Lasso from the Edit menu to undo your last action.

Smoothing a selection

Another way to include unselected areas within a selection is to use the Smooth command.

To smooth a selection:

1 Choose Modify from the Select menu and Smooth from the submenu. The Smooth Selection dialog box appears.

2 Enter **5** in the Sample Radius box, then click OK.

Adobe Photoshop uses a method of averaging to add stray pixels to a selected area. You may lose some pixels at the edge of your selection. If that's the case, try using the Grow command again.

MAGNIFYING THE IMAGE

To make selecting the claws easier, you're going to zoom in before you continue adding to the selection. The title bar tells you that, right now, you're looking at a 1:1 view of the image.

In Adobe Photoshop, the view ratio is 1 monitor pixel to 1 image pixel, not the actual physical size of the image. Images are always displayed at a resolution of 72 pixels per inch (ppi), which is the standard Macintosh monitor resolution. An image with a resolution higher than 72 ppi appears bigger on the screen than its actual size. For example, a 3-inch by 4-inch image with a resolution of 144 pixels per inch (which is approximately twice the monitor resolution) takes up a 6-inch by 8-inch area on the screen when viewed at a 1:1 ratio. The same image with a resolution of 300 ppi (four times the monitor resolution) would appear to be 24 inches by 32 inches.

You use the *zoom tool* to increase and decrease the image's view ratio. Changing the view ratio modifies how the image appears on the screen, but it doesn't change the actual size of the image.

To increase the magnification of the view:

1 Click the zoom tool in the toolbox and move the pointer into the image. Notice that the pointer turns into a magnifying glass with a plus sign.

2 Position the magnifying glass in the black area between the two claws, and click.

1:1 view   *2:1 view*

The image is enlarged by one order of magnification. The title bar now shows a 2:1 view ratio. Each click of the zoom tool increases the magnification by a factor of 2.

Increasing the magnification makes it easier to add the claw tips to the selection.

To add the top claw to the selection:

1 Click the lasso tool in the toolbox.

2 Since you are adding to the selection, hold down the Shift key while you use the lasso to trace the top claw tip. Be sure you start dragging the lasso inside the current selection border, and close the lasso at the same point that you started it.

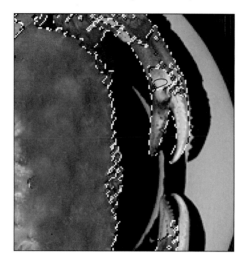

Don't worry if your selection border isn't perfect; the general shape of the claw is all that's important for this selection.

3 Continue to use the lasso tool to add any small unselected areas within the top claw.

If you accidentally include part of the plate or background in the selection, use the Command key with the lasso tool to subtract the unwanted areas.

Moving around in the image

When you're working in a magnified view, you can't see the entire image. One way to move around in the image is to use the standard scroll arrows and scroll bars. Another way to scroll is to drag sections of the image into view using the *hand tool*.

To add the bottom claw tip to the selection:

1 Click the hand tool in the toolbox and move the pointer into the image area. Notice that the pointer turns into a hand.

2 Position the hand in the black area between the claws and drag upward to display all of the bottom claw.

3 Click the lasso tool, then hold down the Shift key and use the lasso to outline the claw tip and include the areas within the claw that aren't selected.

Again, don't worry about exactness. If you're unhappy with the outline, choose Undo Lasso and retrace the area.

Once you've added the claw, you'll notice that the selection border is not quite correct where the bottom claw intersects the shell. You need to smooth out the selection border. Zooming in again will help you to see this area more clearly.

4 Choose Zoom In from the Window menu (or press Command-plus).

The Zoom In command does the same thing as clicking the zoom tool, except that the magnification factor is 1 instead of 2. The view ratio is now 3:1.

5 If necessary, use the hand tool to move down in the image until you can see the intersection of the crab's back and claw.

6 Use the lasso tool and the appropriate key command to add or subtract areas to correct the selection border.

 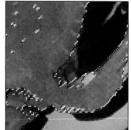

Adding a selection   *New selection*

Zooming out in an image

Using the zoom tool with the Option key allows you to reduce the view ratio. Each click of the Option-zoom tool combination reduces the magnification by a factor of 2.

To zoom out in an image:

1 Click the zoom tool and hold down the Option key as you move the pointer into the image area. Notice that the pointer appears as a magnifying glass with a minus sign.

2 Click to reduce the image magnification to 2:1.

3 Choose Zoom Out from the Window menu (or press Command-minus).

The Zoom Out command does the same thing as the Option-zoom tool combination. The image view is now back to its original 1:1 ratio.

Using zoom shortcuts

Here are some techniques you can use to zoom in, zoom out, or move around in an image while you're using another tool.

To try out the zoom shortcuts:

1 Click any one of the selection tools (rectangular or elliptical marquee, magic wand, lasso).

2 Press the Command key and the spacebar.

The zoom-in magnifying glass appears. Pressing Command-spacebar has the same effect as clicking the zoom tool or choosing Zoom In from the Window menu.

3 Release both keys and press the Option key and the spacebar.

The zoom-out magnifying glass appears. Pressing Option-spacebar has the same effect as holding down the Option key and clicking the zoom tool or choosing Zoom Out from the Window menu.

4 Release the Option key so you're holding down only the spacebar.

The hand tool appears. Pressing the spacebar has the same effect as clicking the hand tool.

5 Use one of the shortcuts to zoom in or zoom out, then double-click the zoom tool.

You are quickly returned to the 1:1 view of this image (this works no matter what the magnification is).

One convenient way to use these shortcuts is to put your ring finger on the Option key, your middle finger on the Command key, and your index finger on the spacebar. When all three fingers are pressed down, the zoom-out icon appears. If you lift your ring finger and release the Option key, the zoom-in icon appears. If you lift your ring and middle fingers so that only the spacebar is pressed, the hand icon appears. Once you get used to these key combinations, you'll be amazed at how quickly you can move to exactly the part of the image you want to work in.

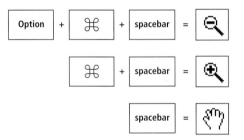

Fine-tuning the selection

Using the selection and magnification techniques you've learned, you're now ready to make final adjustments to the crab selection.

To select the rest of the crab:

1 While you're in the 1:1 view, note any areas in the crab that are still unselected.

Pay particular attention to the back of the shell and the crab legs on the left side. If you see any small areas enclosed by marquees, these areas need to be added to the selection. You might also want to check the outside edges to see if the selection border makes any noticeable detours into the background.

2 Use the lasso tool and the zoom techniques to adjust the selection border until you're satisfied with the results.

Small imperfections aren't important. Just have fun trying out the tools, commands, and shortcuts. When your selection border resembles the following illustration, you're ready to move on.

3 If necessary, double-click the magic wand tool in the toolbox to return to 1:1 view.

You can also use the Zoom Factor dialog box to magnify and reduce the image.

4 Choose Zoom Factor from the Window menu.

5 Type **2** and make sure the Magnification option is selected, then click OK.

The view ratio changes to 2:1.

6 Choose Zoom Factor from the Window menu.

7 Type 1– (minus). The Reduction option is selected. (Entering a minus sign after the number selects the Reduction option; entering a plus sign after a number selects the Magnification option.)

8 Click OK to change the zoom factor to 1:1.

SAVING A SELECTION

You can see that making a selection, especially one as intricate as the crab, can take some time. When you think you might use a complex selection

again, it's wise to save it. *If you don't save a selection, it is lost when you begin making your next selection.*

At the beginning of this lesson you loaded a pre-saved selection of the shell. Now, you're going to save your crab selection, since you'll use it later in this lesson.

To save a selection:

1 Choose Save Selection from the Select menu. Click OK in the Save Selection dialog box.

Remember that selections are saved in channels. Adobe Photoshop creates a new channel (and names it #5) to save the selection. In Lesson 4, you'll learn how to give channels descriptive names.

Even though it's saved, the crab is still the current selection. To verify that the crab selection has been saved, you're going to deselect it, then load the saved selection.

2 Choose None from the Select menu (or press Command-D).

The selection border disappears and there is no current selection in the image.

3 Choose Load Selection from the Select menu.

The Load Selection dialog box appears.

4 Choose #5 from the Channel pop-up menu, then click OK.

The selection is loaded and the selection border again appears around the crab. If you want to try this a few more times, choose the Load Selection command again and alternate between loading the shell selection (#4) and the crab selection (#5).

5 Choose None from the Select menu to deselect your last-loaded selection.

The saved selection can be reused in this image as many times as you want. However, to be sure the selection is available the next time you open this file, you must also save the file.

TIP: IF YOU HOLD DOWN
THE OPTION KEY AND
CLICK THE LASSO TOOL,
YOU CAN CREATE
STRAIGHT-EDGED
SELECTIONS.

6 Choose Save from the File menu (or press Command-S).

7 Choose Load Selection from the Select menu and #5 from the Channel pop-up menu, then click OK.

To enhance the colors in the crab image, you will adjust the contrast of the crab selection.

8 Choose Adjust from the Image menu and Brightness/Contrast from the submenu.

Brightness controls the intensity of light in the selection. *Contrast* controls the tonal gradations in a selection. You'll explore this feature in more detail in Lesson 5.

9 Drag the Contrast slider to the right until it reads +20 (or type **20** in the text box), then click OK.

The area inside the crab selection increases in contrast.

10 Choose Save from the File menu (or press Command-S).

Subtracting a saved selection

Now you'll increase the sharpness and clarity of the background elements in the image.

To select the background elements:

1 Choose Inverse from the Select menu.

The selection now encompasses everything that was not previously selected—that is, the entire image except for the crab itself. At first glance, you might not think anything has changed, since the selection border is still around the crab. But notice that the outside of the image also contains a selection border. It's the area between the marquees that is selected.

Now you will subtract the shell from the current selection.

2 Choose Load Selection from the Select menu.

3 Choose #4 from the Channel menu, then click the Subtract from Selection button.

You can also add saved selections to the current selection, and select the intersecting pixels of a saved selection and the current selection.

4 Click OK and note that the shell is subtracted from the rest of the background.

Now you'll apply the Sharpen filter to the rest of the background.

5 Choose Sharpen from the Filter menu and Sharpen from the submenu.

The Sharpen filter increases the overall contrast of the pixels in the selection, increasing the clarity of the background.

6 Choose Sharpen from the Filter menu again.

Undoing all your changes

When you work with filters, you may find that you want to back up and start over. As you already know, you can undo your last action using the Undo command. Adobe Photoshop also provides a quick way to return to your last-saved version of a file when you want to undo all the changes you've made.

To retrieve the last-saved version of a file:

1 Choose Revert from the File menu. A dialog box appears asking you to confirm your choice.

2 Click Revert to revert to the last-saved version.

The saved version of the file retains any selections you saved in the original file. However, when you revert to a file, it opens without any current selection.

CROPPING AN IMAGE

Right now, the plate is slightly off center. Using the cropping tool, you'll delete some of the right part of the image. You use the cropping tool to select a part of an image and discard the rest.

To crop the image:

1 Choose Show Rulers from the Window menu (or press Command-R) to display the rulers.

2 Click the cropping tool in the toolbox and move the pointer into the image area. Notice that the pointer turns into the cropping icon.

3 Place the pointer in the upper-left corner of the image.

4 Drag all the way down and to the right until the right edge of the cropping marquee is at the 5½-inch mark on the top ruler and about the 5¾-inch mark on the left ruler.

If you want to change the size of the cropping area, position the pointer on one of the corner square boxes and drag.

5 Move the pointer outside the cropping selection. The pointer appears as the international symbol for "No," indicating that clicking in this area cancels the cropping action.

6 Move the pointer inside the cropping selection. The pointer turns into a pair of scissors, meaning that clicking in this area confirms the cropping.

7 Click the scissors pointer.

The cropped image appears in a resized window. The pixels outside the cropping selection are deleted. In addition to changing what you see, cropping an image also reduces its file size.

8 Choose Save from the File menu (or press Command-S).

And there you are! By using the selection tools and menu commands, you have fine-tuned this photograph. It's ready to be used in one of Gourmet Visions' brochures or advertisements.

In the next part of the lesson, you will combine your new knowledge of selection and painting techniques to finish the cover of the Creole Classics cookbook.

OPENING MORE FILES

You will leave the *02Work1* image open on your screen, open the *02Final* file, and then open the *02Begin* file, which is the painted crab that you worked on in Lesson 1.

To open additional files:

1 Choose Open from the File menu, open the Lesson 2 folder, then open *02Final.*

2 Choose Zoom Out from the Window menu to reduce the *02Final* image.

3 Resize the window if necessary, then drag the window to the upper-right corner of your screen.

4 Open the *01Work* file in the Projects folder.

If you prefer, you can use the *02Begin* file in the Lesson 2 folder.

COPYING A SELECTION FROM ONE FILE TO ANOTHER

The first thing you'll add to the painted crab image is a copy of the lemon slice from the original crab image. Because Adobe Photoshop lets you have several documents open at one time, it's easy to copy a selection from one file to another, or to sample colors from one image to use in another image.

To copy the lemon slice:

1 Click the *02Work1* window to make it active, or choose 02Work1 from the Window menu.

TIP: WHEN STARTING A SELECTION MARQUEE FROM THE CENTER, BE SURE TO RELEASE THE MOUSE BEFORE YOU RELEASE THE OPTION KEY.

2 Click the marquee tool in the toolbox and make sure Elliptical is selected for the shape in the Marquee Options palette.

You can soften the effect of a pasted selection by smoothing the selection's hard edges. *Feathering* a selection blurs the edges by building a gradual transition boundary between the selection and the surrounding pixels. The Feather option in the Marquee Options palette specifies how far inside *and* outside the selection border the feathering extends. You'll learn more about feathering in Lesson 5.

3 Enter 2 in the Feather text box.

4 Collapse the Marquee Options palette by double-clicking the Options palette tab.

5 Position the cross hair in the center of the middle lemon slice. Hold down the Option key as you drag to start the marquee from the center.

If your selection is the right size but in the wrong place, hold down the Command and Option keys as you drag the selection border. This Command-Option-drag shortcut works any time you want to reposition a selection border.

6 Choose Copy from the Edit menu. The lemon selection is copied to the Clipboard.

7 Click the close box in the upper-left corner to close the *02Work1* file.

8 Make sure *01Work* or *02Begin* is the active window.

9 Choose Paste from the Edit menu.

The lemon appears in the center of the *01Work* or *02Begin* file.

Floating selections and layers

When selections are pasted, they are *floating selections*. This means they can be moved without affecting the underlying pixels. (Once a selection is deselected or "defloated," it merges with the pixels in the target layer.) See the *Adobe Photoshop User Guide* for more information on floating and defloating selections.

To create a layer for a floating selection:

1 Drag the lemon until it is in the red area to the left of the painted crab.

The selection is floating because it sits on a plane above the current target layer—in this case, the Painting layer. If you deselect the lemon, the floating selection will merge with the Painting layer.

To prevent the lemon from deleting part of the underlying painted crab, you can turn a floating selection into its own layer. Creating new layers for added elements protects the underlying image from change and gives you the flexibility to experiment.

2 Make sure that the Layers palette is open.

Notice the Floating Selection thumbnail in the Layers palette.

3 Choose Make Layer from the Layers palette pop-up menu. The Make Layer dialog box appears.

4 Type **Lemons** for the new layer name and click OK.

The New Layer thumbnail appears in the Layers palette list.

Notice that the selection marquee disappears from the lemon slice. Making a layer from a floating selection deselects or "defloats" the selection. The lemon slice is now on its own layer; the rest of the new layer is transparent. Use the move tool in the toolbox to drag the lemon on the layer.

5 Click the move tool in the toolbox and position it over the lemon.

6 Drag the lemon down and to the bottom left of the painted crab.

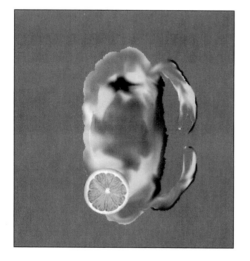

Using the move tool in a layer moves everything on the layer.

7 Choose Save As from the File menu, type **02Work2** as the name of the new file, open your Projects folder, then click Save.

USING THE RUBBER STAMP TOOL

Now that the lemon is pasted into the image, you're going to duplicate (or clone) it using the *rubber stamp tool*. The rubber stamp tool samples, or picks up, an area of the image, then duplicates that area as you paint.

To clone the lemon:

1 Double-click the rubber stamp tool in the toolbox and move into the image area. Notice that the pointer becomes a rubber stamp. The Rubber Stamp Options palette also appears.

Cloning, or exact duplication of the sampled area, is the default setting for the rubber stamp tool.

2 Press the Option key, then click the rubber stamp in the upper-left corner of the lemon slice to set the sampling point.

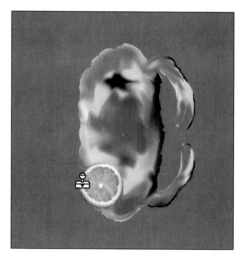

You may need to move some of the palettes out of the way.

The *sampling point* is the starting point of the area you want to duplicate.

3 Position the pointer above, and slightly to the right of, the top of the crab, hold down the mouse button, and begin tracing the top half of the lemon slice.

As you paint, a cross hair appears, showing you the part of the original sample that's being applied.

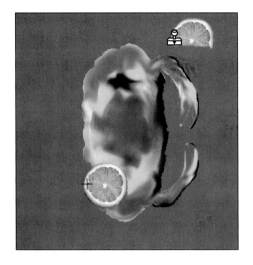

Watch your sampling point (the cross hair) as you drag the rubber stamp tool. If you want to start over, choose Undo from the Edit menu.

Sampling works in the target layer, so you won't get any crab in the painted area. If you want to sample from all the layers at once, choose the Sample Merged option from the Rubber Stamp Options palette, as you did when you were using the smudge tool.

Painting with an aligned sampling point

By default, the rubber stamp tool paints with the Clone (aligned) option. This means that Adobe Photoshop remembers how far the sampling point is from the location where you began painting. For example, in the lemon slice you just painted, the sampling point is about 3 inches down and 2 inches to the left of the painting point.

If you move the rubber stamp pointer and begin painting again, the distance between the sampling point and the painting point will be the same (that is, the sampling point will be 3 inches down and 2 inches to the left of where you're painting). Each time you stop and then resume painting, the sampling point moves to maintain this distance. If this

seems confusing, move the rubber stamp to the left of the new lemon and start painting again. You will see the cross hair moving in the red background, which is the location of the new sampling point.

Painting with a non-aligned sampling point

The non-aligned Clone option applies a sampled image from the same initial sampling point, no matter how many times you stop and resume painting.

 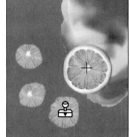

Sampling point   *Painting with non-aligned Clone option*

To paint with a non-aligned sampling point:

1 Choose Clone (non-aligned) from the Option pop-up menu in the Rubber Stamp Options palette.

2 If you changed it, reset the sampling point at the top left of the far-left lemon by Option-clicking a new sampling point.

3 Paint a lemon in the upper-left and lower-right corners of the crab.

No matter where you place the rubber stamp, you always begin painting from the same sampling point. With the clone (aligned) option, when you move to a different location you keep the same angle and distance as that of the original sampling point.

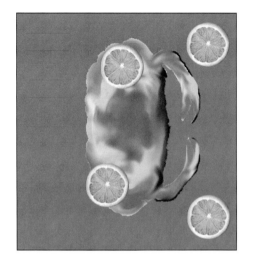

You can also use the rubber stamp tool to paint using the last-saved version of the file, much like the Erase to Saved option in the Eraser Options palette. You can paint with a pattern or use an impressionistic effect.

4 Choose Save from the File menu (or press Command-S).

5 Notice the Lemons layer thumbnail in the Layers palette shows the new lemons.

SELECTING WITH A FIXED MARQUEE

Although the lemons look like they're floating in space, their placement will add cohesiveness to the final design. To make the image more attractive, you're going to eliminate some of the unneeded areas using the Crop command.

When you used the cropping tool, you dragged to indicate the marquee for the section you wanted to crop. This worked fine, since you didn't need to be very precise in the area you selected.

In cropping the area for the final book cover, you want to match the exact dimensions needed for the final art. To do this, you're going to use a *fixed marquee* to select the area to be cropped with the Crop command.

To specify a fixed marquee:

1 Double-click the marquee tool in the toolbox. The Marquee Options palette appears.

2 Choose Rectangular from the Shape pop-up menu.

3 Select Fixed Size from the Style pop-up menu, then enter **240** for the width, press the Tab key, and enter **290** for the height.

4 Change Feather to 0.

5 Click anywhere in the image to make the fixed marquee appear.

6 Hold down the Command and Option keys to freely move the marquee. Drag the marquee until its left edge is about 1¼ inches from the left edge of the window and its top is about 1 inch from the top of the window.

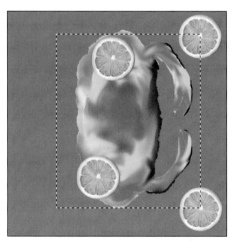

7 Choose Crop from the Edit menu.

The cropped image appears in a resized window.

8 Choose Save from the File menu.

You can also set a marquee to have a specific height-to-width ratio, or to select a single row or column. (The elliptical marquee tool can also use a fixed-size or constrained-ratio setting.)

FILLING A SELECTION

Now you are going to create the blue border that appears in the left part of the cookbook cover. You'll start by creating a new layer using the New Layer icon on the Layers palette.

To fill a selection:

1 Click the New Layer icon at the bottom of the Layers palette. The New Layer dialog box appears.

2 Name the new layer **Border,** and click OK.

3 Click the eyedropper tool in the toolbox.

4 Click to sample a dark blue- or purple-gray color from the image for the new foreground color (or you can sample the color from the final image).

5 Click the marquee tool in the toolbox.

6 Make sure that Fixed Size is selected in the Style menu. Type **54** for the width. The height should remain 290.

7 Click in the image, and press the Option, Command, and Shift keys to reposition the border in the left part of the window.

The Shift key constrains the horizontal movement as you're dragging.

8 Choose Fill from the Edit menu.

The Fill dialog box appears. By default, the Fill command uses the foreground color for the fill (later you'll learn how to fill selections using a pattern).

9 Make sure the Foreground Color option is selected, the opacity is set to 100 percent, and the mode is set to Normal, then click OK.

The fixed marquee fills with the purple-gray color.

Selections act as *masks*—the shape of the selection limits the painting area.

10 Choose Save from the File menu (or press Command-S).

OPENING AN EPS FILE

You can also fill a selection using a pattern. Several patterns are included in your Adobe Photoshop software. One of these patterns, *Intricate Surface*, has been copied to your Lesson 2 folder.

To open an EPS file:

1 Choose Open from the File menu and select the *Intricate Surface* file in the Lesson 2 folder.

The EPS Rasterizer dialog box appears.

The Adobe Photoshop patterns are all in Encapsulated PostScript language file (EPS) format. The EPS format is used by many illustration and page-layout applications. When you open an EPS file in Adobe Photoshop, the image is *rasterized*—that is, the mathematically defined lines and curves of the *vector* image are converted to the points (or pixels) displayed in Adobe Photoshop. See the *Adobe Photoshop User Guide* for more information on using EPS files.

2 Click OK to accept the default settings.

FILLING WITH A PATTERN

Filling with a pattern consists of two steps: first you define the pattern, which stores it in the *pattern buffer* (similar to a Clipboard for patterns), then you fill using this stored pattern. *There can only be one defined pattern at a time.* When you next define a pattern, it replaces the current pattern in the pattern buffer.

To define a pattern:

1 Choose All from the Select menu (or press Command-A).

This selects the entire contents of the *Intricate Surface* file.

2 Choose Define Pattern from the Edit menu.

The pattern is copied to the pattern buffer.

3 Click the close box to close the *Intricate Surface* file and don't save changes.

4 Choose Fill from the Edit menu (or press Shift-Delete).

5 Click Foreground Color in the Contents pop-up menu, select Pattern, make sure the opacity is set to 100 percent.

6 Choose Darken from the Mode menu, and click OK.

The Opacity and Mode options in the Fill dialog box produce the same effect as changing the opacity and mode settings in the Options palette for a tool. The Darken option fills only pixels that are lighter than the fill color.

7 Choose None from the Select menu (or press Command-D).

8 Choose Save from the File menu (or press Command-S).

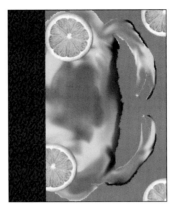

CREATING A GRADIENT FILL

To add a little interest to the blue border area, you're going to create a thin gradient fill along the right edge of the patterned area.

A gradient fill displays a gradual transition from the foreground color to the background color. You use the *gradient tool* to create a gradient fill.

A *linear* gradient fill creates a gradient from one point to another in a straight line (you can create *radial* gradient fills, too). The gradient begins at the point where you start to drag and ends at the point where you release the mouse. You will use a special marquee to select the area for a linear gradient fill.

To create the gradient fill:

1 Click the New Layer icon in the Layers palette. The New Layer dialog box appears.

2 Type **Blend** as the name of the new layer, then click OK.

3 Double-click the marquee tool in the toolbox.

4 In the Marquee Options dialog box, select the Single Column option from the Shape pop-up menu. This marquee selects a single column of pixels that is the exact height of the image.

5 Click to the right of the border to display the marquee.

A single column of pixels is selected. Before you position it, you'll expand the selection to create a wider line.

6 Choose Modify from the Select menu and Expand from the submenu.

7 Enter **4** pixels, then click OK.

The column selection expands four pixels on either side of the original selection for a column nine pixels wide.

8 If you need to adjust the position of the marquee, hold down the Command and Option keys and drag, or use the arrow keys to nudge the selection marquee so that the right edge of the marquee is flush with the blue rectangle.

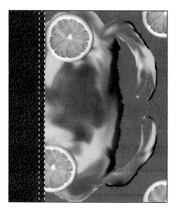

9 Make sure that the purple-gray is the foreground color and white is the background color.

10 Click the gradient tool in the toolbox.

11 Hold down the Shift key to keep the line straight as you draw, then drag from the bottom to the top of the selected area.

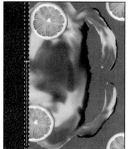 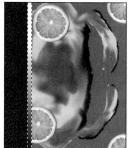

Drag from bottom to top   *Resulting gradient fill*

The gradient fills the selected area, starting with purple-gray (the foreground color) at the bottom and ending with white (the background color) at the top.

12 Choose None from the Select menu (or press Command-D).

13 Choose Save from the File menu (or press Command-S).

MERGING LAYERS

Now that the border is complete, you will *merge* the patterned border and the gradient blend layers. When you've finalized the characteristics and positioning of elements in several layers, you can merge the layers. Merging layers keeps your file size manageable, especially when you are working with large documents.

To merge layers:

1 Click the zoom box in the Layers palette to see all the layers.

2 Hide all the layers except the Border layer and the Blend layer by clicking the eye icons of the Background layer, the Red Overlay layer, the Paint layer, and the Lemons layer.

The Merge command combines all the layers that are visible in the Layers palette.

3 Choose Merge Layers from the Layers palette pop-up menu.

The two layers are merged and take the name of the layer closest to the bottom of the stack. The size of the file is reduced by about 260K.

Remember that the number on the right of the file size box in the lower-left corner of the window reflects the size of the file, including layers.

Deleting layers

Another way of conserving disk space is to delete unnecessary layers. The *02Work2* image is based on the crab image you worked with earlier. It is still the Background layer.

To delete a layer:

1 Show all the layers by pressing the Option key and clicking any visible eye icon.

2 Click the Background layer to highlight it and make it the target layer.

3 Drag the Background layer thumbnail down to the Trash icon in the bottom of the Layers palette (or choose Delete Layer from the Layers palette pop-up menu).

4 Choose Save from the File menu (or press Command-S).

ADDING TYPE TO THE IMAGE

The final design element you'll add to your book cover is a title. You will use the *type tool* to enter the type.

To add type to the image:

1 Make sure that the Border layer is the target layer.

2 Click the New Layer icon in the Layers palette, type **Text** for the layer name, then click OK.

Creating a new layer for each element provides an incredible amount of flexibility. You will be able to edit the text at any time during the design process.

3 Click the Switch Colors icon in the toolbox to make white the foreground color.

4 Click the type tool in the toolbox.

5 Click a starting location for the type slightly to the left of the crab. The Type Tool dialog box appears.

6 Choose Helvetica Bold from the Font menu.

7 Type **42** in the Size box.

8 Click in the text box at the bottom of the dialog box, then type **Creole** in the first line of the text box, press Return, and type **Classics** in the second line.

TIP: WITH THE MOVE TOOL SELECTED, YOU CAN USE THE ARROW KEYS TO MOVE LAYERS OR SELECTIONS ONE PIXEL AT A TIME. PRESS THE SHIFT KEY AND THE ARROW KEYS TO MOVE LAYERS OR SELECTIONS FIVE PIXELS AT A TIME.

When you want type to extend over more than one line, you must press Return to indicate where you want the type to break.

Type Tool	
Font: B Helvetica Bold ▼	OK
Size: 42 points ▼	Cancel
Leading:	
Spacing:	Alignment
Style	⊙▤ ○▥
☐ Bold ☐ Outline	○▤ ○▥
☐ Italic ☐ Shadow	○▤ ○▥
☐ Underline ☒ Anti-Aliased	
Creole	
Classics	
Show: ☒ Font ☒ Size	

9 Click OK.

When you create type, it appears as a floating selection above the target layer. To reposition the text you can use the text tool but you have to be careful to position the text tool inside the text. If the cursor is positioned outside the text, Adobe Photoshop thinks you want to type in more text. If you use the move tool, you don't need to worry where you position the tool.

10 Choose None from the Select menu (or press Command-D).

The Floating Selection becomes part of the Text layer.

11 Click the move tool, then drag the type to position it so that the *s* at the end of *Classics* is between the two claws.

As long as you have the move tool selected in the toolbox, you can move the selection in pixel increments by pressing the arrow keys.

12 Click the arrow keys to adjust the positioning of the selection.

MAKING SELECTIONS IN A LAYER

The word *Creole* needs to be moved over about two letters to the left. You can't use the move tool because it would move both words at the same time.

To select parts of a layer:

1 Make sure that the Text layer is the target layer.

2 Click the lasso tool in the toolbox.

3 Drag a selection marquee around the word *Creole*. You don't need to worry about accuracy, because once the selection is moved, Adobe Photoshop will only select the contents of the marquee on the target layer.

4 Press the mouse button, then press the Shift key, and drag the selection about two letters to the left.

Once you begin moving the selection, the selection marquee "hugs" the letters, so that you can easily see that only the text is selected. The Shift key constrains the movement from left to right.

5 Choose None from the Select menu (or press Command-D).

6 Choose Save from the File menu (or press Command-S).

And there you are! In only two lessons, you've come a long way. Just compare this final image with the crab-on-plate you started with to gauge exactly how much you've learned.

SAVING A FILE WITH LAYERS

Once you have finished creating a composite image, you should create a *flattened* version of the file. Flattening a document merges all the layers to create a smaller file.

Saving layered documents

When you are sending files out for proofs, you may want to save two versions of the file, one version with all the layers intact so you can easily edit the file later, and a flattened version to send to the printer.

The Save a Copy command allows you to create a flattened version of your file while saving the original source file.

To save a copy of your file:

1 Choose Save a Copy from the File menu.

2 Name the file *02WorkL (L* for *Layers)* and save it into your Projects folder.

When you use the Save a Copy command, the original file remains open on your screen.

Flattening layers

Flattening an image merges all the visible layers into the background and discards hidden layers.

To flatten layers:

1 Make all the layers visible (you can press the Option key and click twice in the far-left column of the Layers palette).

Look in the lower-left corner of the document window and notice that the file size is about 1.06 megabytes for the image with the layers.

2 Choose Flatten Image from the Layers palette pop-up menu.

The layers are merged into one, drastically reducing the file size.

3 Choose Save from the File menu (or type Command-S).

The Save a Copy command copies the open document to a new file, leaving the original open on your screen. You can save a copy of the file including the layers and then flatten the original file. Or, if you prefer, you can flatten the file as you are saving the copy. You'll learn how to flatten as you save a copy in Lesson 12.

4 Click the close box in the upper-left corner to close the *02Work2* file.

5 Click the close box for the *02Final* file.

With the knowledge you've gained in these first two lessons, you're well on your way to becoming an experienced Adobe Photoshop user. In the next lesson, you'll review what you've learned and put your skills to use by editing another culinary creation.

Lesson

3

LESSON 3: PROMOTIONAL PIECE

This lesson gives you a chance to practice the commands and techniques you learned in the first two lessons of *Classroom in a Book*. Nothing new is introduced in this lesson (although you will learn some alternative ways to perform tasks you're already familiar with). You'll probably be amazed at how dramatically you can transform an image using the knowledge and experience you already have.

This lesson provides step-by-step instructions that you can follow at your own pace. If you find that you can't remember how to do something, or need to remind yourself of a shortcut, refer back to Lessons 1 and 2. It should take you about 45 minutes to complete this lesson.

In Lesson 1, most of your efforts were directed toward *painting* the crab and producing an artistic version of the image. In this lesson, you'll use many of the same tools and commands to *edit* an image. You'll start with an attractive, if rather traditional, image of crawdads. You'll end up with a crisper, flashier version of the same subject as it will appear on a table-top promotional piece Gourmet Visions has created for a French restaurant that specializes in exotic seafood.

Especially in this lesson, feel free to try out different colors and settings as you edit the image. Use the ending image as a guide, but don't feel restricted to reproducing an exact replica.

BEGINNING THIS LESSON

Again, in this lesson, you'll throw away the preferences file, then set up two images on the screen: the file you begin with and the final version of the image.

To reset the program's defaults:

1 Quit Adobe Photoshop.

2 Locate and drag the *Adobe Photoshop 3.0 Prefs* file to the Trash.

If you can't find the file, choose Find from the desktop File menu, enter **Adobe Photoshop 3.0 Prefs** in the text box, and click Find.

3 Choose Empty Trash from the Special menu.

To begin this lesson:

1 Launch the Adobe Photoshop application.

2 Choose Open from the File menu, then open the *03Final* file in the Lesson 3 folder as your reference file.

3 Click the zoom box in the upper-right corner of the Layers palette to see all the layers.

This file contains four layers: the Background layer with the pattern, the Foreground layer with the crawdad image, the Drop Shadow layer, and the Text layer.

4 Zoom out to reduce the *03Final* image, resize the window if necessary, then drag the window to the upper-right corner of your screen.

5 Open the *03Begin* file in the Lesson 3 folder and choose Show Rulers from the Window menu to turn on the rulers in this file.

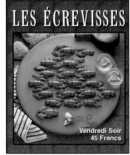

Source file (03Begin)   *Ending image (03Final)*

6 Collapse the Brushes/Options palettes and the Picker/Swatches/Scratch palettes by clicking the zoom box in the upper-right corner or by double-clicking on any palette tab.

DUPLICATING A LAYER

This image starts with only one layer—the Background. The first thing you'll do is duplicate the Background layer. Duplicating a layer allows you to experiment on a copy of the original scanned image.

To duplicate a layer:

1 Make sure the Layers palette is open.

2 Choose Duplicate Layer from the Layers palette pop-up menu to copy the Background layer.

3 Type **Foreground** for the name of the new layer, check that the destination is *03Begin*, then click OK.

A new layer thumbnail named *Foreground* appears above the Background layer. Both layers are identical.

MAKING A COMPLEX SELECTION

The next thing you're going to do to edit this image is select the crawdads and increase the contrast of the selection. Because the crawdads are very complicated to select, you will start by creating an elliptical selection of the plate, then use it later to help complete the selection.

To make selections:

1 Double-click the marquee tool.

2 Choose Elliptical from the Shape menu in the Marquee Options palette.

3 Make sure that the Foreground is the target layer.

4 Select the plate, including the crawdads, part of the wine bottle, and part of the glasses.

Selecting an elliptical image can be tricky. Remember that if you press the Option key you can start the selection from the middle, and if you use the Command and Option keys you can move the selection marquee without moving the pixels inside the selection. Don't worry about getting an exact fit.

5 Use the Command key and the elliptical marquee to deselect the two glasses. (If you press the Option key *after* you click the mouse, you can make a selection from the center.)

6 Choose Save Selection from the Select menu, then click OK.

7 Choose None from the Select menu (or press Command-D).

Now you'll select parts of the plate and use the Inverse command to select the crawdads.

8 Click the magic wand tool and position it below the bottle in the light gray area of the plate, then click.

This selects a large portion of the plate; however, you will have to use other selection tools and commands to select the entire plate.

9 Choose Similar from the Select menu.

Notice that the selection now includes the area between the crawdads. The Similar command, you might remember, selects pixels of similar color anywhere in an image, whereas the Grow command selects *adjacent* pixels within the tolerance level.

Unfortunately, the selection also includes a lot of areas that you don't need. You'll delete these areas in a minute.

10 Choose Grow from the Select menu.

This increases the selection so that all the gray areas around and between the crawdads are included in the selection.

11 Choose Inverse from the Select menu. This inverses the selection so that the crawdads are selected, as well as a lot of areas outside the plate.

Intersecting a selection

Now you'll combine this selection with the elliptical selection you saved earlier.

To intersect a selection:

1 Choose Load Selection from the Select menu.

2 Choose #4 from the Channel menu, click the Intersect with Selection option, then click OK.

The selection that remains is the area common to both the saved selection and the recent current selection.

3 Use the lasso tool with the Command key to subtract the rest of the unneeded areas outside the crawdads, including the flower and the rim of the plate.

When you're finished, your selection should look like the following illustration.

4 Choose Hide Edges from the Select menu.

Hide Edges hides the selection marquee so that you can see the edges of the selection.

5 Choose Adjust from the Image menu and Brightness/Contrast from the submenu.

6 Drag the sliders to the right to increase the brightness to +10 and the contrast to +28, then click OK.

7 Use the Undo command (or press Command-Z) to toggle back and forth and see the effects of the image adjustment. Make sure that you have the brightness and contrast settings applied when you finish experimenting.

8 Choose Show Edges from the Select menu.

9 Choose None from the Select menu (or press Command-D).

10 Choose Save As from the File menu and type **03Work** for the file name.

11 Locate and open the Projects folder, then click Save.

FILLING A SELECTION

In the final image, you want the board on the table to be a similar green to the bottle. You will colorize the selection using the Fill command.

To make the selection:

1 Make sure the Foreground layer is the target layer.

2 Click the magic wand tool.

3 Make sure the tolerance in the Magic Wand Options palette is set to 32.

If the palettes are in your way, move or collapse the palettes, then move them back when you are finished with this section.

4 Position the wand in the blue board at the bottom of the plate and click.

You'll need to use other selection techniques to finish selecting the board.

5 Choose Grow from the Select menu (or press Command-G).

6 Choose Modify from the Select menu and Smooth from the submenu, then enter **2** for the sample radius and click OK.

The Smooth command includes a few more stray unselected pixels.

7 Use the lasso tool with the Shift key to add areas to the selection that you need. (Or use the Command key to subtract areas you don't need.)

8 Feel free to zoom in and out as needed.

When you're finished, your selection should look like the following illustration.

Next, you're going to fill the selection by sampling a color from the bottle.

9 Use the eyedropper to sample the green in the neck of the bottle.

10 Choose Fill from the Edit menu, make sure that Foreground Color is selected, then choose Color from the Mode pop-up menu and click OK. (You may need to scroll down in the pop-up menu.)

The Color mode changes the color of the selection, but leaves the highlights and shadows intact.

11 Choose None from the Select menu (or press Command-D).

DEFINING THE BACKGROUND PATTERN

In Lesson 2, you filled a selection with a pattern supplied with the Adobe Photoshop software. Now you're going to create a pattern from elements in this image. The pattern you're going to use consists of a series of square tiles.

To create the pattern:

1 Click the Background layer in the Layers palette to make it the target layer.

2 Hide the Foreground layer by clicking the eye icon in the far-left column of the Layers palette.

This image is the same as the foreground except for the blue board and the brightness of the crawdads.

3 Click the zoom tool and zoom in on the lower-right corner of the image.

4 Collapse the Layers palette if necessary.

5 Double-click the marquee tool, set the shape to Rectangular, and make sure that the style is set to Normal.

6 Position the cross hair in the blue area of the table edge.

7 Hold down the Shift key to constrain the selection to a square, then drag to create about a 1⅛-inch square selection (the bottom edge of the selection will extend below the board). Refer to the illustration below.

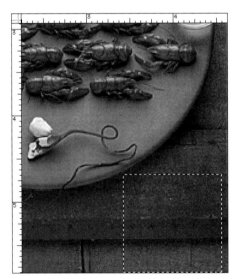

To make the pattern "tile" large enough, you need to remove the table from the bottom part of the selection.

8 Double-click the rubber stamp tool.

9 Make sure that the Rubber Stamp option is set to Clone (aligned) and Option-click in the upper-left corner of the rectangular selection to sample the blue board.

10 Paint the bottom of the selection to fill the square selection with blue.

Now you'll colorize this texture using a reddish-brown from the crawdads.

11 Click the eyedropper tool, then sample a reddish-brown from the crawdads. Use the final file as a reference.

12 Choose Fill from the Edit menu, make sure Foreground color is selected and that Color is still selected in the Mode menu, then click OK.

The rectangle takes on a reddish-brown tone but retains the texture of the blue board.

TIP: YOU CAN HOLD DOWN THE SHIFT KEY AND CLICK IN EACH CORNER OF THE SELECTION TO PAINT IN A STRAIGHT LINE FROM POINT TO POINT.

Adding a border

Now you need to add the border around the edge of the tile.

To add the border:

1 Use the eyedropper to sample the brown that's between the tiles in the reference file (or use a darker color in the crawdads image).

2 Click the airbrush tool, then click the Brushes palette tab and select the third brush from the left in the second row of the Brushes palette.

3 Click the Options palette tab, make sure the pressure is set to 50 percent, then paint along the edges of the tile selection. Hold down the Shift key as you paint to stroke in a straight line.

4 Click the paintbrush tool and select the third brush from the left in the first row of brushes in the Brushes palette.

5 Use the paintbrush to add depth to the top-left corner of the tile.

6 Choose Define Pattern from the Edit menu.

This stores the pattern in the pattern buffer.

FILLING WITH A PATTERN

Now you're ready to fill the entire Background layer with the new pattern.

1 Zoom out to 1:1 view.

2 Choose All from the Select menu.

A marquee appears around the entire image.

3 Choose Fill from the Edit menu.

4 Click Foreground Color under Contents and select Pattern.

5 Make sure the opacity is set to 100 percent, change the mode to Normal by scrolling to the top of the pop-up menu, then click OK.

The background fills with the custom pattern.

6 Choose None from the Select menu (or press Command-D).

7 Click the eye icon in the far-left column of the Layers palette to show the Foreground layer.

You can't see the new background because the Foreground layer is the same size as the background and obscures the image underneath. You will delete part of the top layer, but first save the file.

8 Choose Save from the File menu (or press Command-S).

DELETING PART OF A LAYER

You will delete some of the Foreground layer so that the background can show through.

To delete part of a layer:

1 Click the Foreground layer thumbnail to make it the target layer.

2 Double-click the marquee tool, then set a fixed-size marquee of 304 pixels by 304 pixels.

3 Click in the image, then use the Command and Option keys to reposition the marquee so that it looks like the illustration below.

The selection is against the right edge of the image. That's OK; you'll center the image later.

4 Choose Inverse from the Select menu, then press the Delete key.

The area inside the selection marquee is deleted, thus becoming transparent and showing the Background layer underneath.

CREATING A BORDER FROM A SELECTION

Now you'll use a selection marquee to create a border around the image on the top layer.

To create a border from a selection:

1 Choose Inverse from the Select menu again so that the image of the plate and crawdads is selected.

2 Choose Modify from the Select menu, then choose Border from the submenu.

3 Enter 2 for the number of pixels, then click OK.

A two-pixel selection border appears around the edge of the foreground image.

4 Choose Fill from the Edit menu.

5 In the Fill dialog box, change the pattern fill to Black in the Contents pop-up menu, make sure the opacity is 100% and the mode is Normal, then click OK.

6 Choose None from the Select menu (or press Command-D).

7 You should see a two-pixel black border around the foreground image.

8 Click the move tool and reposition the foreground image so it's centered from left to right against the background and the top edge of the crawdad image is about 1¼ inches from the top of the window.

9 Choose Save from the File menu (or press Command-S).

CLONING PART OF THE IMAGE

To change the visual balance of the crawdads, you're going to add one more crawdad in the upper-right corner of the plate. To do this, you will again use the rubber stamp tool.

To clone a crawdad:

1 Click the zoom tool, then zoom in on the top six rows of crawdads.

2 Click the rubber stamp tool.

3 Choose the Clone (non-aligned) option in the Rubber Stamp Options palette.

4 Click the Brushes palette tab and choose the second brush from the left in the second row.

5 Option-click to set the sampling point on the center crawdad in the third row.

6 Move the rubber stamp to the right of the top crawdad and begin painting. (Watch the sample point in the original crawdad.)

7 Continue painting until you have duplicated the crawdad. Don't worry if you add other shadows from other crawdads.

If you run out of room, choose Undo and try again.

To clean up the image:

If necessary, zoom in and use the Erase to Saved option to clean up the areas around the edges of the crawdad.

1 Double-click the eraser tool, then click the Erase-to-Saved checkbox in the Eraser Options palette.

2 Click the Brushes palette tab and click the smallest brush in the first row.

3 Drag through areas that you want to touch up to revert them to the last-saved version of the file.

4 When you've finished, the image should look something like this.

5 Choose Save from the File menu (or press Command-S).

CREATING A DROP SHADOW FOR TYPE

As a final touch to this table-top promotion, you're going to add type with a drop shadow. You'll create the drop shadow first.

To add the type:

1 Zoom out to 1:1 view.

2 Click the Layers palette tab, then click the New Layer icon in the bottom of the Layers palette.

3 Type **Drop Shadow** for the name of the new layer and click OK.

4 Set the colors back to their defaults by clicking the Default Colors icon in the toolbox.

The type at the top of the file with the restaurant name has already been formatted for you as an Adobe Photoshop file. You will copy the type into the *03Work* file.

5 Choose Open from the File menu, then open the *03Text* file in the Lesson 3 folder.

6 Choose All from the Select menu, and choose copy from the Edit menu, then close the file.

7 In the *03Work* file, make sure the Drop Shadow layer is the target layer, then choose Paste from the Edit menu.

8 Deselect the text.

The floating selection becomes part of the Drop Shadow layer.

9 Click the move tool and position the text at the top of the page and centered over the inset photo, as in the illustration below.

Entering more type

Now you'll enter the text in the lower-right corner of the file.

To enter more text:

1 Click the type tool and then click the insertion point below the plate in the lower-right corner of the inserted photo.

2 In the Type Tool dialog box, choose Helvetica Bold from the Font menu, set the size to 18 points, and click the right alignment setting.

3 Type **Vendredi Soir** in the first line of the text box, press Return, then type **45 Francs** in the second line. (*Vendredi Soir* means "Friday Night" in French.)

4 Click OK to display the type.

5 Click the move tool and drag to position the selected text in the lower-right corner of the inset image as show in the illustration below.

6 Choose None from the Select menu (or press Command-D).

7 Choose Save from the File menu (or press Command-S).

ADDING THE TYPE

You'll use layers to create and position a duplicate of the drop shadow as the top layer of type for the headline and the body text.

1 Select Duplicate Layer from the Layers palette pop-up menu to create a new layer for the text, then name the new layer **Text** and click OK.

You won't be able to see the text because it's an exact copy of the drop shadow.

2 Choose Fill from the Edit menu, choose White from the Contents pop-up menu, and make sure the mode is set to Normal.

3 Click the Preserve Transparency button, then click OK to fill the text with white.

The Preserve Transparency button allows you to fill a layer with color, without affecting the transparent areas of the layer.

4 Click the move tool, then use the arrow keys to nudge the Text layer about two pixels up and two pixels to the left.

5 Click the Drop Shadow layer thumbnail to make it the target layer.

6 Slide the layer opacity triangle until the layer opacity for the drop shadow is 75 percent.

7 Choose Save a Copy from the File menu.

8 Type **03WorkL** for the file name and save it in the Projects folder.

This saves a copy of the file with the layers intact.

9 Choose Flatten Image from the Layers palette pop-up menu to flatten the file.

10 Choose Save from the File menu to save the flattened version of the file.

11 Choose Close from the File menu to close both files.

Give yourself a pat on the back! In a short time, you have enhanced the look of the crawdad image. With this experience behind you, you're ready to explore some of the more advanced aspects of Adobe Photoshop in Lessons 4 and 5.

Lesson

4

Lesson 4: Paths, Masks, and Channels

This lesson builds on your knowledge of using selections as masks and in layers, and expands on the concept of channels that was introduced when you first saved selections. It also introduces a new tool that allows you to draw paths you can convert into selections.

In this lesson, you'll begin with a new, empty file. Using some new as well as some familiar tools, you'll draw in the new file, copy a selection from a photograph into this file, and then manipulate the selection to create a final, almost cartoon-like image. It should take you about 60 to 90 minutes to complete this lesson.

In this lesson, you'll learn how to do the following:

• open a new file

• use the pen tool to draw paths

• use the Quick Mask mode

• use the Commands palette to assign function keys and buttons

• use the Color Range command

• save, name, and view a channel

• posterize an image

• stroke a path

• use layer modes

At the end of this lesson, you'll have an eye-catching display sign for red peppers, sure to attract the attention of Gourmet Visions' produce customers.

The following images show the photograph you'll borrow from and the final image.

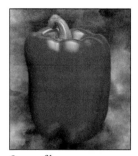

*Source file
(04Pepper)*

*Ending image
(04Final)*

BEGINNING THIS LESSON

In previous lessons, you've begun with an existing Adobe Photoshop image and modified it. In this lesson, you'll create a new file starting with a blank window. Because you're starting from scratch, you'll probably find it especially helpful to refer to the final image as you work through this lesson.

To reset the program's defaults:

1 Quit Adobe Photoshop.

2 Locate and drag the *Adobe Photoshop 3.0 Prefs* file to the Trash, then empty the Trash.

If you can't find the file, choose Find from the desktop File menu, type **Adobe Photoshop 3.0 Prefs** in the text box, and click Find.

3 Restart the Adobe Photoshop program.

To begin this lesson:

1 Choose Open from the File menu, then open the *04Final* file in the Lesson 4 folder.

2 Click the zoom box in the upper-right corner of the Layers palette.

The final file contains four layers: the white Background layer, the Peppers layer, the Graphic Border layer containing all the border elements, and the Text layer.

In this lesson, you may find it helpful to enlarge the thumbnails in the Layers palette.

3 Choose Palette Options from the Layers palette pop-up menu.

4 Click the third choice from the top to increase the thumbnail size, then click OK.

The thumbnails have increased in size.

5 Choose Zoom Out from the Window menu, then drag the window to the upper-right corner of your screen.

6 Choose Show Rulers from the Window menu to turn on the rulers in the reference file.

OPENING A NEW FILE

Now you're ready to open a new, blank Adobe Photoshop file.

To open a new file:

1 Choose New from the File menu (or press Command-N). A dialog box appears so you can set the name and size for the new file.

2 Type **04Work** for the name of the file, and make sure inches is selected in the pop-up menus, then enter 6 inches in the Width box and 5 inches in the Height box. The other options should be left at their default values—Resolution at 72, Mode at RGB Color, and Contents at White.

You can create a new file with the contents of the Background layer filled with transparency, white, or the current background color.

3 Click OK to create the file.

An empty window appears that contains one layer —the white Background layer.

Organizing the palettes

For this lesson you will rearrange the default palettes into different groups.

To organize the palettes:

1 Drag the Brushes palette tab on top of the Picker/Swatches/Scratch group of palettes.

2 Click the Scratch palette tab, then drag the Scratch palette tab on top of the Options palette.

The Scratch and Options palettes are now a palette group.

3 Close the Scratch/Options group by clicking the close box in the upper-left corner of the palette.

4 Collapse the Picker/Swatches/Brushes palette by double-clicking any of the three palette tabs.

5 Leave the Layers/Channels/Paths palette group open, but click the zoom box to reduce the size of the palette.

6 Arrange the palettes so that you can see the bottom of your window.

CREATING A NEW LAYER

The first element you'll add to the image is the graphic border, so you'll start by creating a new layer. When the background of a design is a solid color like white, it's often a good idea to create a new layer for each additional graphic element. Creating a new layer for the border gives you the flexibility to move the border layer and to insert elements behind it.

To create a new layer:

1 Make sure the Layers palette is open, then click the New Layer icon.

2 Type **Graphic Border** as the name of the new layer, then click OK.

3 Choose Save As from the File menu, then open your Projects folder and click Save.

USING THE PEN TOOL

To draw the graphic border, you're going to use the *pen tool*. The pen tool lets you create smooth-edged *paths* with precision. In this lesson, you'll use the pen tool as a drawing tool. In the next lesson, you'll learn how to use the pen tool as a selection tool. You'll start by creating the bottom part of the border.

To set palette options:

1 Make sure that the Graphic Border layer is the target layer.

2 Click on the Paths palette tab to display the Paths palette.

The five tools across the top of the palette are used to create and edit paths. As in the Layers palette, when you create a path, the path name and thumbnail appear in the scroll box below the tools.

You can alter the size of the thumbnails just as you did in the Layers palette.

3 Choose Palette Options from the Paths palette menu.

4 Choose the third option from the top and click OK.

To draw a straight line path:

1 Click the pen tool (the second tool from the left).

You may need to move the Paths palette to the upper-right corner of your screen. Use the rulers in the final image as a guide for placing your points.

2 Move the pointer to the lower-left corner of the *04Work* window and click.

The solid square that appears is a smooth *anchor point*. This point is selected until you click the next point.

3 Move the pointer up and to the right until the ruler markers are at about 4 inches in the left ruler, and three-quarters of an inch in the top ruler, then click again.

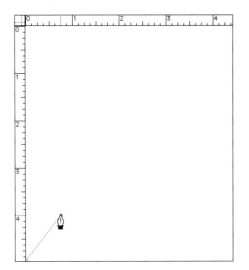

The second anchor point is selected, and the first anchor point changes to a hollow square. A line connects the two anchor points. The name and thumbnail of the current work path appear in the Paths palette. The selected path is highlighted, making it the *target path*. You can only edit one path at a time.

TIP: TO MOVE AN
ANCHOR POINT ONE
PIXEL AT A TIME, CLICK
TO SELECT THE ANCHOR
POINT, THEN PRESS THE
ARROW KEYS ON YOUR
KEYBOARD.

You'll be drawing the shape in the illustration below.

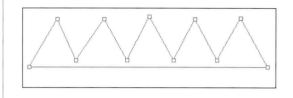

Move the pointer until it's near the bottom of the window and slightly before the 1½-inch marker on the top ruler, then click.

Don't worry about the exact location; you'll learn how to edit the points in a minute. If your line has curves and additional lines coming out of it, you're probably dragging instead of clicking. You must *click* to draw straight lines with the pen tool.

You can use Undo to remove the last anchor point, or press Delete twice to erase the entire path if you want to start over.

4 Continue clicking until you've drawn the bottom border (there are five triangles in the border). Your last click should be in the bottom-right corner of the window.

5 To close the path, move the pen tool from the last point outside the bottom of the window. A small loop appears next to the pointer when you place it on the first anchor point. This loop tells you that the next click closes the path.

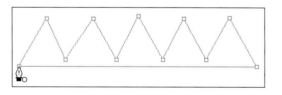

6 Click the first anchor point again.

The Work Path thumbnail reflects the changes that you have made so far.

Editing a straight path

When the anchor points in a path are visible, that path is selected. Using the tools in the Paths palette, you can adjust the anchor points to change the shape of a selected path.

To edit the straight path:

1 Click the arrow tool at the left of the Paths palette.

2 Drag an anchor point to change its location.

You may need to move a palette to see the bottom of the window.

If the anchor points aren't visible, click anywhere on the path to display them. Experiment with moving the anchor points until you have the border you want.

3 If the line along the bottom of the path is not quite at the window's bottom edge, drag the lower-right and lower-left anchor points down. You don't want any space between the bottom of the path and the bottom of the window.

SAVING A PATH

Just as it's a good idea to save selections in case you want to reuse them, it's also a good idea to save paths that you might want to use again in the image.

To save a path:

1 Choose Save Path from the Paths palette pop-up menu. The Save Path dialog box appears.

2 Name the path **Border Path** and click OK.

The path name is updated in the Paths palette. In order for this path to be a permanent part of this file, you must also save the file.

3 Choose Save from the File menu (or press Command-S).

You can only display one path at a time. To deselect or hide a path, click away from the path name in the Paths palette.

TIP: TO EDIT A POINT WHILE THE PEN TOOL IS SELECTED, HOLD DOWN THE COMMAND KEY TO DISPLAY THE ARROW POINTER. PRESS THE SHIFT KEY TO CONSTRAIN THE DIRECTION LINES AS YOU DRAW.

4 Deselect the *Border Path* by clicking in the white area below the Border Path thumbnail in the Paths palette. The Border Path is hidden in the document window.

DRAWING A CURVED PATH

The top part of the border in the final produce poster contains both straight and curved segments. Before you create the actual border, you'll open another file and practice drawing curves with the pen tool. If you are already familiar with using the pen tool to draw curves, skip to the next section.

Drawing a curved segment is slightly different from drawing a straight segment. When you draw a straight path with the pen tool, you *click* to set the anchor points. When you draw a curve with the pen tool, you *drag* in the direction you want the curve to be drawn. You'll practice this next.

Time-out for an Adobe Teach movie

If your system is capable of running Adobe Teach movies, you can see a preview of the techniques taught in this section.

Depending on the amount of memory you have, you may have to close the Adobe Illustrator program while you watch the movie.

To play the movie:

1 From the Finder, locate the Adobe Teach folder and open it.

2 Double-click the file named *Adobe Teach 2*.

3 When you see the splash screen, choose Start from the Movie menu.

4 You can use the Rewind command in the Movie menu to rewind the movie and start it again.

5 For more information on playing the Adobe Teach movies, see the "Getting Started" section of this book.

6 Choose Close from the File menu.

7 Return to the Adobe Photoshop program.

And now, back to the lesson

1 Choose Open from the File menu, then open the *04Paths* file in the Lesson 4 folder.

You'll see two gray curves, which you'll use to trace using the pen tool.

2 Click the Layers palette tab.

The curves are on the *Template* layer. You'll do your practice drawing on the *Practice* layer.

3 Click the Paths palette tab, then click the pen tool in the Paths palette.

4 Move the pen tool pointer to the left end of the practice curve A.

5 Press the mouse button and drag straight up about half an inch.

6 Release the mouse button.

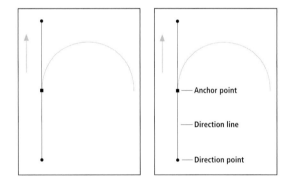

As you drag, a *direction line* appears. The two *direction points* at either end of the line move in opposition to each other around the anchor point. The length and slope of the direction line determine the length and slope of the curve.

7 Position the pen at the end of the curve and drag down about half an inch until the pen tool curve conforms to the shape of the gray curve in the *04Paths* file.

A curve appears between the two anchor points.

8 Click the pen tool in the Paths palette to indicate that you have completed the path.

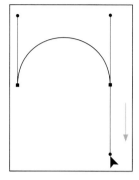

Try another curve:

1 Move the pen tool to the beginning of the second curve. Drag up about half an inch.

2 Position the pen tool on the second anchor point and drag down about half an inch to align the curve to the template.

This completes the first segment of the more complex curve.

3 Move the pen to the third anchor point, then press and drag up another half-inch to create the second curve.

4 Finish tracing the outline by positioning the pointer on each numbered point and dragging to create the curves.

If you want to start over, press the Delete key once to delete the last segment and twice to delete the whole curve.

5 Click the pen tool in the toolbox to indicate that you have completed the path.

Editing a curved path

Once you've drawn a curved path, you can use the anchor points and direction lines to edit the shape of the path.

As you read along, try out these curve-editing techniques on either of the paths that you just created:

1 Click the arrow tool in the Paths palette.

2 To move individual anchor points, select them with the pointer, then drag to a new position, just as you did when you were editing the straight path.

3 To move a segment of a path, click a line segment with the arrow tool, then drag it to the new position.

4 To change the height or length of a curved path, drag the direction points. Try dragging the second direction point up and notice how the curve gets taller; dragging the same direction point down shortens the curve.

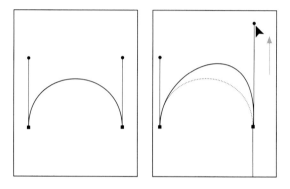

5 To change the slant of the curve, drag the direction points to the left and right.

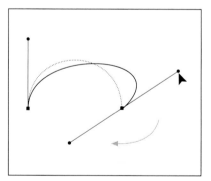

6 To move the entire path, use the arrow tool to drag a selection marquee around the path to select the anchor points. Once the path is selected, you can drag it anywhere in the document window.

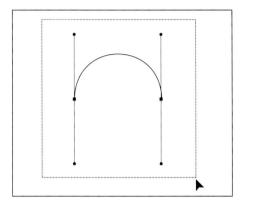

7 To deselect the path, click in the white area away from the path in the document window. The direction lines disappear but you can still see the path. To reselect a path, simply click on the path.

Take a minute to practice drawing curves. After you finish practicing, close the *04Paths* file without saving changes.

8 Click the close box in the upper-left corner of the *04Paths* window, then click Don't Save.

DRAWING THE TOP BORDER

Now you're ready to add the rest of the border. Although you can have multiple paths in a file, only one path is visible at a time. Once a path is saved and is the target path, any additions, deletions, or editing changes you make are saved under that path name. This means that as you draw the top border, it becomes part of the Border Path.

The top border consists of both straight segments and curved segments. First you'll set the anchor points for the straight segments.

To begin the top border:

1 Click the *Border Path* thumbnail in the Paths palette to display the Border Path.

The Border Path is now the target path and everything you draw becomes a part of that path.

2 Click the pen tool in the Paths palette.

3 Click inside the upper-right corner of the window to begin adding to the path.

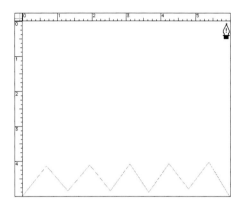

4 Press the Shift key, then click the upper-left corner to make the first straight segment run across the top of the window.

5 Move the pointer down along the left edge of the window to about the 2½-inch marker on the left ruler, press the Shift key, and click once more.

To draw the curved path segment:

1 Move the pointer so that it is at the 1¼-inch marker on the left ruler and at the 2½-inch marker on the top ruler.

2 Drag the pointer up and to the right.

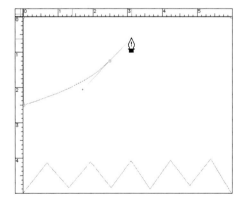

As you drag, the direction line appears.

3 Position the pen so that it's at about the 5¼-inch marker on the top ruler and at the three-eighths inch marker on the left ruler, then drag a short distance to the right to set another point.

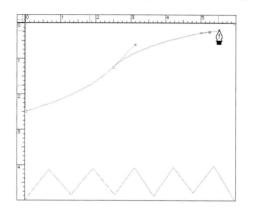

4 Move the pointer slightly down and to the right edge of the window, then click to add a straight segment to the path.

5 Close the path by clicking the first anchor point in the upper-right corner of the window.

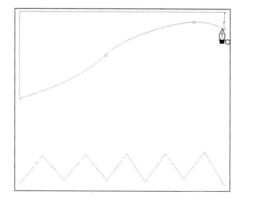

6 Click the arrow pointer in the Paths palette and click the anchor point in the middle of the curve to make the direction line reappear.

7 Drag the direction points to adjust the slope of the curve until it looks similar to the path shown below.

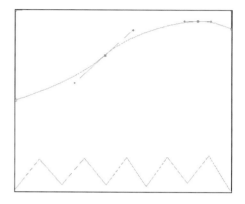

Notice that the slope of the direction line for the first anchor point is rather steep; the slope of the direction line for the second anchor point is flatter.

8 Repeat step seven for editing the other anchor points if needed.

Only the top part of the path is currently selected. This is because the path consists of two *subpaths*.

In this example, the two parts of the border are the *path*; the top part of the border and the bottom part of the border are each called *subpaths*.

9 Click anywhere in the window outside the paths to deselect the top subpath.

You don't have to save again because the new part of the path is automatically saved as part of the *Border Path*. To see that both borders are part of the Border Path, you're going to deselect the path and then make it visible again.

10 Click anywhere in the white area of the Paths palette (don't click the path name). You will still see the path in the path thumbnail.

The path disappears from the *04Work* window and the highlight disappears from the Border Path name in the Paths palette.

11 Click Border Path in the Paths palette.

The path (with both subpaths included) appears in the window.

FILLING THE PATH

Paths, like selections, can be filled with the foreground color or a pattern. To fill this path, you're going to learn a new way to create a color.

To fill the path:

1 Uncollapse the Swatches palette by double-clicking the Swatches palette tab.

2 Click the medium blue swatch in the fourth row of the Swatches palette (the sixth swatch from the right).

3 Click the Picker palette tab to display the Picker palette.

The Picker palette contains a foreground and background color selection box, a color bar you can use to select colors, and three sliders.

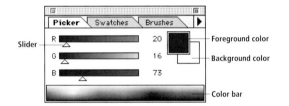

Although you might think of the new foreground color as "blue," it actually consists of a mix of the three primary colors—red, green, and blue (often abbreviated as *RGB*). The numbers to the right of the sliders in the Picker palette show the values for each component: 92 for red (R), 106 for green (G), and 166 for blue (B).

4 Drag the red slider to the left until it reads about 20, the green slider until it reads about 16, and the blue slider until it reads about 73.

As you move the sliders, the color in the foreground color selection box changes to reflect the new values. Don't worry about selecting exactly the same values. The resulting color should be a deep, rich blue.

You will use the Fill Path button at the far left of the bottom of the Paths palette to fill the border. (You may need to move a palette to see the button).

5 Click the Fill Path button.

The path is filled with your custom foreground color.

Note: If only one subpath is filled with color, the subpath was selected in the document window. To fill the entire path with color, deselect the path in the document window by clicking in the white area, then click the Fill Path button again.

Once you fill a path with a color, the colored pixels become part of the target layer. The outline of the border is stored in the Paths palette.

4 Click the zoom tool, and zoom in on the left side of the pepper.

5 Click the pencil tool and select the second brush from the left in the top row of the Brushes palette.

6 Using this fine brush, color the edges of the pepper green.

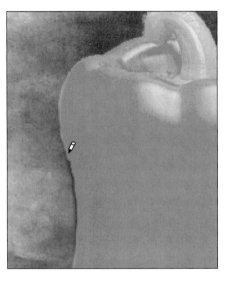

Use short strokes, so you can easily undo part of the painting if necessary. The areas you paint turn green, adding them to the mask. Don't worry about outlining the exact shape of the pepper.

7 Use the Spacebar to access the hand tool then move around in the image and paint until all the red edges and highlights of the pepper have been added to the mask.

8 Use the spacebar and the Option key to zoom out.

9 Click the Standard mode control in the toolbox to leave Quick Mask mode.

10 Choose Inverse from the Select menu to make the pepper the selected area.

USING THE COMMANDS PALETTE

In the last few lessons, you've used the Inverse command quite a bit. You've found that often it's more useful to select the areas you don't want, and then inverse the selection. The Inverse command does not have a preassigned Command-key shortcut.

Adobe Photoshop allows you to assign function-key shortcuts and buttons to any command in a menu, submenu, or palette pop-up menu using the Commands palette. If your keyboard does not have function keys, you can still use this palette.

You're going to use the Inverse button and assign a function key and button to the Save Selection and Load Selection commands using the Commands palette.

To use the Commands palette:

1 Choose Palettes from the Window menu and Show Commands from the submenu.

The Commands palette appears. If you don't have function keys, you can use the Commands palette buttons to choose frequently used commands.

Commands	▶
Undo	F1
Cut	F2
Copy	F3
Paste	F4
Hide Brushes	F5
Hide Picker	F6
Hide Layers	F7
Show Info	F8
Hide Commands	F9
Fill	⇧F5
Feather	⇧F6
Inverse	⇧F7

Many function keys already have commands assigned to them.

The Inverse command is currently assigned to the Shift-F7 key combination.

2 Click the Inverse button to activate the Inverse command.

3 In the *04Pepper* window, try out the Shift-F7 function key and Inverse button. Make sure the pepper is selected when you've finished experimenting.

Now you'll assign the Save Selection command to a function key.

To assign a function key:

1 Choose New Command from the Commands palette pop-up menu. The New Command dialog box appears.

2 Choose Save Selection from the Select menu in the document menu bar.

3 Choose F10 from the Function Key pop-up menu.

4 Choose Red from the Color menu, then click OK.

The Save Selection command appears as a red button on the Commands palette.

5 Press F10 (or click the Save Selection button), then click OK to save the pepper selection.

Now assign the Load Selection command to the F11 function key.

To create another function key command:

1 Choose New Command from the Commands palette pop-up menu.

2 Choose Load Selection from the Select menu in the document menu bar.

3 Choose F11 from the Function Key pop-up menu.

4 Choose Blue from the Color menu, then click OK.

You'll use your new command in the next part of the lesson.

You can reassign current function key commands by choosing Edit Commands from the Commands palette pop-up menu. You can also save and load separate sets of commands for different types of projects.

WORKING WITH CHANNELS

Quick Mask mode temporarily creates a mask, but unless you save the mask as a selection, the mask disappears when you make another selection. You needed to save this mask in a channel because you will to use it again when you duplicate the pepper a second time.

The channels that Adobe Photoshop assigns to images are analogous to the plates used in the printing process. For example, images created using the default RGB mode have three channels—one for the red color, one for the green color, and one for the blue color.

As mentioned in Lesson 2, saved selections are also stored in channels. The channels you create to store selections are sometimes called *alpha channels*. A file can have as many channels as needed, but each channel increases the file size by about one-third.

To display the channels in an image:

1 Click the Channels palette tab in the Layers/Channels/Paths group of palettes. The Channels palette pops to the front.

You are currently looking at the composite channel (RGB) that shows all the color information for the image. The eye icons indicate that you are viewing the channel. You can show or hide a channel by clicking in the eye icon column, just as you do with the Layers palette.

2 Click the eye icon for the red channel.

The image changes so that now you're looking only at the blue and green information, although any editing changes would still affect the red channel. Viewing and editing individual channels lets you make very specific and subtle adjustments to an image. You'll learn more about using individual channels in Lesson 7.

3 Click the left column for the red channel again to return to the composite view of the image.

Anytime the red, blue, and green channels are all visible, you are automatically looking at the composite view of the image.

ADDING NEW CHANNELS

Although you may not realize it, you already know how to create new channels. Anytime you save a selection, Adobe Photoshop automatically creates a new channel (remember channel #4 and the New channel in the Save Selection dialog box?). Now you're going to learn how to name the channels you create. The alpha channels you create are 8-bit grayscale channels within the document.

To name a channel:

1 Click the zoom box in the upper-right corner of the palette to expand the palette to full size.

Notice that a channel, assigned the number 4, appears in the Channels palette (any channels you create are automatically numbered sequentially).

When you clicked the new Save Selection button, you created a channel that was named #4.

2 Choose None from the Select menu to deselect the marquee.

3 Click #4 in the Channels palette to view the new channel.

Clicking a channel name makes it the only visible and editable channel. The #4 grayscale channel appears, showing you the mask you created. If you've worked with traditional masks, this image probably looks familiar. The white areas are transparent and are affected by any changes you make. The black areas are opaque and are protected from change.

4 Choose Channel Options from the Channels palette pop-up menu.

As in the Quick Mask mode, you can reverse these black-and-white settings by clicking the Selected Areas option in the Channel Options dialog box. Leave the setting at Masked Areas for now.

5 Name the channel **Pepper** and click OK.

The name appears in the Channels palette.

Editing a channel

After examining a saved selection in a channel, you may find that it needs to be cleaned up. You can use the painting and editing tools to edit a mask in its channel.

To edit the channel:

1 Reset the foreground and background colors to the default colors of black and white.

2 Click the paintbrush tool, and select a medium brush with hard edges from the Brushes palette.

3 Use black paint to eliminate any white speckles you see in the black areas of the channel.

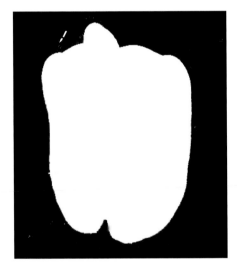

4 If needed, use the eraser tool to clean up the white areas of the channel. The eraser uses the background color of white.

5 Click RGB in the Channels palette (or press Command-zero) to return to the composite view.

6 Click F11 (or click the Load Selection button in the Commands palette), choose Pepper from the Channel submenu, then click OK.

The shape of the selection marquee changes slightly after you edit a channel.

You've already saved selections using the Save Selection command and button. Another way to save a selection is to click the Save Selection button at the bottom of the Channels palette.

Although it's a good idea to save complex selections in additional channels, channels do increase the size of your file. If you don't have much disk space, you might want to delete channels or save them to another file before saving your document.

7 Choose Save As from the File menu.

8 Type **04Work2** as the file name.

9 Open the Projects folder, then click Save.

10 Collapse the Brushes palette.

DRAGGING A SELECTION FROM ONE FILE TO ANOTHER

Now you're ready to paste the pepper selection into your *04Work* file. In addition to using the Copy and Paste commands to duplicate selections, you can *drag and drop* selections from one file to another.

To drag a copy of the pepper:

1 Position the *04Work2* window to the right of the *04Work* window so that the two windows are side by side and you can see some of the contents of both windows (they can overlap).

2 Click the *04Work2* window to make it the active window, then click the move tool in the toolbox.

3 Click the move tool, then position it over the pepper selection.

4 Drag the pepper selection from the *04Work2* window to the middle of the *04Work* window. (You will not see the pepper, just a rectangular outline of the selection. Don't worry about positioning the pepper right now.)

The *04Work* window becomes the active window and the pepper appears in front of the border as a floating selection.

5 Click the Layers palette tab to bring the Layers palette to the front of the group.

The pepper needs to go behind the border. To work with both elements independently, you will create a new layer.

Dragging a selection to create a new layer

In Lesson 2, you learned how to use the Make Layer command to turn a floating selection into a new layer. You can also create new layers by dragging the Floating Selection thumbnail to the New Layer icon.

1 Drag the Floating Selection thumbnail in the Layers palette to the New Layer icon at the bottom of the Layers palette.

2 In the Make Layer dialog box type **Pepper 1** for the layer name and click OK. The Pepper 1 layer thumbnail appears as the target layer.

In your final image you want the pepper to be *behind* the border. Use the Layers palette to move the Pepper 1 layer below the Graphic Border layer.

3 Drag the Pepper 1 layer thumbnail down until it's between the Graphic Border and Background thumbnails in the Layers palette.

The border appears in front of the pepper.

ROTATING A SELECTION

In addition to dragging, another way to change the position of a selection or layer is to use the Rotate command. Since the pepper is in its own layer, you don't need a selection marquee around the pepper. (In a layer, the painted areas are automatically selected when you select the layer.)

To rotate an area:

1 Choose *04Final* from the Window menu to use the final file as reference for the amount of rotation to use.

2 Click the *04Work* file and make sure the Pepper 1 layer is the target layer.

3 Choose Rotate from the Image menu and Free from the submenu.

A box appears around the pepper with four corner handles.

4 Drag the upper-left handle down until the pepper is tilted at a slight angle (use the angle of the left pepper in the final image as a guide).

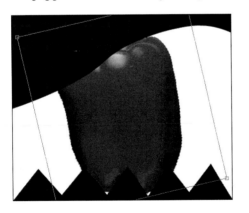

Be patient! It takes a few seconds for Adobe Photoshop to show you a preview of the new orientation. You can keep adjusting the handles until you have the angle you want.

If you move the cursor around in the image and pass it over the rotation box, you'll notice two cursors. When you're inside the box, you see a *gavel icon*. When you're outside the box, you see the *No icon*. Clicking when the gavel icon is visible (inside the box) confirms the rotation; clicking when the No icon is visible (outside the box) lets you change your mind and cancel the rotation.

5 Click with the gavel icon inside the pepper to rotate the image.

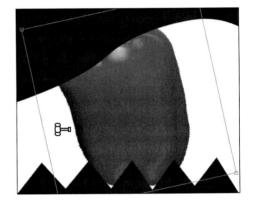

6 Click the move tool in the toolbox.

7 Drag the pepper down until it is almost one-quarter of an inch from the left ruler and the tip of the pepper stem is slightly below the 2½-inch marker on the left ruler.

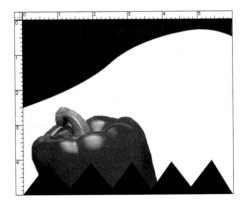

8 Choose Save from the File menu (or press Command-S).

POSTERIZING THE IMAGE

The Posterize command lets you change the number of gray levels (or brightness values) for an image. In effect, this produces large, flat areas in an image.

To posterize the pepper:

1 Choose Map from the Image menu and Posterize from the submenu. The Posterize dialog box appears.

2 Drag the dialog box so you can see how the pepper changes.

3 Type **3** for the number of levels and click the Preview option.

4 Click OK to posterize the layer.

DRAGGING AND DROPPING THE SECOND PEPPER

Now follow the same steps to drag and drop a copy of the second pepper into the image, rotate it, and posterize it.

To drag and drop the pepper:

1 Choose *04Work2* from the Window menu.

2 The pepper should still be selected, but if it isn't, click F11 (or click the Load Selection button in the Commands palette), and click OK.

3 With the move tool, drag the pepper selection from the *04Work2* window to the middle of the *04Work* window.

4 This time, create a new layer by double-clicking the Floating Selection thumbnail.

5 Type **Pepper 2** for the layer name, then click OK.

6 The new layer (Pepper 2) appears directly above the Pepper 1 layer and becomes the target layer.

7 Choose *04Work2* from the Window menu, then choose Close from the File menu.

8 Make sure that the *04Work* file is selected, then choose Rotate from the Image menu, then Free from the submenu.

9 Drag the upper-right corner of the rotate box to rotate the pepper using the final file as a reference, then click the gavel to rotate the pepper.

10 Position the pepper so that the tip of the stem is at about the 4¼ inches from the left ruler and about 1¼ inches from the top ruler (part of the pepper will extend beyond the right edge and bottom of the window).

11 Choose Map from the Image menu and Posterize from the submenu. Posterize the selection using 3 Levels, then click OK.

Working in layers

By creating a new layer for each graphic element, you give yourself a lot of flexibility in designing your document. Experiment with switching the order of the pepper layers.

To rearrange the layers:

1 Click the zoom box in the Layers palette to show all the layers.

2 Drag the Pepper 2 layer thumbnail down between the Pepper 1 and Background layers.

The left pepper moves in front of the right pepper.

3 Drag the Pepper 2 layer thumbnail back above the Pepper 1 layer thumbnail.

Merge the two pepper layers to conserve disk space.

4 Click the eye icon for the Background and Graphic Border layers to hide them. You should only see the two pepper layers.

5 Choose Merge Layers from the Layers palette pop-up menu.

The layers take on the name of the bottom layer. To edit the layer name, double-click the layer thumbnail.

6 Double-click the Pepper 1 layer thumbnail in the Layers palette. The Layer Options dialog box appears. You'll be using this dialog box more in Lesson 5.

7 Type **Peppers** for the new layer name, then click OK.

8 Option-click the eye icon next to the Peppers layer to show the rest of the layers.

DRAWING A NON-CONTIGUOUS PATH

The path you drew for the border consisted of a set of continuous connected lines. You can also draw a path that is a series of segments. To finish the border on this image, you're going to draw a non-contiguous path.

To draw the path:

1 Click the Graphic Border layer thumbnail in the Layers palette to make it the target layer.

The lines will become part of the Graphic Border layer.

2 Click the Paths palette tab, then click the pen tool in the Paths palette.

3 Click the white area in the Paths palette (below the Border Path) to deselect the current path as you begin a new border.

4 Click in the lower-left corner of the image, about one-quarter of an inch to the left of the first triangle.

5 Click the next point near the tip of the first triangle. This creates the first path segment.

6 Click the pen tool in the Paths palette to end that segment.

7 Click slightly to the right of the first triangle tip, then click near the bottom of the triangle.

8 Click the first point in this segment to close the segment. You will see the loop that indicates closing a path.

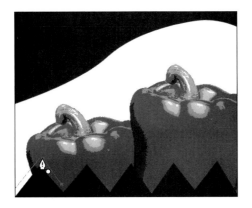

There are two ways to end a path segment; you can either click the first anchor point in the segment, or click the pen tool before beginning the next segment. If you don't end a segment, a line will always be drawn between the last two points you clicked.

9 Continue drawing the segments until you've outlined the bottom border.

The exact location of the segments isn't important; use your own creative judgment.

10 Choose Save Path from the Paths palette pop-up menu and type **Lines** for the Path name, then click OK.

The new path thumbnail appears in the Paths palette.

11 Choose Save from the File menu (or press Command-S).

STROKING A PATH

Stroking a path allows you to paint color along the path border. You can choose to apply the paint with any of the painting tools in the toolbox and any of the brush shapes in the Brushes palette.

To stroke the path:

1 Click the eyedropper tool, then click in the pepper stem to sample the green as the new foreground color.

2 Click the paintbrush tool in the toolbox.

3 Double-click the Brushes palette tab, then double-click the second brush from the left in the top row of the Brushes palette to display the Brush Options dialog box. Make sure the diameter is set to 3, set the hardness to 0, and make sure the spacing to 25 percent, then click OK.

4 Click the Stroke Path button at the bottom of the Paths palette.

The path is outlined in green paint.

5 Click a blank area in the Paths palette scroll box to deselect the path.

Since changes to the current path are automatically saved, if you don't deselect the path you'll add to the *Lines* path the next time you begin drawing with the pen tool.

FILLING A SUBPATH

You might remember that when you created the *Border* path it consisted of two subpaths—the top border and the bottom border. To achieve more balance in this image, you're going to fill the top subpath with a different color.

To fill a subpath:

1 Click the Layers palette tab.

2 Make sure that the Graphic Border layer is the target layer.

3 Click the Paths palette tab, then click the Border Path thumbnail to make it the target path.

4 With the arrow tool in the Paths palette selected, click the edge of the top subpath to display its anchor points.

5 Click the Picker palette tab, then create a foreground color with an R value of about 199, a G value of about 199, and a B value of about 38.

6 Click the Fill Path button on the Paths palette.

The khaki color replaces the dark blue of the former fill in the top subpath.

7 Choose Save from the File menu (or press Command-S).

FILLING A SUBPATH WITH A PATTERN

Paths are independent of layers. You can use paths with different layers to experiment with various design elements. In the next section, you will create a new layer, and use the Border subpath to create a fill with a pattern.

1 Click the Layers palette tab, then click the New Layer icon.

2 Type **Border Pattern** for the name, then click OK.

The new layer becomes the target layer.

3 Click the Paths palette tab and make sure the Border Path is selected.

4 Press the Option key, then click the Fill Path button in the Paths palette.

The Fill Path/Subpath dialog box appears.

The Fill Path and Stroke Path buttons in the Paths palette use the previously defined settings to fill and stroke paths. If you press the Option key, you can access the dialog box.

5 Select White from the Contents menu, then click OK.

The top border is filled with white. You'll now fill the white border with a black pattern.

6 Choose Open from the File menu, then open the *Intricate Surface* file in the Lesson 4 folder. Accept the EPS Rasterizer default values and click OK to display the file.

7 Choose All from the Select menu to select the entire image.

8 Choose Define Pattern from the Edit menu to copy the pattern to the pattern buffer, then close the file, without saving changes.

9 Choose Fill Subpath from the Paths palette pop-up menu to access the Fill Path dialog box (or you can Option-click on the Fill Paths button).

10 Choose Pattern from the Contents menu, make sure that the opacity is set to 100 percent and the mode is set to Normal, then click OK.

The new layer fills the white border with a black pattern, obscuring the layer underneath. Experiment with turning the Border layer off and on.

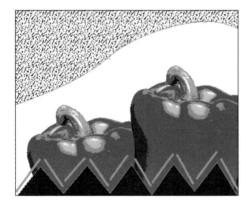

11 Click the Layers palette tab, then click the eye icon for the Border Pattern layer to hide it.

You can create different elements in separate layers to explore a variety of design effects.

Using Layer Modes

The Mode menu in the Layers palette is similar to the painting modes you worked with in Lesson 2. The layer modes blend colors between layers, instead of within one selection.

To use the layer modes:

1 Click the left column for the Border Pattern to show the layer.

2 Make sure the Border Pattern layer is the target layer.

3 In the Layers palette, click Normal in the Mode menu and choose Lighten.

The Lighten option blends the layers so that only pixels that are darker than the underlying color are changed. The white from the original pattern remains, and the black pixels in the pattern are lightened to the khaki green.

Since you are using different layers, you can easily experiment with different layer modes.

4 Try the Darken mode and some of the other modes in the Layers palette.

For a complete explanation of the effects of the different modes, see the *Adobe Photoshop User Guide.*

5 Make sure that the Lighten mode is the final mode you selected.

Now you'll merge the Graphic Border layer and the Border Pattern layer. First make sure only those layers are visible in the Layers palette.

6 Click the eye icons for the Background and Pepper layers in the left column of the Layers palette.

7 Choose Merge Layers from the Layers palette pop-up menu.

8 View all the layers by Option-clicking the eye icon.

9 Choose Save from the File menu (or press Command-S).

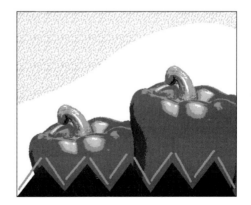

ADDING GRADIENT TYPE

In Lessons 2 and 3, you added opaque type to the images. In this image, you're going to fill the type with a gradient, then change the opacity of the type layer.

To add the type:

1 Click the type tool in the toolbox.

2 Click the insertion point in the upper-left corner of the image.

3 Choose Times Bold Italic from the Font pop-up menu and enter **42** points for the type size.

4 Enter **45** for the Leading option and **13** for the Spacing option, and make sure the Alignment option is set to Left.

If you've used the type tool in other applications, you're probably familiar with these two options. Leading, or *line spacing*, is the measurement from baseline to baseline. Spacing, or *kerning*, controls the spacing between letters.

5 Type **pimientos** in the first line of the text box, press Return, insert three blank spaces, and type **rescos** in the second line. Both words should be in lowercase. (You'll add the *f* for *frescos* in a minute.)

The blank characters in the second line are there to space the type correctly, and leave room for the *f*, which will be in a different style and type size. (You can only choose one font and style at a time.)

6 Click OK to close the dialog box.

The text appears as a floating selection that is filled with the current foreground color.

7 Double-click the Floating Selection thumbnail, type **Text** for the new layer name, then click OK.

8 The selection marquee disappears and the Text layer becomes the target layer.

9 Click the move tool and position it over the bottom of the *p* in *pimientos*, then drag until the bottom of the letter is at the three-quarters-inch marker on the left ruler and the half-inch marker on the top ruler.

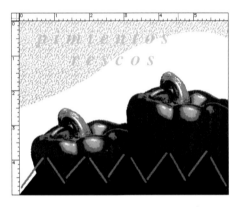

Filling type with a gradient

To fill the type, you must first choose the foreground and background colors for the gradient.

To fill the type:

1 Use the eyedropper to sample the bright red surrounding the highlights in a pepper for the foreground color.

2 Hold down the Option key and sample the blue in the bottom border for the background color.

3 Click the gradient tool.

4 Click the Preserve Transparency checkbox in the Layers palette.

Since there is no selection marquee, using the Preserve Transparency option protects the transparent areas of the text layer from being filled with the gradient.

5 Drag diagonally from the top of the *m* in *pimientos* to the bottom of the *c* in *rescos*.

The type is filled with the gradient.

6 Drag the Opacity slider on the Layers palette to 80 percent.

You should be able to see the border pattern through the gradient fill.

COMBINING FONTS IN TYPE

You often want the type in a design to be uniform and easy to read, so that the type does not distract from the graphic impact of the image. Sometimes, however, you can use the type as a design element itself, by combining different fonts, styles, and sizes. In this display sign, the type is more graphic than informational. You're going to complete the sign by adding the flowing *f* in the second line of type.

To add the remaining character:

1 Click the type tool, then click the insertion point to the left of the *r* in *rescos*.

2 Set the font to Times Italic, and the size to 90 points. Leading and Spacing should be blank.

3 Type a lowercase **f** in the text box, and click OK.

4 Turn off the Preserve Transparency option to see the text in the foreground color.

The Preserve Transparency option prevents a selection of a transparent area from being filled with a color.

5 With the move tool, drag the *f* until its top edge is under the left edge of the *m* in *pimientos*.

Use the placement in the reference file as a guide. None of the letter should extend below the top border.

6 Choose None from the Select menu (or press Command-D).

Since the floating selection was above the text layer, it becomes part of the text layer when it's deselected.

7 Choose Save from the File menu (or press Command-S).

8 Choose Save a Copy from the File menu, name the file **04WorkL** (*L* for *Layers*), make sure the Projects folder is open, then click Save.

9 Choose Flatten Image from the Layers palette pop-up menu.

The layers are merged and the size of the file is reduced. You still have a copy of the file with layers, in case you want to make changes later.

10 Choose Close from the File menu and close each open file.

You've come a long way! In just four lessons you've learned how to create a very professional-looking piece of art. Along the way, you've built up quite a working knowledge of paths, masks, and channels.

Lesson

5

Lesson 5: Manipulating Selections and Layers

This lesson marks your leap from beginning to experienced Adobe Photoshop user. In this lesson, you'll make selections from five different files and paste them into a new file to create a composite image. As part of building this image, you'll refine your pasting and selecting skills, work more with multiple layers, and learn more about using the pen tool, stroking, and filling. It should take you about two hours to complete this lesson.

Source file (05Aspg)

In this lesson, you'll learn how to do the following:

- scale a selection
- change the hue and saturation of a selection
- apply filters to selections
- stroke a selection
- increase the canvas size of an image
- make selections using the pen tool
- defringe a selection
- adjust a selection's brightness and contrast
- flip a selection
- reduce the size of an image
- paint with a pattern

Source file (05Plate)

Source file (05Veg)

At the end of this lesson you'll have created the cover for an informative food brochure that Gourmet Visions is distributing as a public service to its customers. The source graphics for this cover art include both line art and full-color continuous-tone images.

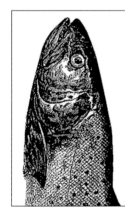

Source file (05Fish)

Ending image (05Final)

BEGINNING THIS LESSON

As in the last lesson, you will throw away your preferences file, then open a new file and the final image for this lesson.

To reset the program's defaults:

1 Quit Adobe Photoshop.

2 Locate and drag the *Adobe Photoshop 3.0 Prefs* file to the Trash, then empty the Trash.

If you can't find the file, choose Find from the desktop File menu, enter **Adobe Photoshop 3.0 Prefs** in the text box, and click Find.

3 Launch the Adobe Photoshop program.

To begin this lesson:

1 Choose Open from the File menu, then open the *05Final* file in the Lesson 5 folder.

2 Choose Show Rulers from the Window menu (or press Command-R).

3 Make sure that the Layers palette is visible, then click the zoom box in the upper-right corner of the palette.

The final file contains seven layers: the white Background layer, the Square layer containing the textured graphic element, the Asparagus layer, the Veggies layer, the Fish layer, the Border layer and the Text layer.

4 Choose Zoom Out from the Window menu, then drag the window to the upper-right corner of your screen.

5 Choose New from the File menu, type **05Work** for the file name, and enter **4.6** inches for the width and **4.6** inches for the height.

6 Leave the resolution at 72, the mode at RGB Color and the contents White, then click OK.

7 Choose Save As from the File menu, open the Projects folder, then click Save.

Organize the palettes

In this lesson you will create one palette group that contains all the palettes that you will use during the lesson.

To reorganize the palettes:

1 Click the Picker palette tab, then drag the Picker palette tab on top of the Layers/Channels/Paths palette.

2 Close the Swatches/Scratch palette by clicking the close box in the upper-left corner.

3 Drag the Options palette tab on top of the Layers/Channels/Paths palette to add it to the group, then drag the Brushes palette on top of the palette group.

4 Click the Layers palette tab.

If you are working with a small monitor, it may be easier to consolidate palettes into one or two groups.

5 Choose Palettes from the Window menu and Show Commands from the submenu.

CREATING THE TEXTURED SQUARE

Your first step is to design a graphic element for the bottom half of the cover. The graphic starts as a straightforward selection from a photograph of asparagus and ends as an interesting textured pattern.

To copy the selection from file to file:

1 Choose Open from the File menu, then open the *05Aspg* file in the Lesson 5 folder.

2 Drag the window to the right of the *05Work* window (it will temporarily cover the *05Final* file).

3 Click the rectangular marquee tool and press down the Shift key as you select about a three-quarter-inch square section of the asparagus from the upper third of the bunch.

The exact location of the selection doesn't matter; in fact, the final effect will be unique to the selection you make. Just be sure the selection includes some light and dark areas. If you need to change the selected area, hold down the Command and Option keys and drag the selection border.

4 Drag the selection from the *05Aspg* file to the *05Work* window. The selection is copied into the *05Work* file.

5 Choose *05Final* from the Window menu to bring it in front of the *05Aspg* window, then click the *05Work* window to make it active.

6 You want to leave the Background layer solid white, so double-click the Floating Selection thumbnail in the Layers palette, type **Square** for the name of the new layer, then click OK.

A new layer named *Square* appears in the Layers palette and the image is deselected.

7 Click the move tool and drag the image until it's near the upper-right corner of the window.

8 Use the up arrow and right arrow keys to move the layer until it's flush with the top and right edges of the window.

Each press of an arrow key moves the selection one pixel. This lets you get to the exact edge of the window without inadvertently losing part of the layer outside the top or right side of the window.

SCALING THE IMAGE

Scaling lets you extend or shrink the length and width of a selection or layer element. Depending on the effect you're trying to achieve, you can keep the original proportions or distort the selection as you scale.

You're going to scale the selection so that it fills the entire window. Don't worry about the fact that this area is only a small part of the final image—you'll learn how to add the extra space later in this lesson.

To scale the selection:

1 Choose Effects from the Image menu and Scale from the submenu.

A box appears around the selection with four corner handles (you might remember these handles from the Rotate command).

2 Drag the lower-left handle down and to the left until the selection fills the window. A preview of the scaled selection appears.

3 Click with the gavel icon to confirm the scaling.

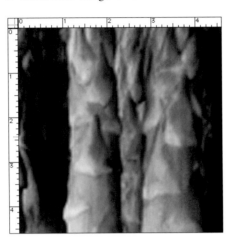

4 Choose Save from the File menu (or press Command-S).

ADJUSTING THE HUE AND SATURATION

Right now, the selection just looks like some stretched-out stalks of asparagus. For the food brochure, you'd like the background texture to be a bit more abstract. To achieve this touch of unreality, you're going to change the hue, saturation, and lightness of the selection.

Hue is the name of the color that places it in the correct location in the color spectrum. For example, a color with a blue hue is distinguished from a yellow, red, or green color.

Saturation refers to the clarity or degree of hue in a color. A neutral white, gray, or black doesn't have any saturation, so saturation is also a measure of how much a color differs from neutral gray. Less saturation produces a color closer to neutral; more saturation produces a color further from neutral.

Saturation is usually described using such words as *faint, pale, vivid,* or *strong*. For example, a selection might be dull red, bright red, or brilliant red depending on its saturation.

Lightness, or *brightness,* describes the intensity of light as it is reflected from, or transmitted by, the color. For example, hair color might be described as light brown, medium brown, or dark brown.

To change the hue, saturation, and lightness:

1 Choose Adjust from the Image menu and Hue/Saturation from the submenu (or press Command-U). The Hue/Saturation dialog box appears.

2 Drag the dialog box down to the bottom of the screen.

3 Drag the Hue slider to the right until it reads +63.

The asparagus takes on more of a neon green hue.

4 Drag the Hue slider all the way to the left until it reads −180.

Now the asparagus is a rather interesting (if unappetizing) purple hue. The hue values (in this case, +63 and −180) reflect the number of degrees of rotation around the color wheel that the new color is from the pixel's original color. A positive value indicates clockwise rotation; a negative value indicates counterclockwise rotation.

If you've used the AppleColor™ Picker, you're already familiar with the idea of the color wheel.

5 Return the Hue slider to 0.

6 Drag the Saturation slider to the right until it reads +56.

The asparagus increases in saturation and takes on an unreal glow as the colors become very intense.

7 Drag the Saturation slider to the left until it reads −56.

TIP: FOR A BRIEF
DESCRIPTION OF
EACH INSTALLED
FILTER, CHOOSE
ABOUT PLUG-IN FROM
THE APPLE MENU;
THEN CHOOSE THE
FILTER FROM THE
SUBMENU. CLICK TO
CLOSE THE
DESCRIPTION BOX.

The asparagus decreases in saturation and is now an almost gray, dull green. Dragging the Saturation slider to the right shifts the color *away* from the center of the color wheel. Dragging the slider to the left shifts the color *toward* the center of the color wheel. If you want to, take a few minutes to experiment with changing the hue and saturation in this Preview mode. It doesn't matter what values you end up with.

As this practice has shown you, you can invent a wide variety of colors by adjusting hue and saturation from the starting point of the selection's original color. Sometimes, however, when you want to dramatically change the color of a selection, it's easier to start from zero than to modify an existing color.

Colorizing the selection

The Colorize option lets you use the Hue and Saturation sliders to change a selection's color based on rotation from the 0-degree point on the color wheel (which is red). When you're using the Colorize option, positive numbers indicate counterclockwise motion and negative numbers indicate clockwise motion around the wheel.

To use the Colorize option:

1 Select the Colorize option.

The window turns red to indicate that the value you're specifying is a specific number of degrees from red in the color wheel. The hue is set to 0 and the saturation is set to 100.

2 Type **+41** into the Hue text box and leave the saturation at 100 percent.

The asparagus takes on a gold color, since gold is approximately 41 degrees from red (in a counterclockwise direction) on the color wheel.

3 Set the lightness to –27.

Changing the lightness setting provides a more muted golden color. Now this selection is close to the color needed for the final image.

4 Click OK to change the hue and lightness.

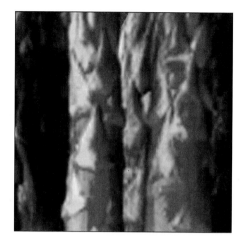

5 Choose Save from the File menu (or press Command-S).

FILTERING THE SELECTION

Filters provide one of the easiest and quickest ways to create visually exciting results. Adobe Photoshop comes with a wide variety of filters that let you produce some stunning special effects. Plug-in filters for Adobe Photoshop are also available from third-party companies.

As the final step in creating your background texture, you're going to use a filter to add *noise* (pixels with randomly distributed color values) to the image.

To apply a filter:

1 Choose Noise from the Filter menu and Add Noise from the submenu. The Add Noise dialog box appears.

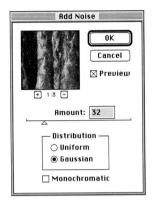

Several Adobe Photoshop filters let you preview the filter effect before applying the filter. Use the plus and minus buttons to change the preview box zoom ratio. If the section that you want to see is not visible, move the cursor inside the preview box to activate the hand tool. Drag the hand to move the preview.

2 Click the minus button two times to zoom out the preview thumbnail.

3 Make sure the amount is set to 32 and click the Gaussian option.

The Gaussian option distributes color values of noise along a bell-shaped curve. This multicolored effect is just what you want for the final background texture. (Click the Monochromatic checkbox if you want noise that only uses colors in your image.)

4 Click OK to apply the filter. Now you want to tone down the noise effect slightly.

5 Choose Stylize from the Filter menu and Diffuse from the submenu. The Diffuse dialog box appears.

6 Click Lighten Only, then click OK.

The Diffuse filter shuffles pixels to make a selection look less focused. The Lighten Only option replaces dark pixels with lighter pixels. As you can see, applying multiple filters allows you to create an even wider assortment of unique effects.

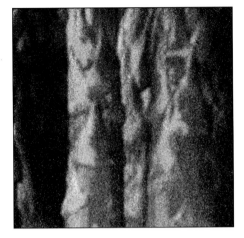

7 Choose Save from the File menu (or press Command-S).

STROKING A SELECTION

In the last lesson, you learned to stroke a path, which outlined the path with color. You can also stroke a selection to add a strip of color around the edge of the selection. You achieved this same effect in Lesson 3 by using the Select/Modify/Border command, but stroking a selection is faster.

Before you add the border, you're going to add a plate to the selection, then you'll stroke the entire image.

To copy the plate:

1 Make sure the Square layer is the target layer.

2 Choose Open from the File menu, then open the *05Plate* file in the Lesson 5 folder.

3 Double-click the magic wand tool and set the tolerance to 64, then click the magic wand anywhere in the gray area outside the plate.

Because of the distinct color differences, this produces an almost perfect selection of the entire background.

4 If you need to add to or subtract from the selection, use the lasso with the Shift key or the Command key. The silverware should not be included in the selection.

5 Choose Inverse from the Select menu (or click the Inverse button in the Commands palette) to select the plate.

6 Move the *05Plate* window to the right of the *05Work* window, then drag the selection from the *05Plate* file to the *05Work* file.

The plate is very large in relation to the rest of the image. This is because the resolution of the *05Plate* file is 144, while the resolution of the *05Work* file is 72. You'll learn more about resolution and resizing when you're cutting and pasting in Lesson 10.

7 Drag the selection down and to the right until you can't see the knife and fork (the top of the plate and the left edge of the plate should both be at about the 1-inch mark on the rulers).

8 Choose *05Plate* from the Window menu, then choose Close from the File menu to close the file.

9 Choose All from the Select menu to select the entire square image.

Now you're ready to add the border.

To stroke the selection:

1 If necessary, click the default colors icon to set the foreground color to black.

2 Choose Stroke from the Edit menu. The Stroke dialog box appears.

3 Enter **4** for the width and click the Inside option. Leave the opacity at 100 percent and the mode at Normal.

4 Click OK to stroke the selection.

A black border appears around the image. Since the selection fills the entire image, you want to start stroking from the inside edge of the selection and move in for a width of four pixels.

5 Choose Save from the File menu (or press Command-S).

TIP: YOU CAN ALSO
HOLD DOWN THE
COMMAND KEY WHILE
THE PEN TOOL IS
SELECTED TO DISPLAY
THE ARROW POINTER.

CHANGING THE CANVAS SIZE

As a final step in creating this part of the cover, you're going to add space around the image, so you will have room to add the vegetables that overlap the outside of the textured square. To add space, you increase the *canvas size*. The canvas area appears in the background color.

This increase in canvas size is an interim step toward the final size of the image (which will be the actual size of the brochure). As you're working with an Adobe Photoshop file, it's always a good idea to keep the file size as small as possible. Using a file that's bigger than you need slows down your procedures, especially when you're applying special effects like scaling and filters.

To add the canvas around the image:

1 Choose Canvas Size from the Image menu. The Canvas Size dialog box appears.

2 Enter **5.6** inches for the width and **5.6** inches for the height of the new canvas.

Look at the file size at the top of the Current Size and New Size boxes. Adding just an inch all the way around the image increases the file size from 321K to 476K.

3 The placement box indicates where you want to position the image in the new canvas area. Make sure the center placement box is selected, then click OK.

The new canvas is added to the edges of the image. As the finishing touch, you're going to create a slightly "underwater" look to this image.

4 Choose Distort from the Filter menu and Ripple from the submenu. The Ripple dialog box appears.

Experiment with the ripple settings while watching the preview thumbnail. Try entering the limit of **–999** or **999**.

5 Enter **30** for the amount and select the Large option to increase the ripple frequency, then click OK.

That's the look you want! The ripple is especially noticeable around the border.

(If you prefer to ripple just the border, choose Select All then use the Command key and the rectangular marquee to subtract the center of the square from the selection. You may need to experiment with the settings to get the look you want.)

Next you will add the asparagus stalks to the image.

6 Click the Layers palette tab, then click the New Layer icon.

7 Type **Asparagus** for the new layer name, then click OK.

8 Choose Save from the File menu (or press Command-S).

MAKING SELECTIONS WITH THE PEN TOOL

In the last lesson, you used the pen tool to draw freehand paths. You can also use the pen tool to draw irregularly shaped paths composed of curves and straight lines. These paths can then be saved as selections. The next element to be added to the brochure cover is an asparagus stalk, which you'll select using the pen tool.

To select using the pen tool:

1 Choose *05Aspg* from the Window menu (or click the window to make it active). If you've closed the *05Aspg* file, reopen it.

You're going to select the center stalk in the asparagus bunch. When you're making a complex selection like this, it's sometimes preferable to start with an approximation of the shape and then zoom in to edit the individual anchor points.

2 Choose None from the Select menu (or press Command-D).

3 Click the Paths palette tab, then click the pen tool.

You may need to move the Paths palette so that you can see the center asparagus stalk.

4 Starting at the very tip of the center stalk, click once to set the first anchor point.

5 Move down along the right edge of the stalk and drag to add a curved segment at the corner of the asparagus tip.

6 Move down about half an inch along the right edge of the stalk, and click to add another segment.

7 Move down about 2 inches and click to add a straight segment.

It's okay if this straight-line path segment cuts off part of the stalk. You'll come back and adjust this point later.

8 Continue adding straight segments until you have moved down the right side of the stalk, across the bottom of the stalk, and up the left edge. Stop when you are about equal with the curved segment on the right side (the second anchor point you clicked).

9 Drag to add a curved segment at this point, across from the other curved segment.

10 Close the path by clicking the first anchor point.

Editing the path

Since it takes a little practice to get used to the pen tool, you might not be totally happy with the selection border you've drawn.

Editing straight segments of the path is simple. You just click the arrow tool in the Paths palette and drag to adjust the anchor points.

The anchor points you use when drawing a curve are *smooth* anchor points (both points at the end of the direction line move in unison when you drag). When you want to modify the two halves of a direction line independently, you change the anchor point to a *corner* point (the direction points move independently). To understand how this works, try experimenting with editing a segment of the path at the top of the asparagus stalk.

To edit a curved segment:

1 Zoom in on the asparagus stalk so you can see the path clearly.

2 Select the arrow tool and click the anchor point for the curved segment (the second point you placed). The direction lines appear.

3 Drag either direction point.

Notice that the handles move in unison around the anchor point.

4 Click the corner tool in the Paths palette (the tool on the far right) and click the anchor point.

This turns the anchor point into a corner point with no direction lines.

5 Click the anchor point and drag to make the direction lines appear again.

6 Drag the top direction point.

Notice that the direction points now move independently, and you're adjusting either the segment on the path from the first anchor point or the segment leading from this anchor point. Once you release the direction point, the anchor point reverts to a smooth point (the direction points move in unison). Clicking the corner tool on an anchor point toggles the anchor point between a smooth point and a corner point.

7 Toggling between a corner point and a smooth point, drag the direction points until the curve is the way you want it.

8 Experiment with using the corner tool to toggle the anchor point of the curved segment on the left side of the stalk as you make adjustments to this curve.

You can also use the corner tool to make corrections to straight-line segments.

To edit a straight segment:

1 Select the corner tool from the Paths palette and click the third point you placed (you may need to scroll down to the one that is below the curved segment).

This turns the smooth point into a corner point so you can use direction lines to adjust the path.

2 Drag to make the direction lines appear, and adjust the point.

3 Toggle the anchor points a few times to see how the direction points switch between moving together and moving independently.

Adding and deleting points in a path

The pen tools with the plus and minus signs in the Paths palette allow you to add and delete points on a path.

To add and delete anchor points:

1 Click the pen+ tool in the Paths palette and move the pointer onto the path between two of the long straight segments along the stalk.

When you are directly over the path, a plus sign appears next to the pen pointer.

2 Click the path.

An anchor point with a direction line appears.

3 Add a few more anchor points to the path.

4 Click the pen- tool in the Paths palette and move the pointer over one of the anchor points you just added.

When you're directly over an anchor point, a minus sign appears next to the pen pointer.

5 Click to delete the anchor point from the path.

If you want to experiment with these tools, add and delete points until the path is the way you want it.

MAKING A PATH INTO A SELECTION

Once you have used the pen tool to make a path, you can convert the path to a selection. Use this capability if you want to copy and paste a selection or use any of the filters or image adjustment commands.

1 Click the Make Selection button that is third from the left in the bottom of the Paths palette.

2 Click the arrow tool, then click anywhere outside the path name in the Paths palette to deselect the path (the marquee will still surround the selection).

3 Click the Channels palette tab, then click the Save Selection button at the far left of the bottom of the Channels palette.

4 Double-click the #4 channel.

5 Type **Asparagus** for the name of the new channel, then click OK.

You will be copying this selection several times, and in case there's a problem with the copying, you wouldn't want to have to select this complex shape again.

6 Return to the composite view by clicking the RGB channel thumbnail.

7 Choose Save As from the File menu, open the Projects folder, and name the new file *05Aspg2* (saving now ensures that the selection is saved as part of the file).

8 Double-click the zoom tool to return to 1:1 view.

9 Click the move tool and drag the asparagus selection to the *05Work* file.

10 Select the *05Aspg2* file, then choose Close from the File menu. It's OK to close the file without saving the path since you've saved the *Asparagus* selection.

CHANGING OPACITY

You can change the opacity of layers and selections. Take a look at the final image. Using the opacity control, you are now going to create the "fade-away" look of the three asparagus stalks.

To position the first asparagus stalk:

1 Click the Layers palette tab.

2 The asparagus appears as a floating selection above the Asparagus layer. Choose Rotate from the Image menu and 90 degrees CW from the submenu.

3 Drag the selection up and to the left until its width is centered around the 1-inch marker on the left ruler and the tip of the stalk is at the 3-inch mark on the top ruler.

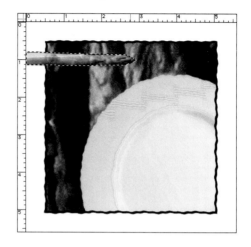

The first asparagus is totally opaque.

4 Click the move tool (or any selection tool in the toolbox).

5 Press the Option key and the Shift key, then drag the selected asparagus spear down until the top of the second stalk is about half an inch below the bottom of the first stalk.

Make sure that you release the mouse button *before* you release the Option key.

A copy of the selection is created.

When you press the Option key and drag you create a copy of the selection. This copying technique only works on floating selections. When you press the Shift key, you are constraining the movement to vertical, horizontal, or 45 degrees.

Changing the opacity of a selection

You can use the Layer palette opacity control to change the opacity of a selection or a layer.

To change the opacity of the selection:

1 Set the opacity in the Layers palette to 70 percent.

When there is a floating selection on a layer, the layer opacity controls only affect the selection.

2 Press the Option and the Shift key again and drag the selection down about half an inch under the second stalk.

3 Set the opacity for the third stalk to 45 percent.

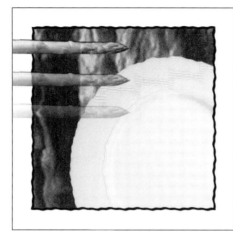

4 Choose None from the Select menu (or press Command-D).

5 Choose Save from the File menu (or press Command-S).

USING LAYER OPTIONS

Normally every pixel in a top layer is visible. Using the Layer Options command, you can indicate which pixels in the layer will replace the pixels in the underlying layer. This allows you to "composite" (or blend) the layer into the underlying image.

You're going to experiment with the Asparagus layer to see how Layer Options work.

Determining which pixels are visible:

1 Choose Layer Options from the Layers palette pop-up menu. The Layer Options dialog box appears.

2 Make sure the Preview option is checked, and drag the dialog box to the bottom of the screen so you can see the changes as you move the sliders.

3 Drag the black triangle under the *This Layer* slider to the right, until it reads 85.

The values of the pixels in a layer can range from 0 (black) to 255 (white). The This Layer slider controls which pixels in the layer are visible.

As you drag the triangle, the objects in the layer begin to break up and parts of them are no longer visible. Dragging the black triangle tells Adobe Photoshop not to display the pixels in the target layer that have values between 0 and 85 (these are the dark pixels).

4 Return the black triangle to 0 and drag the white triangle under the This Layer slider to the left, until it reads 165.

Notice that now the lighter pixels (those with values between 165 and 255) are not visible.

5 Return the white triangle to 255.

6 Drag the black triangle under the *Underlying* slider to the right, until it reads 64.

The Underlying slider determines which pixels in the underlying layer replace the pixels in the target layer. In this case, all the pixels in the underlying layers that have values between 0 and 65 replace the pixels in the target layer. You can see this clearly if you look at the border where it intersects the asparagus stalk. The border in the underlying layer cuts right through the stalks.

7 Return the black triangle to 0 and experiment with the white triangle under the Underlying slider, to see how the lighter pixels in the underlying image replace the pixels in the target layer.

Look at the border area again to see how the white canvas area replaces the bottom half of a stalk as soon as you begin to move the white triangle to the right.

The Layer Options dialog box also contains opacity and mode settings that affect the target layer. The opacity setting in the Layer Options dialog box controls the opacity of the entire target layer. The opacity setting on the Layers palette allows you to control the opacity of *selections*, as well as the opacity of the layer.

8 When you've finished exploring, click the Cancel button.

See the *Adobe Photoshop User Guide* for more information on Layer Options and opacity controls.

USING THE FEATHERING COMMAND

As you learned in Lesson 2, feathering blurs the edges of a selection by building a transition boundary between the selection and the surrounding pixels. You can feather the edges as you make a selection by using the Feather Radius option in the Marquee Options palette, as you did in Lesson 2.

You can also feather a selection after it is made, but before you copy and paste it. Feathering is apparent only when you modify a selection by cutting, moving, pasting, or filling it.

Anti-aliasing is another technique that softens the edges of a selection. See the *Adobe Photoshop User Guide* for a discussion and comparison of feathering and anti-aliasing.

To feather a selection:

1 Choose Open from the File menu, then open the *05Veg* file in the Lesson 5 folder.

In this file, both the radish and the tomato have been saved as selections.

2 Choose Load Selection from the Select menu and Radish from the Channel pop-up menu, then click OK.

3 Zoom in twice on the radish so you can see the feathering effect more clearly. The feathering will be particularly clear on the radish tail.

4 You may need to use the hand tool to see the tail of the radish.

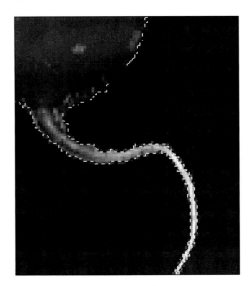

5 Choose Feather from the Select menu. The Feather Selection dialog box appears.

6 Enter **3** for the feather radius, then click OK.

This is too much feathering. You can see that the white section of the tail is no longer in the selection.

7 Double-click the zoom tool to zoom out to a 1:1 view.

8 Choose Undo Feather from the Edit menu, choose Feather again, enter **1** for the Feather Radius, then click OK.

9 To see the effects of the feathering more clearly, click the move tool, then drag the radish about half an inch to the left. You'll see the smooth transition border around the background of the radish.

10 Zoom in to see the feathering at the border of the selection, then double-click the zoom tool to return to a 1:1 view.

11 Choose Undo Move from the Edit menu.

This time, instead of dragging the selection to copy it to the new file, you'll use the Copy and Paste Layer commands.

12 Choose Copy from the Edit menu.

13 Choose *05Work* from the Window menu, then choose Paste Layer from the Edit menu.

14 In the Make Layer dialog box, type **Veggies** for the new layer name, then click OK.

The copied radish is dramatically out of proportion to the asparagus stalks. To make the relative sizes of the vegetables more realistic, you need to scale the radish layer.

MEASURING SCALING PERCENTAGES WITH THE INFO PALETTE

The Info palette provides information about the location of the pointer in the window and the color values of the pixel at the current pointer location. You'll learn more about using this palette to measure color in Lesson 7.

Depending on the tool you're using, the Info palette provides more than just the x and y coordinates of the pointer. It can also tell you dimensions, distance, angle of rotation, and percentage of scaling. You're going to use this scale information as you scale the radish selection.

To display the Info palette:

1 Choose Palettes from the Window menu and Show Info from the submenu (or click the Show Info button on the Commands palette). The Info palette appears.

2 Move the pointer around in the window and watch the x and y values change.

The pointer location is given in the current ruler units.

3 Choose Effects from the Image menu and Scale from the submenu.

The width and height measurements appear. They are the size of the selection

The radish is surrounded by the Effects box with four corner handles. Notice that two angle measurements appear at the bottom of the Info palette.

```
┌─────────────────────┐
│ ▦              ▦     │
│ ┌──────┐            │
│ │ Info │          ▶ │
│ └──────┘            │
│    R:      255      │
│ ⌇ G:      235      │
│    B:      140      │
│                     │
│    C:       3%      │
│ ⌇ M:       5%      │
│    Y:      56%      │
│    K:       0%      │
│    X:    2.528      │
│ ⌗ Y:    2.972      │
│    W:    2.069      │
│ ⌐ H:    2.694      │
│  ΔW:   100.0%      │
│  ΔH:   100.0%      │
└─────────────────────┘
```

4 Hold down the Shift key to constrain the scaling, and drag the lower-left handle up until the Info palette reads about 55 percent.

5 Click inside the selection with the gavel icon to confirm the scaling.

6 Click the move tool and then drag the radish to the upper-right corner of the background, so that the edges of the leaves slightly overlap the top border of the textured area. (Use the final image as a placement reference.)

ADJUSTING BRIGHTNESS AND CONTRAST

As the final step in adding the radish to the brochure cover, you're going to adjust the brightness and contrast of the selection, as you did in Lesson 2.

Brightness, as mentioned earlier, describes the intensity of light reflected from or transmitted through an image. *Contrast* is a measure of the tonal gradation between the highlights, midtones, and shadows in the selection or image.

To adjust the brightness and contrast:

1 Choose Adjust from the Image menu and Brightness/Contrast from the submenu (or press Command-B). The Brightness/Contrast dialog box appears.

2 Make sure the Preview option is selected, then drag the dialog box down, so you can see the changes as you move the sliders.

3 Experiment with brightness by dragging the slider to the left to decrease it, and to the right to increase it.

You can see that the radish gets dull, or more vivid, depending on the direction in which you drag.

4 Type in **24** to increase the brightness.

5 Experiment with the contrast by dragging its slider to the left to decrease it, and to the right to increase it.

Decreasing the contrast makes the green of the leaves closer to the red of the radish itself (both colors become more neutral). Increasing the contrast makes these two areas stand out more sharply.

6 Set the contrast to 24.

7 Click OK to put the settings into effect.

8 Choose Save from the File menu (or press Command-S).

DEFRINGING A SELECTION

When you paste a smooth-edged selection, some of the pixels surrounding the selection border are included with the selection. *Defringing* a selection replaces the color of any fringe pixels with the colors of nearby pixels in the selection that contain pure colors (pure colors don't contain any of the background color). You are going to defringe the tomatoes as you complete your assembly of vegetables for the brochure cover.

To defringe a selection:

1 Choose 05Veg from the Window menu.

2 Drag the *05Veg* window to the right so you can see both the *05Work* window and the *05Veg* window.

3 Click the *05Veg* window, and choose Load Selection from the Select menu.

4 In the Load Selection dialog box, select Tomato from the Channel menu, then click OK.

5 Drag the tomato selection to the *05Work* file.

You defringe a selection after it is pasted.

6 Marquee zoom in on the tomato.

7 Choose Hide Edges from the Select menu to hide the selection borders so you can see the changes as you defringe.

Look closely at the edges of the tomato (especially the green stem borders at the top). You can see that some of the black background from the *05Veg* file has been copied.

8 Choose Matting from the Select menu and Defringe from the submenu. The Defringe dialog box appears. Move the box if necessary so you can see the tomato.

9 Enter **2** for the width and click OK.

If the change was too subtle for you to see, choose Undo Defringe and Redo Defringe to look at the results again. The black around the edges of the selection is removed.

10 Choose Show Edges to display the selection border, then zoom out to the 1:1 view.

11 Click the move tool and drag the tomato until it is just about one-quarter inch under the bottom stalk of asparagus and overlaps the edge of the plate.

The Defringe command only works on a marqueed selection.

FLIPPING A SELECTION

You need to add one more tomato to the image. In addition to pasting and defringing this selection, you're going to add a little visual interest by flipping the second selection.

To flip a selection:

1 Click the *05Veg* file and drag another copy of the tomato over to the *05Work* file.

2 Choose Matting from the Select menu and Defringe from the submenu, then leave the width at 2, and click OK.

3 Choose Flip from the Image menu and Horizontal from the submenu.

The Horizontal option flips the selection along the vertical axis from left to right. You can see that the stem in the top selection is now pointing in the opposite direction and the tomato is angled to the left.

4 Drag the tomato down so that it is under the first tomato, leaving about three-eighths of an inch between the bottom of the first tomato and the red top of the second tomato.

5 Choose None from the Select menu (or press Command-D).

6 Change the opacity of the layer to 85 percent by using the Layers palette opacity slider.

Since the radishes and the tomatoes are on the same layer and there is no floating selection, all the elements on the layer change to 85 percent opacity.

7 Choose Save from the File menu (or press Command-S).

8 Select the *05Veg* window, then choose Close from the File menu. Do not save changes.

ADDING COLOR TO A BLACK-AND-WHITE IMAGE

The final healthy food group you're going to add to the brochure cover is protein—that is, the fish. The original fish image is a line-art drawing that you'll add color to after you copy it to the brochure cover file.

To fill using a mode:

1 Choose Open from the File menu, then open the *05Fish* file in the Lesson 5 folder.

2 Click the magic wand tool in the white area to select the background.

3 Choose Inverse from the Select menu.

4 Drag the *05Fish* window to the right of the *05Work* file.

5 Drag the fish selection to the *05Work* file.

6 Select the *05Fish* file, then choose Close from the File menu.

The floating selection of the fish image reflects the 85 percent opacity of the underlying layer.

7 Position the pointer on the fish's mouth and drag down until the top of the head is at the 2¾ inch marker on the left ruler, and the mouth is at the 3¾ inch marker on the top ruler.

8 Create a new layer for the fish image by double-clicking the Floating Selection thumbnail in the Layers palette.

9 Type **Fish** for the new layer name, then click OK.

The fish now reflects the 100 percent opacity of the new layer.

10 Click the Picker palette tab to change the foreground color. Set the R slider to 54, the G slider to 0, and the B slider to 61 to produce a dark violet color.

11 Choose Fill from the Edit menu. Make sure the Foreground Color option is selected, and the opacity is set to 100 percent.

12 Choose the Lighten mode from the Mode menu, click the Preserve Transparency checkbox, then click OK.

The Lighten mode fills only pixels that are darker than the foreground color. The lighter pixels do not change. Since there is no selection, the Preserve Transparency option protects the transparent areas of the layer from being filled with color.

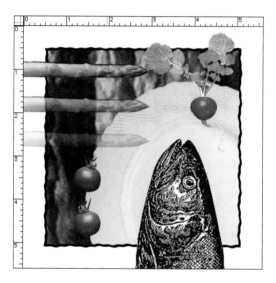

CHANGING THE IMAGE SIZE

With this selection completed, you have finished adding art to the brochure cover. Now you only need to add the top border and the type.

You have been working with the art as a 5.6-inch square image. In order to complete this project, you must resize the image so that it reflects the size of the art in the final brochure cover.

To resize the image:

1 If necessary, set the background color to white. The canvas you'll add appears in the background color.

2 Choose Image Size from the Image menu. The Image Size dialog box appears.

3 Make sure the Constrain Proportions option is checked and the Constrain File Size option is turned off.

If you constrain the file size when you resize an image, Adobe Photoshop makes sure that no pixel information is lost. This means that if you make an image smaller, the resolution is increased. If you make the image larger, the resolution is decreased. You'll learn more about the relationship between image size and resolution in Lesson 8.

Sometimes, especially when printing a color image, it's important that you keep all the pixel information, and you will want the File Size option to be on. In this case, it's okay to lose some information when you make the image smaller.

4 Enter **3.2** in the Width box.

Since the Proportions option is on, Adobe Photoshop automatically enters 3.2 in the Height box. Notice that the file size drops from 476K to 155K.

5 Click OK to resize the image.

With the art at the right size, you're ready to add the top border and type. In order to make room for these elements, you need to increase the canvas size until it approximates the actual size of the final brochure cover—3.5 inches wide and 5.6 inches high.

To increase the canvas size:

1 Choose Canvas Size from the Image menu, and enter 3.5 in the Width box and 5.6 in the Height box.

2 Click the bottom square in the placement box, then click OK to add the canvas at the top of the image.

Canvas Size		
Current Size: 74K		**OK**
Width: 3.833 inches		**Cancel**
Height: 3.806 inches		
New Size: 100K		
Width: 3.5	inches ▼	
Height: 5.6	inches ▼	
Placement:		

LINKING LAYERS

You need to add about half an inch of white space to the bottom of the image. Instead of adding more canvas, you will move all the elements in the image up a quarter-inch. You can only select and edit one layer at a time, so you will use the *Link Layers* feature to link several layers together. Linking layers allows you to move more than one layer at a time.

To link layers for moving:

1 Click the Layers palette tab, then click the zoom box to view all the layers.

2 Click in the second column in the Layers palette next to the Square layer. You will see the move icon appear next to the thumbnail and the target layer thumbnail.

3 Click in the Move column for the *Asparagus* and *Veggies* layers.

The four layers are now linked so that they can be moved as a unit.

4 Click the move tool in the toolbox, then position the cursor in the document window.

5 Press the Shift key, then drag up on the image until you see the bottom of the fish shape move up about a quarter-inch.

6 Click the move icon in the Fish layer of the Layers palette to turn linking off.

Your image should look similar to the image below.

PAINTING WITH A PATTERN

Creating the top border begins with making a selection. Since you know the exact size you want the selection to be, you will use a fixed marquee to select the area.

In Lesson 2, you used the rubber stamp tool with the aligned options to duplicate areas within an image. In Lessons 2 and 3, you defined a pattern and then filled an area with that pattern. Now you're ready to combine these procedures by using the rubber stamp tool to duplicate a pattern in a selection.

To create the top border:

1 Click the New Layer icon and type **Border** for the layer name. Click OK.

2 Double-click the marquee tool, then use the Fixed Size style in the Marquee Options palette to create a rectangular marquee with a width of 190 and a height of 30.

TIP: TO SEE ALL THE
PALETTE TABS IN A
LARGE GROUP OF
PALETTES, DRAG THE
SIZE BOX IN THE
LOWER-RIGHT
CORNER OF A PALETTE
GROUP TO THE
RIGHT.

3 Click the white area in the window to make the marquee appear, then hold down the Command and Option keys and drag the marquee up to the top edge of the image.

4 Use the rulers to center the marquee in the window.

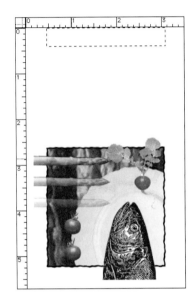

5 Choose Open from the File menu, then open the *Waves* file in the Lesson 5 folder and click OK to accept the ESP Rasterizer default settings.

6 Choose All from the Select menu, then choose Define Pattern from the Edit menu to copy the selection into the pattern buffer.

7 Choose Close from the File menu to close the *Waves* file.

8 Double-click the rubber stamp tool to display the Rubber Stamp Options palette, and choose Pattern (aligned) from the Option pop-up menu.

9 Click the Brushes palette tab, then choose the far-right brush in the top row of the Brushes palette (the largest brush with hard edges).

10 Starting from the left side of the selection, paint the pattern with the rubber stamp tool (you'll probably need two passes to fill the selection).

The selection marquee acts as a mask to keep the pattern inside the rectangle.

FILLING A PATTERN WITH A GRADIENT

As you might remember from Lessons 2 and 4, a gradient fill displays a gradual transition from the foreground to the background color. You can create an interesting effect when you use gradient fills with a pattern.

To fill the pattern:

1 If you changed the foreground color, use the eyedropper to reset it by sampling the dark purple from along the back of the fish.

2 Double-click the gradient tool and make sure the opacity in the Gradient Options palette is set to 100 percent.

3 Choose Darken from the Mode menu in the Gradient Options palette.

4 Place the cross hair for the starting point at the center of the bottom edge of the border.

5 Drag up to the top of the window.

Notice that the gradient begins with the foreground color at the point where you click and ends with the background color at the end of the line you drag.

6 Choose None from the Select menu (or press Command-D).

If you had chosen the Normal mode, the waves would not have shown through the gradient.

7 Choose Save from the File menu or (press Command-S).

ADDING TYPE

Now you'll add the brochure title. After entering the type, you will adjust the spacing of individual characters by editing the type in a layer.

To create the type:

1 Click the Layers palette tab, then click the New Layer icon.

2 Type **Text** for the new layer name, then click OK.

3 Click the eyedropper tool, then sample the dark red from the edge of the radish for the new foreground color.

4 Click the type tool, then click the insertion point about half an inch below the border to display the Type Tool dialog box.

5 Choose Times Roman from the Font pop-up menu.

6 Set the type size to 36 points, and the spacing to 1, and choose the Center alignment option.

7 In the text box, type **Eating for**, press the Return key, type **Your Health**, then click OK.

8 Choose None from the Select menu (or press Command-D).

9 Click the move tool, then position the text in the center of the cover.

EDITING TYPE IN A LAYER

To complete the project, you'll make some adjustments to the spacing in the type.

To edit type in a layer:

1 Make sure the Text layer is the target layer.

2 Press Command-spacebar to zoom in on the *Y* in *Your.*

3 Use the lasso tool to select the *Y*, then click the right arrow key twice to move the *Y* two pixels to the right.

The letter spacing of the *Y* was rather wide; moving it to the right improves the look of the type.

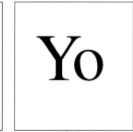

4 Deselect the type, then save the file.

MAKING FINAL ADJUSTMENTS

If you need to make any final adjustments to any element in any layer, be sure to make the appropriate layer the target layer. You know you can click the layer thumbnail to make it the target layer, but there is also a shortcut.

To select a layer:

1 Double-click the zoom tool to return to a 1:1 view.

2 Click the move tool, then press the Command key.

The cursor turns into a pointing hand.

3 Position the cursor over the wave border at the top of the document window and click.

The Border layer becomes the target layer.

4 Position the cursor over the textured square, press the Command key, and click. The Square layer becomes the target layer.

5 Try selecting another layer by pressing the Command key, then clicking on the fish. The Fish layer becomes the target layer.

6 Make any final adjustments that you need to any of the layers.

7 Choose Save a Copy from the File menu, name the copy **05WorkL**, and open the Projects folder.

8 Choose Flatten Image from the Layers palette pop-up menu to flatten the file for printing.

9 Choose Save from the File menu to save the flattened version of the file.

10 If you want to, you can print the image.

11 Choose Close from the File menu to close the files.

You should be proud! Not only have you created a very sophisticated piece of art, you've also learned a great deal about Adobe Photoshop in a couple of hours. In the next lesson, you'll take some time to review what you've learned in Lessons 4 and 5.

Lesson

6

Lesson 6: Wine Label

This lesson gives you a chance to practice the commands and techniques you learned in the fourth and fifth lessons of *Classroom in a Book*.

The step-by-step instructions in this lesson provide all the information you need to complete the project; however, detailed explanations of procedures are not included. If you find that you want more precise instructions, or can't remember how to do something, refer back to Lessons 4 and 5. It should take you about 45 minutes to complete this lesson.

In this lesson, you'll create a wine label for a new vineyard whose wines are going to be stocked by Gourmet Visions markets. As you create the label, you'll combine the selection, masking, and manipulation techniques you already know in a new and interesting way.

Source file (06Star)	Source file (06Grapes)
Source file (06Type)	Ending image (06Final)

There are four source files for this lesson—a line drawing, a star graphic, a file containing saved text, and a wine bottle drawing.

At the end of the lesson, you'll use the wine label with the wine bottle drawing to create an illustration that could be used for an advertisement or point-of-purchase display.

In this lesson, feel free to experiment with placement and pasting settings. Use the final image as a guide, but don't feel you must reproduce the label exactly. These review lessons are your opportunity to explore the features of Adobe Photoshop.

BEGINNING THIS LESSON

Again, in this lesson, you will open a new file to work in and open the final image to use as a visual reference.

To begin this lesson:

1 Quit Adobe Photoshop, then throw away the *Adobe Photoshop 3.0 Prefs* file to make sure all settings are returned to their default values. The *Adobe Photoshop 3.0 Prefs* file is located in the Preferences folder in your System folder.

2 Choose Open from the File menu, then open the *06Final1* file in the Lesson 6 folder.

3 Click the zoom box in the top-right corner of the Layers palette to expand the palette to full size.

The final file contains five layers: the white Background layer, the Border layer, the Grapes layer, the Star layer, and the Text layer.

4 Zoom out to reduce the image, resize the window if necessary, then drag the window to the upper-right corner of your screen.

5 Create a new RGB Color file named **06Work** that is 4.3 inches wide and 5.6 inches high with a resolution of 72. Be sure the units of measurement in the New dialog box are set to inches, and click OK.

6 Turn on the rulers in the window.

7 Choose Save As from the File menu, then open the Projects folder, and click Save.

To organize the palettes:

1 Drag the Picker palette on top of the Brushes/Options palette.

2 Drag the Swatches palette on top of the Brushes/Options palette, then close the Scratch palette.

3 Collapse the new palette.

4 Click the zoom box in the Layers palette to reduce the size of the palette.

5 Create a new layer and name it **Border**.

DEFINING THE PATTERN

The first step in creating this label is to define the pattern you'll use for the top and bottom borders.

To define the pattern:

1 Choose Open from the File menu, then open the *06Grapes* file in the Lesson 6 folder.

You will use this file in two different ways during this lesson. First, you'll select part of the grapes to use as the basis of your pattern. Later, you'll copy the entire bunch of grapes to serve as the main design element in the label.

2 Use the rectangular marquee to select a half an inch square area near the top of the grapes.

Since this selection does not have to be precise, you can use the normal marquee setting with the rectangular marquee tool.

3 Choose Define Pattern from the Edit menu.

MAKING A FIXED-SIZE SELECTION

You're going to use a fixed marquee to define the selection for the top border. You want the marquee to be exactly as wide as the image.

To select the border area:

1 Select the *06Work* file.

2 Double-click the marquee tool in the toolbox, then choose the Fixed Size option from the Style pop-up menu in the Marquee Options palette, enter a width of 310 and a height of 46.

TIP: THE LAST FILTER YOU APPLIED APPEARS AT THE TOP OF THE FILTER MENU. TO REAPPLY A FILTER WITH THE SAME SETTING QUICKLY, CHOOSE THIS COMMAND TO BYPASS THE DIALOG BOX.

3 Click anywhere in the image to display the marquee, hold down the Command and Option keys, and drag the marquee to the top edge of the window.

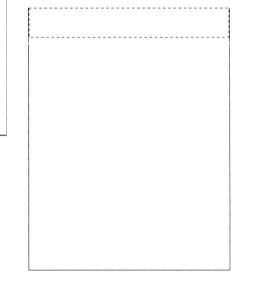

PAINTING WITH THE RUBBER STAMP TOOL

Now you're ready to paint the border using the pattern that's currently stored in the pattern buffer.

To paint the selection:

1 Double-click the rubber stamp tool, then choose the Pattern (aligned) option in the Rubber Stamp Options palette.

2 Click the Brushes palette tab, then choose any hard-edged brush and paint with the pattern.

CREATING A MARBLE EFFECT

To distort the grapes and produce the marble-like effect in the border, you're going to apply a filter to the selection.

To apply the filter:

1 Choose Distort from the Filter menu and Wave from the submenu. The Wave dialog box appears.

2 Enter **7** for the Number of Generators option, and change the type to Triangle, then click OK.

The pattern takes on a marble-like texture. If you want to experiment with the other settings in the Wave dialog box, go ahead and do it now. You can also try applying the same filter setting more than once to see how the selection changes.

ADDING COLOR TO A PATTERN

Now you're ready to make the border dark green.

To fill the pattern:

1 Click the Picker palette tab, set the R slider in the Picker palette to 0, set the G slider to about 84, and set the B slider to about 43 to select the foreground color.

2 Choose Fill from the Edit menu (or press Shift-Delete), make sure the Foreground Color option is selected and the opacity is set to 100 percent, choose the Darken mode to fill the pattern, then click OK.

DUPLICATING A SELECTION

You will duplicate the border selection by dragging the border in the same way that you drag-copied the asparagus in Lesson 5.

To duplicate the selection:

1 Click the move tool and press the Shift key to constrain the selection.

2 With the Shift key still down, hold down the Option key and drag the selection to the bottom of the image.

A copy of the selection moves as you drag.

3 Choose Save from the File menu (or press Command-S).

CLEANING UP A SCANNED IMAGE

You may have noticed the smudges around the cluster of grapes in the *06Grapes* file. These types of imperfections are frequently found on scanned images. You're going to use Quick Mask mode to clean up these areas before pasting the bunch of grapes into your *06Work* file.

To edit the scanning marks:

1 Select the *06Grapes* file.

2 Double-click the magic wand tool, make sure the tolerance is set to 32, then click to select the white background area.

Notice that neither the grapes nor the smudged areas are part of the selection (which you will invert before you copy and paste). You need to add the smudged areas to the selection.

3 Click the Quick Mask mode control in the toolbox.

All the protected areas appear in light red. If someone else has been using the program, the selected areas might be another color. If the background (instead of the grapes) is selected, open the Quick Mask dialog box and select the Color Indicates Masked Areas option.

4 Make sure the default background and foreground colors are set, then use the eraser to remove the color over the smudged areas.

Since the color indicates a masked area, you are removing these areas from the mask. You will still see the dark smudges.

5 Click the Standard mode control (to the left of the Quick Mask mode control in the toolbox).

6 Choose Inverse from the Select menu. Only the grape cluster is included in the selection. For safety's sake, you might want to save this selection before closing the file. If you do save the selection, save this file as *06Grape1* and put it into your Projects folder before closing it.

7 Drag the *06Grapes* window to the right of the *06Work* window.

8 Click the move tool, drag the Grapes selection to the *06Work* window, then close the grapes file. Don't save your changes unless you are saving under the new name.

ROTATING THE SELECTION

You're ready to rotate the floating selection.

To rotate the selection:

1 Make sure that the *06Work* file is the active window.

2 Choose Rotate from the Image menu and Arbitrary from the submenu.

The Arbitrary option allows you to enter an angle and direction of rotation.

3 Enter **30** degrees CW, then click OK.

4 Double-click the Floating Selection thumbnail to create a new layer, type **Grapes** for the name, then click OK.

SCALING UP A SELECTION

To achieve the correct balance in the final wine label, you need to increase the size of the selection slightly.

To scale up the selection:

1 Open the Info palette by choosing Palettes from the Window menu and Show Info from the Submenu.

2 Choose Effects from the Image menu and Scale from the submenu.

3 Hold down the Shift key to constrain the proportions, then drag the upper-right handle on a diagonal off the window until the measurement in the Info palette reads about 112 percent.

4 Click with the gavel icon to confirm the scaling.

5 Drag or use the arrow keys to center the image horizontally and position the tip of the stem about a quarter-inch from the top border.

6 Save the file.

FILLING THE DARK AREAS OF A SELECTION

As a final step in modifying the grapes, you're going to fill the black areas in the Grape layer with color.

To fill the grapes:

1 Use the eyedropper to sample a green area of the grapes in the *06Final1* image.

2 Click the Picker palette tab, then fine-tune the color by setting the sliders in the Picker palette to read R equal to 184, G equal to 194, and B equal to 125.

3 Click the Swatches palette tab.

4 Position the cursor in the white area at the bottom of the Swatches palette until you see a paint-bucket icon, then click to add this color to the palette.

5 You will be changing the color of the Grapes layer, so make sure that the Grapes layer is highlighted in the Layers palette.

6 Choose Fill from the Edit menu and use the foreground color and an opacity of 100 percent. Change the mode to Lighten, and click the Preserve Transparency checkbox, and click OK.

7 Drag the *Grapes* layer thumbnail below the *Border* layer thumbnail in the Layers palette.

CENTERING A SELECTION

Now you're ready to add the star seal to the label. To do this you will create a new layer, make a solid-colored selection in the center of the label, and copy a star selection from another file into this image.

To center a selection:

1 Click the New Layer icon, type **Star** for the name, and click OK.

2 Set the rectangular marquee to the Fixed Size option enter **64** pixels for the width and **80** pixels for the height.

3 Press the Option key, then use the x and y coordinates in the Info palette to set the cross hair for the marquee in the center of the window. The x value should be about 2.2 and the y value should be about 2.8.

If you don't see the coordinates, click the mouse button.

4 Click to create a fixed size rectangle. Refer to the illustration below for positioning.

TYPING IN VALUES FOR A COLOR

In most cases, you have been setting a foreground color by sampling a color from an open window or changing the sliders in the Picker palette.

In Lesson 1, you also learned how to choose a color from the Color Picker. When you need to be very precise in setting color values (for example, when you are doing four-color separation), you can also type color values into the Color Picker. This is sometimes easier than trying to move the Colors palette sliders to an exact location.

To type the numerical values for a color:

1 Click the foreground color selection box in the toolbox to display the Color Picker.

The CMYK color-value text boxes are located to the right of the bottom half of the color slider.

2 Double-click in the C text box, then enter the following values:

Cyan 5%
Magenta 19%
Yellow...........95%
Black...............1%

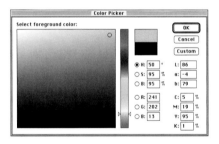

The colors will fluctuate widely as you are entering the values. When you've finished typing, the new foreground color will appear in the top of the color selection box to the right of the color slider.

3 Click OK to close the Color Picker.

4 Fill the selection using an opacity setting of 100 percent and the Normal mode. Make sure Preserve Transparency is turned off.

5 Save the *06Work* file.

SAVING A PATH AS A SELECTION

The next step in creating the seal is to trace the star using the pen tool.

To create the star path:

1 Choose Open from the File menu, then open the *06Star* file in the Lesson 6 folder.

2 Zoom in twice, then resize the window (using the zoom box in the upper-right corner) so you can see the entire star.

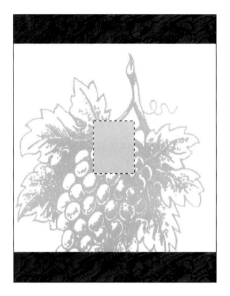

3 Click the Paths palette tab, then click the pen tool.

4 Use the pen tool and click to create a straight-line outline around the star shape.

5 Choose Save Path from the Paths palette pop-up menu.

6 Type **Star Path** for the path name, then click OK.

7 Click the Make Selection button, which is third from the left in the bottom of the Paths Palette.

8 Use the arrow point in the Paths palette to click anywhere outside the path thumbnail to deselect the path (the selection will still have a marquee around it).

9 Choose Save As from the File menu and type **06Star1** for the file name. Open the Projects folder and click Save.

To copy the star:

1 Choose Copy from the Edit menu, then choose Close from the File menu to close the *06Star* file. Don't save the changes.

2 Make sure the *06Work* file is active, then choose Paste from the Edit menu.

3 Dim the star by setting the layer opacity to 80 percent.

4 Choose Multiply from the Layer Mode menu.

The Multiply mode will drop the white out of the star selection.

5 Choose None from the Select menu (or press Command-D).

The star becomes part of the layer containing the yellow square.

6 Save the file.

EMBOSSING THE SELECTION

To create the "raised" effect on the seal, you're going to apply the Emboss filter. The Emboss filter suppresses the color within the selection and traces the outside of the selection with black.

To emboss the seal:

1 Use the fixed size rectangular marquee tool to select the yellow area in the image.

Unless you've changed it, the fixed marquee should still be set, and you can simply click over the square to make the selection.

2 Choose Stylize from the Filter menu and Emboss from the submenu. The Emboss dialog box appears.

3 If necessary, set the options to their default values of an angle of 135 degrees, a height of 3 pixels, and an amount of 100 percent.

4 Click OK to apply the filter.

It's all right that the selection turns gray! The Emboss filter removes the color, but you'll put it back in a moment.

REAPPLYING COLOR TO AN EMBOSSED SELECTION

You will use the Colorize option that you learned about in Lesson 5 to return the color to the seal.

To return the color to the selection:

1 Choose Adjust from the Image menu and Hue/Saturation from the submenu.

2 Click the Colorize option in the dialog box and set the hue to 52, the saturation to 90, and the lightness to 0, then click OK.

3 Save the file.

EDITING THE LABEL TYPE

For the finishing touch, you're going to add the type to the wine label. This type, which uses the Palatino font, is provided in a separate file. You will save and load the type as a selection, then add a gradient.

To add and edit the type:

1 Choose Open from the File menu, then open the *06Type* file in the Lesson 6 folder.

2 Choose All from the Select menu, then choose Copy from the Edit menu.

You will need to paste the contents of the selection into the channel to create a selection of the text.

3 Choose Save Selection from the Select menu, then click OK.

4 Click the Channels palette tab, then click #4 in the Channels palette to display the new channel.

Are you surprised that the image is blank? If so, remember that to save the contents of a selection you copy it to the Clipboard; the Save Selection command saves only the shape of the selection border.

5 Choose Paste from the Edit menu to paste the text copy in the channel.

6 Choose Map from the Image menu and Invert from the submenu.

7 Choose None from the Select menu (or press Command-D).

Remember that the white areas are part of the selection and the black areas are not.

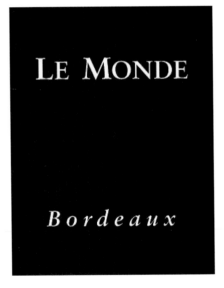

LOADING A SELECTION FROM ANOTHER FILE

You can load the selection from the type file directly into your wine label. Both files—the active window and the file with the selection—must be exactly the same size.

To load a selection from another file:

1 Click on the *06Work* file to make it the active window.

2 Click the Layers palette tab, then create a new layer.

3 Type **Text** for the new layer name.

4 Choose Load Selection from the Select menu.

5 Choose *06Type* from the Document pop-up menu. (You can only load selections from open documents.)

6 Make sure that the #4 selection is selected, then click OK.

The selection from the *06Type* file is loaded into the wine label file.

7 Select the *06Type* file and choose Close from the File menu. Don't save changes.

ADDING A GRADIENT FILL TO TEXT

Now you're ready to add the gradient fill to the type.

To fill the type:

1 Choose a dark purple from the Swatches palette or mix your own color to select a new foreground color.

2 Click the gradient tool and place the cross hair between the *M* and the *o* in *Monde*.

3 Press the Shift key and drag straight up about halfway to the top of the window.

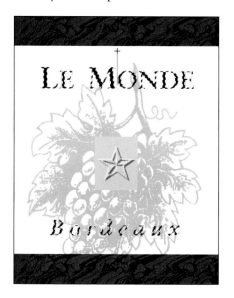

5 Save the file.

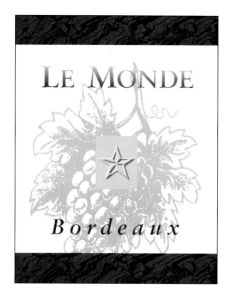

4 Choose None from the Select menu (or press Command-D).

The type is filled with the color. Notice that the *Bordeaux* text is filled with the solid purple. When you create a gradient, the blend starts where you click and the selected area before the click point is filled with the foreground color. Notice also that there is no pure white in the *LE MONDE* text. This is because the background color for a fill begins where you end the line you drag. In this case, the pure background color is halfway to the top of the window.

Excellent job! The wine label is complete. As a final exercise, you will use the wine label and a drawing of a wine bottle to create another illustration.

OVERLAYING THE LABEL ON A WINE BOTTLE

The new illustration that you create could be used for advertisements, brochures, or point-of-purchase displays.

To open the final reference file:

1 Choose Open from the File menu, then open the *06Final2* file in the Lesson 6 folder.

2 Zoom out and position *06Final2* in the top-right corner of your screen.

3 Select the *06Work* file.

4 Choose Save a Copy from the File menu, type **06WorkL** for the name, open the Projects folder, then click Save.

To overlay the label on a wine bottle:

1 Choose Flatten Image from the Layers palette pop-up menu to flatten the layers of the wine label file.

2 Choose Image Size from the Image menu, then make sure that the Constrain File Size option is turned off.

3 Choose Percent from the Width pop-up menu, enter 34 in the Width box, then click OK.

The wine label file size is reduced by 34 percent.

4 Move the *06Work* window to the right of your screen.

5 Choose Open from the File menu, then open the *06Bottle* file in the Lesson 6 folder.

6 Double-click the zoom tool to view the window in 1:1 view if necessary.

This file was created in Adobe Illustrator, then saved as a Adobe Photoshop 3.0 file.

Dragging a layer

You can drag an entire layer from one file to another.

To drag a layer:

1 Make *06Work* the active window.

2 Click the move tool, then drag the wine label image to the *06Bottle* window.

A new layer is created in the *06Bottle* image named *Layer 1*.

3 Double-click the Layer 1 layer thumbnail, and in the Layer Options dialog box type **Label** for the new name and click OK.

4 Position the label on the wine bottle.

5 With the Label layer as the target layer, choose Overlay from the Mode menu on the Layers palette.

The Overlay mode blends the colors in the target layer with the underlying layers, preserving the highlights and shadows. In this case it gives the illusion of three dimensions.

6 Choose Save As from the File menu, type **06Work2** for the name of this new file, and save it into your Projects folder.

7 Choose Close from the File menu to close the files. Don't save the changes.

Nice going! You should really feel that you're getting to be an experienced Adobe Photoshop user by now. With the completion of this review project, you've accomplished a great deal and have a real understanding of the Adobe Photoshop software's editing capabilities.

The remaining lessons in *Classroom in a Book* move into the more sophisticated features of Adobe Photoshop, including color correction, resolution and resizing, mode conversion, and creating color separations.

Lesson

7

LESSON 7: UNDERSTANDING COLOR

This lesson discusses the Adobe Photoshop features that let you alter and manipulate color in images. You're already familiar with quite a few color manipulation tools from previous lessons. For example, you've used the Fill command to replace color in a selection, the Hue/Saturation command to change color and intensity, and the Brightness/Contrast command to increase and decrease those elements in an image.

In this lesson, you'll learn about the Adobe Photoshop tools designed for *color correction*. Just as there are varying levels of color adjustments you'll need to make, there are a variety of controls that offer you progressively more precise color control.

The lesson begins with a brief introduction to color theory and color models as they are used in Adobe Photoshop. You will then color-correct two images. It should take you about two hours to complete this lesson.

In this lesson, you'll learn how to do the following:

- measure color in a number of models

- display images with different palettes

- correct the color of an image using the Variations command

- use a histogram to measure tonal ranges

- adjust color levels in an image

- adjust curves in an image

- use the Info palette to preview color changes

- color-correct a selection

- use the toning tools and the focus tools

- sharpen detail in an image

- color-correct an individual channel

At the end of this lesson you'll have two color-corrected images of the chef, ready to be used in the Gourmet Visions annual report. The following illustrations show the two images you'll work with in this lesson.

Ending image (07After)   *Ending image (07Final)*

SETTING UP THE PALETTES

Before reviewing color theory, you will throw your preferences file away and set up the palettes.

To reset the program's defaults:

1 Quit Adobe Photoshop.

2 Locate the *Adobe Photoshop 3.0 Prefs* file in the Preferences folder in the System folder, throw it away and empty the Trash.

3 Launch the Adobe Photoshop program.

Organizing palettes

During the review of color theory, you will need the Picker/Swatches/Scratch and Info palettes open on the screen.

1 Close the Layers/Channels/Paths group and the Brushes/Options group.

2 Choose Palettes from the Window menu and Show Info from the submenu.

LOOKING AT COLOR MODELS

A color model is a method for displaying and measuring color. The three main models used in Adobe Photoshop are the RGB model for display, the CMYK model for printing, and the Lab model for both display and printing.

RGB

As you learned in Lesson 1, the human eye perceives color according to the wavelength of the light that reaches it. Light containing the full color spectrum is perceived as white. When no light is present, the eye perceives black.

All monitors display color using a mixture of the primary additive colors of red, green, and blue.

To see an example of additive color:

1 Choose Open from the File menu, then open the *07Add* file in the Lesson 7 folder.

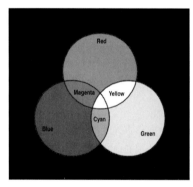

Combining these primary additive colors produces a large percentage of the visible spectrum. You can see that combining red and green produces yellow, combining green and blue produces cyan, and combining blue and red produces magenta. The result of combining all three colors is white (as shown in the center of the wheel).

Measuring RGB color

In RGB color, various brightness values of red, green, and blue light combine to form the colors on the screen. When you're working in the Adobe Photoshop software's RGB mode, you control the range of colors by varying the intensities of the individual RGB components. Up until now, you've been working in the RGB mode. For example, when you selected or modified a color using the sliders in the Picker palette or the values in the Color Picker, you adjusted the red, green, and blue values to display a particular color.

For RGB color images, Adobe Photoshop assigns an intensity value to each pixel ranging from 0 (black) to 255 (white) for each of the RGB components. To see how this works in practice, you're going to experiment using the Swatches palette.

To display the RGB components of a color:

1 Click the eyedropper tool, then click the red circle in the *07Add* file.

In the Picker palette, notice that the color values next to the sliders move to an R value of 255, and G and B values of 0. This indicates that this color contains only a red component; there is no green or blue in this color.

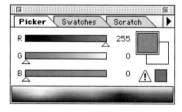

2 Drag the R slider all the way to the left until it reads 0.

The resulting color is black, since none of the components has any value.

3 With the eyedropper, click the green circle in the *07Add* file.

This pure green produces values of 0 for the R and B components and 255 for the G component.

You can preview color changes in the sliders. The red slider currently indicates that if you drag it all the way to the right, you will create yellow.

4 Drag the R slider to the right until it reads 255.

When both the R and G sliders both read 255, the resulting color is yellow. Looking at the B slider, you can see that if you drag it all the way to the right you'll create white.

5 Drag the B slider to the right until it reads 255.

When all three sliders read 255, the resulting color is pure white.

6 Drag all three sliders to the center until their values are about 128.

You can see that when all three components have the same value, the resulting mixture is a gray color.

7 Use the sliders to create magenta and cyan.

You can use the *Add Color* file as a guide. As you move the sliders, watch how the proportions of each component determine the resulting color.

8 Choose Close from the File menu to close the *07Add* file.

CMYK

In Lesson 1 you also learned that the color you see on a printed page is a result of color being absorbed, or subtracted, by the inks on the page. As white light strikes translucent inks, a portion of the color spectrum is absorbed; color that is not absorbed is reflected back to the observer.

To see an example of subtractive color:

1 Choose Open from the File menu, then open the *07Sub* file in the Lesson 7 folder.

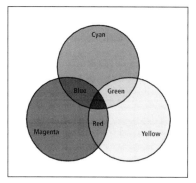

In theory, a mixture of the primary subtractive colors (or *process colors*) of cyan, magenta, and yellow (CMY) should produce black (K). Because of ink impurities, however, these three inks produce a muddy brown, and more black must be added to produce a pure black.

Measuring CMYK color

When you're working in CMYK mode, Adobe Photoshop assigns each pixel a percentage value for each of the process inks. The lightest colors are assigned smaller percentages; darker inks have higher percentages. You can read the value for any color in CMYK percentages in the Picker palette.

Important: Although you can set color values for CMYK colors in Adobe Photoshop, the actual display of the color on your screen is in RGB color (your monitor can only display using additive colors).

To display the CMYK components of a color:

1 Choose CMYK Sliders from the Picker palette pop-up menu.

Adobe Photoshop lets you set color values in a number of color-model systems. For the CMYK model, an additional slider appears and the values for the current color are given as percentages. See the *Adobe Photoshop User Guide* for information on the other color models in the pop-up menu (the Lab Sliders option is explained in the next section).

2 Click any white area in the *07Sub* file.

The sliders move all the way to the left, since in CMYK values pure white contains 0 percent of the process colors (that is, you see white since all the color is reflected back to your eye).

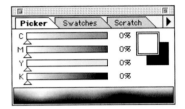

3 Slide the cyan and yellow sliders all the way to the right, until they read 100 percent.

Combining 100 percent of cyan and 100 percent of yellow produces green.

4 Look at the K slider bar to see how adding more black would change the color. Slowly slide the black slider to the right to see the color change in the foreground color swatch.

5 Experiment with the sliders to see if you can produce orange. As you move the sliders, watch how the various combinations of percentages produce different colors.

6 Choose Close from the File menu to close the *07Sub* file.

Out-of-gamut colors

The *gamut* of a color system is the range of colors that can be represented within the color system.

To see the overlay of gamuts:

1 Choose Open from the File menu, then open the *07Gamut* file in the Lesson 7 folder.

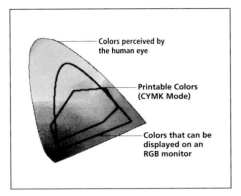

Each of the color models has a different color gamut. When colors that cannot be printed are displayed on the screen (that is, they are outside the CMYK gamut), an alert triangle with an exclamation mark appears in the Picker palette (and in the Color Picker and Info palette).

To display an out-of-gamut color:

1 Click the Swatches palette tab, then click the blue swatch in the top row of the Swatches palette.

2 Click the Picker palette tab, then choose RGB Sliders from the Picker palette pop-up menu to display the colors in the RGB model.

The blue you chose in the Swatches palette is out of the CMYK gamut, so the triangle appears below the color selection boxes. The closest CMYK color equivalent appears next to the triangle.

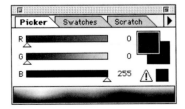

3 Click the triangle.

Adobe Photoshop automatically selects the printable color closest to the color you selected.

The range of printable colors depends on your output device. The availability of printable colors is determined by the printing values you enter in the Printing Inks Setup box. See Lesson 11 for more information on colors, printing, and correcting out-of-gamut colors.

4 Choose Close from the File menu to close the *07Gamut* file.

Lab

L*a*b* is a color model developed by the Centre Internationale d'Eclairage (CIE), an international organization that established specifications for measuring color in 1931. These specifications are the internationally accepted standard for all colorimetric measurements. The Lab model, like other CIE color models, defines color values mathematically, in a way that is device-independent. This means that Lab colors do not vary with different, properly calibrated monitors or printers.

The Lab gamut encompasses both the RGB and CMYK gamuts; it is a standardized color model that comprises all colors. Using Lab color gives you a way to create consistent color documents regardless of the device used to create or print the file.

To see a representation of the Lab model:

1 Choose Open from the File menu, then open the *07Lab* file in the Lesson 7 folder.

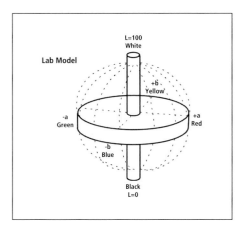

Lab images consist of a luminance, or lightness, component (*L*) and two chromatic components: the *a* component, which ranges from green to magenta, and the *b* component, which ranges from blue to yellow.

To display the Lab components of a color:

1 Drag the Swatches palette tab out of the Picker/Swatches/Scratch palette.

2 Choose Lab Sliders from the Picker palette pop-up menu.

Three sliders appear, one for each of the Lab components. Lab values can range from −120 (on the far left) to +120 (on the far right).

3 Click the blue swatch in the top row of the Swatches palette (the fifth swatch from the left).

4 In the Picker palette, drag the *L* slider to the right until it reads 60 to increase the color's luminance.

Because Lab color lets you adjust lightness separately from the color values, it can be a useful editing tool.

5 Drag the *a* slider to the left until it reads −79 to add green and produce an aqua color.

6 Drag the *b* slider to the right until it reads 0 to remove blue and produce a turquoise color.

7 Pick a new color and drag the sliders around to see how Lab colors are formed.

In the Lab model, you cannot have a color that is green and magenta at the same time, or blue and yellow at the same time.

8 Choose Close from the File menu to close the *07Lab* file.

SELECTING A PALETTE FOR THE COLOR DISPLAY

Each image type in Adobe Photoshop uses a different *color lookup table*, or *color palette*, to store the colors used in the image. To optimize the display for each image, the program stores a different palette for each open file (based on the colors in the image), and displays the active document using its associated palette. Adobe Photoshop uses a technique called *dithering* to simulate the display of colors that are not in the current color palette.

Using the document's individual palette is the preferred method of display because it shows you the colors most accurately. Keep in mind, however, that using the file's individual palette can make the colors in inactive documents look less accurate.

You can choose to display all open documents using the System color palette (rather than the document's individual palette) by clicking the Use System Palette option in the General Preferences dialog box. Choosing the System palette can make the display of colors in the active document less accurate.

MAKING COLOR CORRECTIONS

Color correction allows you to address differences between the original or scanned image and the image as it appears on the screen or in print. Color correction also lets you compensate for some common problems in four-color reproduction, such as the varying contrast between paper and ink and the inability of process inks to match their theoretical performance. In order for your color corrections to be accurate for printing, your system must be calibrated correctly. See Lesson 11 and the *Adobe Photoshop User Guide* for more information on calibrating your system and printing four-color separations.

BEGINNING THIS LESSON

Now you are ready to put some of this theory to work. The first image you'll color-correct is a portrait of a chef.

Important: *Before doing any of the tasks in this lesson, be sure your monitor has been calibrated following the instructions in Lesson 1. If the monitor is not calibrated correctly, you will get some very different results when you color-correct the images.*

Note: *Because of differences in hardware and work environments, some of the corrected files you open from the Lesson 7 folder might not be precisely color-corrected for your system. As you work through the lesson, adjust the color so that the file you're working on matches the color in the final image as it appears on your screen, even if that image is a bit out of balance. The idea is for you to understand the controls and procedures for making color corrections, not to produce a perfectly color-corrected image.*

To begin the lesson:

1 Choose Open from the File menu, then open the *07After* file in the Lesson 7 folder.

2 Zoom out to reduce the image, resize the window if necessary, then drag the window to the upper-right corner of your screen.

3 Choose Open from the File menu, then open the *07Before* file in the Lesson 7 folder.

You will be working entirely in the Background layer for this lesson.

Organizing the palettes

You will create a new palette group that includes the Picker, Swatches, Brushes, and Options palettes.

To create a new palette group:

1 Drag the Swatches palette tab back onto the Picker palette.

2 Drag the Scratch palette tab away from the Picker/Swatches/Scratch group, then click the close box to hide the Scratch palette.

3 Open the Brushes palette, then drag the Brushes palette tab on top of the Picker/Swatches group.

4 Drag the Options palette tab on top of the Picker/Swatches/Brushes group.

5 Since you don't need the new palette group for the first part of this lesson, you can collapse it now by double-clicking any palette tab or clicking the zoom box in the upper-right corner of the palette.

USING THE VARIATIONS COMMAND

The first color correction you're going to make is to adjust the overall color in this portrait. Currently, this image is too light, has too little contrast, and has an unappealing overall blue/magenta cast. This kind of imbalance might result from a poor exposure setting or the use of an incorrect filter or film type when the photograph was shot. Some of these problems could also have been introduced during the scanning process. You're going to correct this image using the Variations command.

Using the Variations command is a quick and easy way to visually adjust the color balance, contrast, and saturation in an image or selection.

To use the Variations command:

1 Choose Adjust from the Image menu and Variations from the submenu. The Variations dialog box appears.

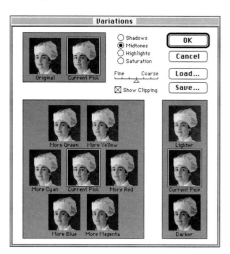

The two thumbnails at the top of the dialog box show you the Original selection and the Current Pick (in this case, they are the same since you haven't made any corrections yet). As you change the settings, the Current Pick shows you the latest version of the corrected image. To color-correct the image, you simply click the thumbnail that looks the closest to the effect you're trying to achieve.

The thumbnails in the bottom-left section let you adjust color balance. The colors are arranged according to their positions on the color wheel; yellow is at 45 degrees, red is at 0 degrees, and so on.

2 Click the More Red thumbnail.

The color balance from the More Red thumbnail becomes the new Current Pick in the center of this section (it's also the new Current Pick at the top of the dialog box). Since you are adjusting color balance, each time you make a choice, all of the thumbnails change. Was this effect too minor for you to see?

3 Click More Red again.

Repeatedly clicking a thumbnail incrementally adjusts the image. Look at the top of the dialog box to compare the Original selection with the Current Pick. You can see a definite change in the image. Unfortunately, this is not the direction you want to go in.

4 Click the Original thumbnail in the upper-left corner of the dialog box to return to your image's original color.

Adjusting the midtones

The Variations command lets you focus the color correction on the dark areas (Shadows), the middle tones (Midtones), or the light areas (Highlights) of the image. In general, the order in which you make color corrections depends on what is wrong with the image. Because this image has a strong color cast, you will begin by correcting the color in the midtones and then adjust the skin tones.

To adjust midtones:

1 Make sure that the Midtones option is selected.

The lower-right section of the Variations dialog box lets you make the image lighter or darker. The Current Pick is in the middle of this section.

2 Click Darker.

Again, all the thumbnails change to show the adjustment. Making the image darker removes its washed-out look.

3 In the left section, click More Green to remove the magenta cast from the image.

With less magenta, the skin tones begin to improve. Since green and magenta are complementary colors, adding more green decreases the magenta in the image.

4 Click More Yellow to remove the blue cast.

Blue and yellow are also complementary colors. Now the image is really coming to life.

Adjusting the highlights and shadows

To increase the contrast in the image, you darken the shadows and lighten the highlights.

To adjust the contrast:

1 Select the Shadows option.

2 Drag the Fine/Coarse slider one notch to the right.

The Fine/Coarse slider determines the increment of change that each click of a thumbnail represents. Moving the slider to the right (toward Coarse) doubles the effect; moving it to the left (toward Fine) halves the effect.

3 Make sure the Show Clipping option is selected.

Clipping (or loss of color) occurs when an adjustment causes a color to exceed its maximum or minimum value. For example, if you increase the contrast too much, light grays are converted to white and dark grays are converted to black. Clipping can also occur when a color exceeds its maximum saturation. Clipped areas are shown in neon colors.

4 Click Darker.

The overall contrast of the image improves. Some of the thumbnails show areas where clipping would occur.

5 Select the Highlights option.

6 Click Lighter.

This final adjustment makes the whites stand out crisp and clear. You can also see that some of the thumbnails show areas where clipping would occur in the white parts of the image.

7 Click OK to apply the corrections to the image.

With just a few simple clicks, you've turned an unacceptable image into a dynamically balanced portrait. If you want to compare your beginning and ending images, choose Undo and Redo from the Edit menu.

8 Choose Save As from the File menu, type **07Work1** as the file name, open your Projects folder, then click Save.

9 Choose Close from the File menu to close both files.

DEVISING A STRATEGY FOR PRECISE COLOR CORRECTION

Using the Variations command is a quick and intuitive way to color-correct an image. Sometimes, however, an image needs more precise adjustments than can be made using the Variations command. Adobe Photoshop offers several additional color-correction tools to help you make more exact color adjustments.

The key to good color reproduction is to produce an image with proper *tonal balance* (correct brightness, saturation, contrast, and density range) and no color deficiencies. Making your color corrections in a specific order can help you achieve this goal.

Here's a suggested strategy for color correction:

• Make sure that your system is calibrated.

• Check the quality of your scan by determining the tonal range of the image.

• Identify the image key type.

• Set the highlight (white) and shadow (black) points in the image.

• Make adjustments to the middle tones.

• Correct for overall color imbalance (such as color cast in skin tones or a green cast from fluorescent lighting).

• Make selective color corrections. For example, you might want to make a sky bluer or take some yellow out of a landscape of trees.

• Apply the Unsharp Mask filter.

Don't worry if none of this makes much sense to you right now. You'll understand most of it by the time you finish this lesson. In Lessons 10 and 11

you will learn how to convert an image to CMYK and correct out-of-gamut colors. Use this strategy as a guide later, when you're working on your own color-correction projects.

PERFORMING PRECISE COLOR CORRECTION

Now you're going to color-correct another image of the chef using this strategy. Once again, you will open a file to refer to as you make the color corrections.

To open the files:

1 Choose Open from the File menu, then open the *07Final* file in the Lesson 7 folder.

2 Zoom out to reduce the image, resize the window if necessary, then drag the window to the upper-right corner of your screen.

3 Choose Open from the File menu, then open the *07Begin* file in the Lesson 7 folder.

Like the earlier portrait, this image appears flat, with little contrast and a decided color cast—in this case, an overall yellow tone.

4 Make sure the *07Begin* window is active.

DETERMINING THE TONAL RANGE IN A SCANNED IMAGE

A *histogram* is a graphic representation of tonal range (brightness and darkness levels) in an image. It plots the number of pixels at each level.

The distribution of pixels can dramatically affect the appearance of an image. If a wide range of levels is used to depict an uninteresting area of the image (such as a dark background or bright highlight), only a narrow range of levels is available for the focus of interest (usually the midtone areas in the image). You use a histogram to check for optimum brightness and contrast as you make color corrections.

To display the histogram:

1 Choose Histogram from the Image menu. The Histogram dialog box appears.

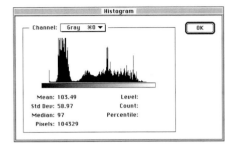

The *x*-axis of the histogram shows the color values of the pixels from the darkest (0) at the far left to the brightest (255) at the far right. The *y*-axis represents the number of pixels with that value. Statistical information about the pixels appears in the lower left of the dialog box.

You can see that there are very few pixels in the shadow and highlight areas of this histogram, which reflects the visual flatness of this image.

2 Move the pointer into the histogram area.

3 Click any spot where there are pixels in the histogram.

The values in the lower right of the dialog box change to display the level of the point (from 0 to 255), the total number of pixels at that point, and the percentage of pixels below that point. If you want the values for a range of pixels, drag the cross hair in the histogram.

A good scanned image should have shadows with RGB values of 10 or less, and highlights with RGB values of 240 or more. A tonal range that encompasses these values contains enough detail to produce good results. In this image, the shadow values start at about 53 and the highlights end at about 224.

4 Click OK to close the dialog box.

This histogram is for information only; you don't make any adjustments using the Histogram command.

5 For comparison, make the *07Final* window active and choose the Histogram command again.

You can see that the pixels in this image cover the entire range of values from light to dark, as you would expect in a color-corrected image.

6 Click OK to close the Histogram dialog box and select the *07Begin* window.

IDENTIFYING KEY TYPE

Before you begin making color corrections, it is useful to identify the type of image you're working with. Image can be classified into one of the *key types,* depending on the visual distribution of tones within the image.

Average images have an equal amount of light and dark tones. High key images have predominantly light tones. Low key images have a majority of dark tones.

Identifying the key type (determining where the detail is in the image) helps you make correct decisions when you're adjusting contrast.

The *07Work* image has an average key tone, with the lighter and darker tones being equally balanced.

ADJUSTING TONAL RANGES WITH THE AUTO LEVELS COMMAND

You can adjust the overall contrast of the image with the Auto Levels command. Automatic tonal correction defines the lightest and darkest pixels in an image as white and black and then equally distributes the colors in between.

To use the Auto Levels command:

1 Choose Adjust from the Image menu and Auto Levels from the submenu.

The overall contrast of the image has changed.

2 Choose Histogram from the Image menu.

Notice that the histogram now shows an overall range of pixel values and reflects the tonal balance of the modified image.

TIP: IF YOU KNOW THE VALUES YOU WANT, YOU CAN TYPE THEM DIRECTLY INTO THE LEVELS TEXT BOXES INSTEAD OF USING THE SLIDERS TO ADJUST CONTRAST.

3 Click OK to close the histogram.

The Auto Levels command clips the white and black values by 0.5 percent to ensure that the program bases its white and black values on more than a single value in the image.

4 Choose Undo Auto Levels from the Edit menu.

Use the Auto Levels command when you're working with average key images. Automatic tonal correction redistributes the values evenly and does not allow for the precise adjustment you can achieve with the Levels command.

ADJUSTING COLOR WITH THE LEVELS COMMAND

Now that the histogram has given you an idea of the tonal balance of this image, you're going to make corrections using the Levels command. Getting a good range of overall density levels is the main step in producing a good color image.

The Levels dialog box includes options that allow you to indicate the pixels in the image that you want to represent the darkest and brightest points (or the end points of the color-value scale). Setting the *black point* (shadow) and the *white point* (highlight) redistributes the pixels in the image and automatically produces a good overall tonal balance. You can also set a *neutral gray* point.

Before opening the Levels dialog box, you're going to use the eyedropper to find the darkest and lightest points. Remember, a pure black point has RGB values all equal to 0, and a pure white point has RGB values all equal to 255.

To find the darkest and lightest points:

1 Be sure you can see the Info palette. If you collapsed it, double-click the Info palette tab. If you closed it, choose Palettes from the Window menu and Show Info from the submenu.

2 Click the eyedropper tool.

3 Move the eyedropper over the piece of hair in front of the chef's ear.

Locate the darkest point in the hair (the point closest to 0 for all RGB values). The values should be about 40 for R, 63 for G, and 28 for B. Make a note of this location.

4 Move the eyedropper around in the bright white area of the chef's smock to the left of the peppers.

Locate the lightest point in the smock (the point closest to 255 for all RGB values). The values should be about 210 for R, 227 for G, and 209 for B. Remember the location of this point.

Now you are ready to adjust the image.

To use the Levels command:

1 Choose Adjust from the Image menu and Levels from the submenu (or press Command-L). The Levels dialog box appears.

Here is the same histogram of the image, showing the compressed shadows and highlights.

2 Click the Preview checkbox, then drag the dialog box down so you can see the top portions of the image.

The Levels dialog box contains an Auto button that works exactly like the Auto Levels command that you tried earlier. To get more control over the white and black points, you will set them using the eyedropper tool.

3 Click the black eyedropper in the Levels dialog box.

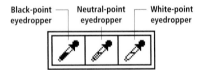

Black-point eyedropper — Neutral-point eyedropper — White-point eyedropper

4 Click the point that you earlier determined to be the darkest point in the image.

Clicking this dark point sets the value of this pixel to 0 (or black) and produces a darker image with more contrast. Notice that the histogram shifts to the left to show the change in pixel distribution. Although this improves the contrast, the image is too dark and the highlights are dull.

5 Click the white eyedropper in the Levels dialog box, then drag the Levels dialog box to the right so you can see the chef's body.

6 Click the point that you earlier determined to be the brightest point in the image.

Setting this white point brings out the brightness of the chef's hat and smock and lightens the image.

In changing the white point, you have lost some of the tone in the white areas (highlights). You need to decrease the contrast in the highlights to bring out some detail.

Decreasing contrast using the Levels command

The Output Levels slider in the Levels dialog box decreases the contrast in an image.

To decrease the contrast:

1 Drag the white triangle for the output levels to the left (the triangle directly below the white end of the gradation bar), until the right text box above the gradation bar reads 239. (You can also type **239** into the Output Levels text box.)

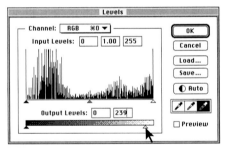

This tells Adobe Photoshop to take all the pixels with values between 239 and 255 and make their new value 239. Redistributing some highlight pixels produces a darker image with less contrast, so that the white areas take on more tone.

In the same way, dragging the black triangle for the output levels redistributes some shadow pixels and decreases contrast, producing a lighter image.

Increasing contrast using the Levels command

The Input Levels slider increases the contrast in an image. Although the contrast is good in this image, you're going to make the background slightly darker (that is, increase the contrast in the shadow areas).

To increase the contrast:

1 Drag the black triangle for the input levels to the right (the triangle directly below the left edge of the histogram), until the left text box above the histogram reads 11.

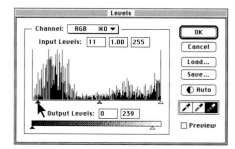

This tells Adobe Photoshop to take all the dark pixels with values between 0 and 11 and make their value 0. Moving the black triangle to the right redistributes the shadow pixels, producing a darker image with more contrast.

2 Click OK to apply the new settings.

3 Press Command-L to display the Levels dialog box again.

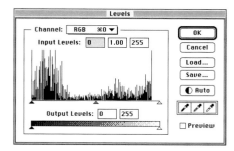

The histogram has changed to reflect the new distribution of pixels in the image. Notice that there are no pixels at the far right of the histogram,

reflecting the removal of some highlight values. The left side of the histogram shows the bunching caused by the redistribution of the shadow pixels.

Adjusting midtones using the Levels command

The *gamma* triangle for the input levels controls the midtone pixels. Although you don't need to adjust the gamma in this image, take some time now to experiment with this control so you'll know how to adjust the midtones in your own images.

To adjust the midtones:

1 Drag the gamma triangle to the right (the gray triangle under the middle of the Input Levels histogram), until the middle text box reads about 0.80.

The midtones in the image, especially those in the face, are darkened, while the highlights and shadows remain the same. In this case, however, this adjustment makes the midtones too dark.

2 Hold down the Option key and click the Reset button to undo the gamma adjustment, then click Cancel to close the dialog box.

As in other color correction dialog boxes, holding down the Option key changes the name of the Cancel button to Reset.

ADJUSTING COLOR WITH THE CURVES COMMAND

Like the Levels command, the Curves command lets you adjust the shadow, highlights, and midtones of an image. However, instead of making the adjustments using just three variables (highlights, shadows, and gamma), you can adjust any point along the gray levels curve for the image. Now you're going to color-correct this same image using the Curves command. To start with the same overexposed image, you must first undo the corrections you just made.

TIP: YOU CAN OPTION-
CLICK THE CURVES
GRAPH TO CHANGE
THE GRAPH TO UNITS
OF TEN INSTEAD OF
UNITS OF FOUR.

To use the Curves command:

1 Choose Revert from the File menu, then click Revert.

If you saved the file after making the color corrections, just reopen the *07Begin* file from the Lesson 7 folder.

2 Choose Adjust from the Image menu and Curves from the submenu (or press Command-M). The Curves dialog box appears.

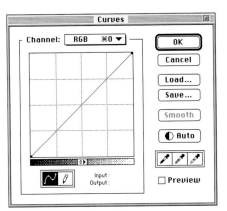

3 Move the Curves dialog box so that you can see as much of the image as possible.

The *x*-axis of the graph represents the original brightness value of the pixels, from 0 to 255 (input levels); the *y*-axis represents the adjusted brightness values (output levels).

The grayscale along the bottom of the dialog box moves from black on the left (0) to white on the right (255).

4 Click the arrows in the bar under the graph. Now the white is on the left and the black is on the right.

5 Move your cursor inside the graph.

The *x*-axis of the graph now represents the original brightness value of the pixels, from 0 to 100 percent (input levels); the *y*-axis represents the adjusted brightness values (output levels).

The grayscale along the bottom of the dialog box moves from white on the left (0) to black on the right (100 percent).

The lines across the graph indicate the *highlight tones* along the bottom border of the box, the *one-quarter tones* (one-quarter of the way between white and black), the *midtones*, the *three-quarter tones*, and the *shadow tones* along the top border.

6 Click the eyedropper tool in the toolbox and hold down the mouse button as you move around in the darkest area of the image (the piece of hair in front of the chef's ear).

As you move the eyedropper with the mouse button pressed, a circle appears on the graph in the Curves dialog box showing you the value of the pixel you're over in the image. The darkest area will appear closest to the upper-right corner of the graph.

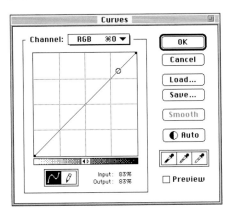

7 Use the eyedropper to locate the brightest point in the chef's smock (the circle will appear closest to the lower-left corner of the graph for the brightest point).

8 Click the black eyedropper in the Curves dialog box, then click the darkest point to set the black point.

9 Click the white eyedropper in the Curves dialog box, then click the brightest point to in the smock to set the white point.

Changing contrast using the Curves command

The line in the Curves graph shows the current relationship between the input values and the output values of the pixels. The diagonal line indicates a value of one to one—that is, every pixel has the same input and output value. To use the Curves dialog box, you click *control points* along this line and change the curve of the line by dragging up or down.

To change the image contrast:

1 Click the Preview checkbox in the Curves dialog box.

2 Move the cross hair along the diagonal line and stop at about the middle of the graph.

Watch the input and output levels at the bottom of the Curves dialog box. You want to position the cross hair on the line so that the input and output values both read about 50 percent.

3 Click and drag the control point up and to the left, and watch how the image gets darker.

The output level is now higher than the input level, indicating that the pixel's value is moving toward black, or becoming darker.

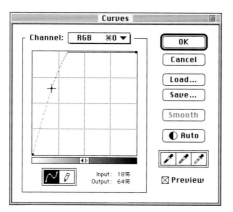

4 Click the same point on the line and drag down and to the right.

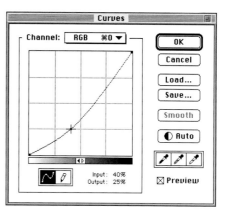

The output level is now lower than the input level, indicating that the pixel's value is moving toward white, or becoming lighter.

5 Click the control point and drag it off the graph to return to the original diagonal line.

Adjusting contrast using the Curves command

The first adjustment you made in the Levels dialog box was to reduce the contrast in the white areas. You then increased the contrast in the dark areas. You're going to drag the curve in this dialog box to make the same adjustments.

To adjust the contrast:

1 Click the small black point on the graph at the bottom-left corner of the line and drag up the edge of the graph, until the output value reads about 7 percent and the input value reads about 0 percent.

TIP: YOU CAN ALSO DISPLAY THE INFO PALETTE OPTIONS FOR MODES BY CLICKING THE EYEDROPPER ICON IN THE INFO PALETTE. TO DISPLAY THE MOUSE COORDINATE OPTIONS, CLICK THE CROSS HAIR IN THE INFO PALETTE.

If you don't see any input or output values, you probably have the pointer slightly outside the graph borders.

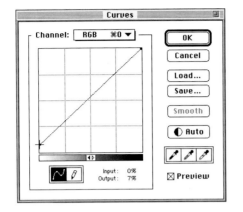

This redistributes the highlight pixels and decreases the contrast in the highlights.

2 Click the small black point at the upper-right corner of the line and drag horizontally along the top border of the graph, until the input value reads 96 percent and the output value reads 100 percent.

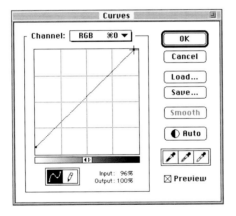

This redistributes the shadow pixels and increases the contrast in the dark areas.

3 Click the midtones area and drag up slightly and to the left to adjust the gamma of the midtones.

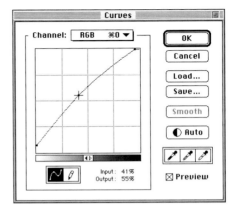

This should be only a slight adjustment. Experiment with this slider until the image looks correct on your screen.

The Levels and Curves dialog boxes also contain a neutral-gray eyedropper. You can use this eyedropper to set a starting point for correcting your middle tones and removing a color cast from the image.

4 Click OK to apply the settings.

USING THE INFO PALETTE AS A DENSITOMETER

A *densitometer* is a tool that reads the percentage (density) of black in a pixel. When you're making color corrections, you can use the Info palette as a densitometer to preview the changes in density before and after an adjustment. As you know, when you move the eyedropper over a pixel, that pixel's values appear in the Info palette.

To set the display for the Info palette:

1 Choose Palette Options from the Info palette pop-up menu. The Info Options dialog box appears.

Using the options in this dialog box, you can display the values for pixels in two different color modes. This can be especially useful when you're working in an RGB image but want to see the CMYK values for the pixels at the same time.

2 Choose RGB Color from the First Color Readout Mode menu and be sure that Show First Color Readout is selected.

In actuality, you have been seeing the RGB colors in the top of the Info palette, even though the First Color Readout Mode menu probably reads Actual Color. The Actual Color mode is the current color mode under the Mode menu—in this case, RGB.

3 Make sure that CMYK Color is selected in the Second Color Readout Mode menu and be sure that Show Second Color Readout is selected.

This dialog box also lets you turn on and off the mouse coordinates displayed in the Info palette, as well as change the measurement units for the mouse coordinates. You don't need to worry about these settings right now.

4 Click OK to close the dialog box.

To compare color values in the Info palette:

1 Click the eyedropper tool and position the eyedropper over the chef's left cheek in the *07Begin* window.

The Info palette shows RGB values of approximately 215 for R, 184 for G, and 147 for B. The CMYK values show the percentage of black in the pixel, about 15 percent for C, 29 percent for M, 39 percent for Y, and 3 percent for K. Unless you have the eyedropper in the exact same location, your values may be slightly different. Since this measurement is only for comparison, the actual values you see in the Info palette don't matter for this example.

2 Activate the *07Final* window and move the eyedropper to the same location (the left cheek) in this image.

Now the values show the color correction. The R value is approximately 231, the G value is 182, and the B value is 163. The CMYK values are about 8 percent for C, 33 percent for M, 30 percent for Y, and 1 percent for K. You can see that the final color-corrected image will have more red, a little less green, and more blue. In CMYK values, the image will have less cyan, about the same magenta, less yellow, and a little less black.

3 Activate the *07Begin* window and click the eye-dropper on the top green pepper in the bowl.

This sets the color as the foreground color so you can use it as a visual color reference.

4 Move into the *07Final* window, press the Option key, and click the same location to set the background color (you may need to drag the window to the left temporarily to show the pepper).

Comparing the color swatches in the foreground and background selection boxes is a quick way to see how a specific color differs in the two images.

ADJUSTING THE COLOR BALANCE IN AN IMAGE

With the highlights, shadows, and midtones corrected, you're now ready to adjust the color balance in this image. For the corrected image, you want to produce balanced skin tones and neutral, or slightly cool, whites and grays in the clothing.

To adjust the color balance:

1 Zoom in on both images so that you're in the 2:1 view.

Zoom in on the *07Final* first, then zoom in on the *07Begin* so that the images overlap and you can see both faces.

2 Drag the Info palette to the lower-right corner of the screen.

3 Make sure the *07Begin* window is active, then choose Adjust from the Image menu and Color Balance from the submenu (or press Command-Y). The Color Balance dialog box appears.

The Color Balance command allows you to change the mixture of color in an image so you can delete unwanted colors or enhance dull or muted colors.

4 Make sure the Preview option is selected, and drag the dialog box down so you can see the adjustments as you make them.

5 Make sure the Midtones option at the bottom of the dialog box is selected.

You can also use this command to change the color balance of the shadows or highlights. The Preserve Luminosity setting prevents changes from darkening the image or changing the color. Leave it checked to maintain the overall color balance in your image.

6 To add red and remove cyan, drag the Cyan/Red slider to the right until the color looks right on your screen (the left text box should read about 20).

7 To add magenta and remove green, drag the Magenta/Green slider to the left. The middle text box should read about −10.

8 To add blue and remove yellow, drag the Yellow/Blue slider to the right (the right text box should read about +30).

Your settings may differ.

9 Do not click OK to apply these settings yet.

COMPARING BEFORE-AND-AFTER COLOR VALUES USING THE EYEDROPPER

Whenever you have a color-correction dialog box open, the Info palette shows you two sets of color values. The values on the left show the original pixel values; the values on the right show the values after correction. To see how this works, you're going to roam around a bit in this image and watch the Info palette values.

Remember, since you are correcting the midtones, the differences will show up only in areas with middle tones.

To compare values in the Info palette:

1 Move the eyedropper over the line of blush on the chef's right cheek.

The Info palette should look something like this.

Again, your values may be different, depending on the exact location of the eyedropper.

Since the values on the left show the original pixels, and the values on the right show the corrected pixels, you can preview the severity of the adjustment. For example, in the Color Balance dialog box you added blue and removed yellow. The values in the Info palette show that you are going

from a B value of about 37 to 48, and a Y value of about 87 to 73. (Your values may differ, depending on the adjustments you made in the Color Balance dialog box.)

2 Move the eyedropper over the shadows in the lower right of the chef's hat.

The Info palette shows the increase in cyan and magenta values and the decrease in yellow values.

3 Press the spacebar to display the hand pointer, and scroll around in the image to see how other areas are affected by these color changes.

As you scroll, look for the changes in the midtones.

4 Click OK in the Color Balance dialog box to apply the color corrections.

5 Choose Save As from the File menu, open the Projects folder, type **07Work** for the name of the file, then click Save.

MAKING SELECTIVE COLOR CORRECTIONS

As with all Adobe Photoshop editing techniques, you can apply color-correction commands to all or part of an image. For this image, you're going to increase the variety of the peppers in the bowl by changing two yellow peppers into orange peppers. First you'll try some color-correction techniques that work with ranges of colors.

To replace a color:

1 Return both images to a 1:1 view, and make sure the *07Work* window is active.

The peppers are currently a bright, almost neon yellow. You will replace the yellow with a warmer orange color.

2 Choose Adjust from the Image menu and Replace Color from the submenu. The Replace Color dialog box appears.

3 Move the dialog box so that you can see your image.

The Replace Color command lets you select a specific color and then adjust the hue, saturation and lightness to correct the color. The dialog box contains a preview box you can use to see the colors you're changing or to see a copy of the entire image.

As you might remember, the sliders in the Hue area reflect the number of degrees of rotation around the color wheel that the new color is from the original color.

4 Click the Preview checkbox.

5 Move the eyedropper out into your image and click in the yellow pepper that is farthest to the right.

Notice that the Sample box at the bottom of the dialog box shows the foreground color. Watch this box to see how the changes you make affect this specific color. You are adjusting the yellow in the peppers.

6 Adjust the Fuzziness slider to include more of the pepper area in the selection mask. Try a value between 70 and 100.

7 Drag the Hue slider to the right until it reads −20 (minus 20).

This makes the peppers a bright orange color—a little too bright to be believable.

8 Drag the Saturation slider to the left until the text box reads −10 (minus 10) to reduce the intensity of the color.

9 Click OK to apply the color correction.

This changes the color of all three peppers. The Replace Color command replaces all the selected color in the image. To replace color in only part of an image, you need to make a selection first.

To make a selection before using Replace Color:

1 Choose Undo Replace Color from the Edit menu.

2 Use the lasso to select the two yellow peppers on the right. You don't need to be precise; just make a rough selection. Be sure to include the right rim of the metal bowl, which shows the reflection of the current peppers.

3 Choose Adjust from the Image menu and Replace Color from the submenu.

4 Click the yellow part of the pepper in the *07Work* file.

5 After selecting the color, type **–20** for the hue.

6 Leave the saturation at 0 (you'll try another method of changing saturation in the next exercise) and click OK.

Only the two peppers on the right are modified. They are both a bright orange color. You'll modify the saturation later.

7 Choose None from the Select menu (or press Command-D).

8 Choose Save from the File menu (or press Command-S).

LIGHTENING, DARKENING, AND DESATURATING AREAS IN AN IMAGE

While the color correction in this image now has a good balance, there are a few areas that need minor corrections. You are going to add some snap to the image by lightening the shadow areas in the peppers, and darkening the shadow tones in the chef's smock. Then, you'll desaturate the peppers you just changed with the Replace Color command. To make these corrections, you'll use the toning tools.

 In Adobe Photoshop you use the *dodge tool* to lighten areas of an image.

 You use the *burn tool* to darken areas of an image.

 You use the *sponge* tool to saturate or desaturate areas of an image.

Dodging and burning-in are familiar techniques to photographers, who use these methods to correct unbalanced areas in a print caused by overexposing or underexposing the negative.

To dodge the shadows in the peppers:

1 Zoom in on the peppers in the *07Work* and *07Final* windows.

Since the changes you're making with this tool are minor, you might want to use the reference file as a guide.

2 Make sure the *07Work* window is active, then click the dodge tool in the toolbox and move into the image area. Notice that the pointer turns into a black circle on a stick.

This icon represents a piece of cardboard taped to a handle that photographers traditionally use as a dodge tool.

3 Double-click the Brushes palette tab, then select the second brush from the left in the second row.

4 Click the Options palette tab, and the Toning Tools Options palette appears, which contains all the options for the dodge, burn, and sponge tools.

5 Make sure that the exposure is at 50 percent and that Midtones is selected in the Mode menu.

Increasing the exposure produces a stronger effect; decreasing it produces a more subtle lightening.

6 Using short strokes, paint with the dodge tool to lighten the midtone areas in the peppers.

The effect is particularly noticeable on the sides of the red and green peppers.

To burn in the shadows on the chef's smock:

1 Zoom out so you can see the entire image in both windows.

2 Choose Burn from the Tool menu in the Toning Tools Options palette.

3 Click the Brushes palette tab, then double-click the brush on the far right in the second row to change the brush options.

4 Set the diameter to 40, the hardness to 0, and the spacing to 25 percent, then click OK.

5 Move into the image area and notice that the pointer turns into a hand with the thumb and index finger touching.

This icon reflects the fact that most photographers use their fingers and hands as burn-in tools.

6 Stroke the burn tool over the shadows in the smock under the peppers to increase the shadows.

If you want to experiment, try using a smaller brush and stroking the right sleeve and collar of the smock. Stroking in white areas won't add shadows. The burn tool builds on the existing pixel values; the white areas don't have any original dark areas to build on.

7 Choose Save from the File menu (or press Command-S).

To desaturate the peppers:

1 Double-click the burn tool in the toolbox.

2 Choose Sponge from the Tool menu in the Toning Tools Options palette.

3 Make sure that Desaturate is selected in the mode menu.

4 Click the Brushes palette tab, then choose the fourth brush from the left in the top row.

5 Move into the image area and notice that the pointer turns into a sponge.

This icon reflects the fact that the sponge tool is often used for "soaking up" the color in an area.

6 Stroke the sponge tool over the bright orange peppers on the right.

The color is desaturated or diluted from the intense hues to more muted tones.

If you desaturate the peppers too much, you can choose Saturate from the mode pop-up menu in the Toning Tools Options palette to increase the color in an area.

BLURRING AND SHARPENING AREAS IN AN IMAGE

Sometimes, areas in an image may be slightly out of focus, or there may be edges that are too sharp (that is, there is a noticeable transition that gives the image that "computer art" look). The focus tools let you correct these minor flaws.

Applying the *blur tool* decreases the contrast between pixels and produces a smoother image. You'll use the blur tool to soften the jagged edges on the peppers.

Applying the *sharpen tool* increases the contrast between pixels and produces more clarity or focus. You'll use the sharpen tool to bring the pepper stems into focus.

To blur the edges of the peppers:

1 Zoom in on the peppers so that both windows are in the 2:1 view.

Notice the jagged edges around the peppers.

2 Make sure the *07Work* window is active, then click the blur tool in the toolbox and move into the image area. Notice that the pointer turns into a water drop.

3 Click the Brushes palette tab, then select the third brush from the right in the top row.

4 Click the Options palette tab, then make sure that the pressure is set at 50 percent and the mode is set to Normal for the Focus Tool options.

Increasing the pressure produces a stronger blurring effect; decreasing the pressure creates a weaker effect.

5 Paint along the edges of the peppers to smooth out the edges.

You can see the blurring most clearly along the edges of the peppers that are outlined by the white smock.

To focus the pepper stems:

1 With the blur tool still selected, press the Option key. Notice that the pointer turns into a triangle.

Holding down the Option key lets you switch between the blur and sharpen tools (you can also hold down the Option key to switch between the dodge and burn tools). When you use this shortcut (instead of choosing the tool from the menu in the Options palette), you must use the same brush and exposure or pressure setting for both tools.

2 Paint the pepper stems to bring them into focus.

3 Choose Save from the File menu (or press Command-S).

4 Return both images to the 1:1 view.

SHARPENING AN ENTIRE IMAGE

Sometimes, a poor-quality original photograph or the scanning process can cause an image to appear slightly out of focus or "soft." You can sharpen an image using the Adobe Photoshop sharpening filters.

To sharpen this image:

1 Make sure that *07Work* is active, then choose Sharpen from the Filter menu and Unsharp Mask from the submenu. The Unsharp Mask dialog box appears.

The Unsharp Mask filter finds areas in the image where abrupt color changes occur, and sharpens them by increasing the contrast between the light and dark pixels.

2 If necessary, set the amount to 50 percent, the radius to 1, and the threshold to 0, then click OK to apply the filter.

The effect of this mask is subtle, and you may not immediately see the difference in the image.

3 Press Command-F to apply the filter a few more times, until the image is "too" sharp.

4 Press Command-Z to undo the last filter application.

When sharpening an image, it's often helpful to overdo the sharpening, and then go back one step to get the correct image. You have now finished your color corrections, and the colors in your file should be close to those in the *07Final* file.

5 Choose Save from the File menu (or press Command-S).

6 Choose Close from the File menu to close the *07Work* file. Leave *07Final* open.

DISPLAYING THE FILE IN CMYK MODE

If you were going to print your images, you would convert this file to CMYK mode. You'll learn about this conversion process in Lessons 10 and 11. For now, you're going to open an already converted CMYK version of this file to make one final color correction.

To open the CMYK file:

1 Choose Open from the File menu, then open the *07CMYK1* file.

While you still have the RGB version of the *07Final* file open, compare the two images. You won't see any difference because your monitor can only display images in RGB color. If you printed the two versions of the file, the differences would be quite apparent.

2 Select the *07Final* file, then choose Close from the File menu.

3 Choose Open from the File menu and open the *07CMYK2* file as your reference file.

4 Move the images side by side.

COLOR-CORRECTING AN INDIVIDUAL CHANNEL

When you made color corrections to this image earlier in this lesson, you applied the color corrections to red, green, and blue channels simultaneously. You can also make color corrections to an individual channel. A channel, you will remember, contains specific color information about the image.

Displaying the histogram for individual channels

Before you make the color correction, you're going to look at the distribution of pixels in each of the color channels.

To display the histogram for individual channels:

1 Make sure that 07CMYK1 is the active window.

2 Choose Palettes from the Window menu, and Show Channels from the submenu.

A CMYK image contains a composite channel and four individual channels, one for each of the process colors.

3 Click the Cyan channel thumbnail in the Channels palette.

Color channels are displayed in grayscale. To view channels in color, you need to change the viewing preferences.

4 Choose Preferences from the File menu and General from the submenu.

5 Click the Color Channels in Color checkbox under Display, then click OK.

The channel thumbnails are now displayed in color.

6 Click the CMYK composite channel thumbnail.

7 Choose Histogram from the Image menu to display the Histogram dialog box.

The pop-up menu at the top of the Histogram dialog box shows that the Gray channel is currently chosen. The Gray channel shows the combined histogram values for all the channels.

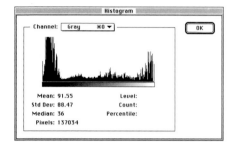

8 Choose Cyan from the pop-up menu to display the pixel values for this channel.

The gradation bar below the histogram appears in cyan to indicate the channel you're looking at. Notice that the cyan channel has a high concentration of pixels in the three-quarter tones.

9 Choose Magenta from the pop-up menu.

The histogram shifts and shows that the greatest concentration of pixels in this channel is in the middle or flesh tones.

10 Choose Yellow from the pop-up menu.

The histogram shifts again to show the yellow pixel values. For both the magenta and yellow channels, the pixels start farther from the right edge of the histogram than they do in the cyan channel. This placement accounts for the blue cast in the bright white fabric of the chef's clothing.

11 Choose Black from the pop-up menu to check this channel's distribution.

12 Click OK to close the Histogram dialog box.

Adjusting colors in the channels

Now you're ready to adjust the cyan channel to remove the blue cast from the image. You'll use the Levels command to make this correction.

To color-correct a channel:

1 Drag the Info palette so you will be able to see it with an open dialog box, then press Command-L to display the Levels dialog box.

2 Drag the dialog box so you can see the image.

3 Choose Cyan from the pop-up menu at the top of the dialog box.

4 Move the eyedropper over the *07CMYK1* file and look at the values in the Info palette.

The values tell you the percentage of the specific color in the image. When you're editing a single channel, only a black (K) value appears in the CMYK readout in the Info palette.

5 Drag the white triangle for the input levels to the left, until the text box reads 185, to remove some cyan from the highlight area.

6 Move the eyedropper over the *07CMYK1* file and look at the values in the Info palette.

The image changes to show the reduction in cyan pixels. This is too much of a correction.

7 For a final adjustment, again drag the white triangle for the input levels to the right, until the text box reads 240.

8 Click OK to apply this correction.

SELECTIVE COLOR CONTROL

Another command that you can use to correct color in an image is a technique performed by high-end scanners called *selective color control.* Selective color control lets you modify colors by changing the amount of ink used to make a specific color.

To modify colors by changing ink percentages:

1 Make sure you are viewing the composite channel.

2 Choose Adjust from the Image menu and Selective Color from the submenu.

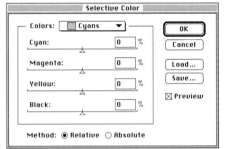

3 Move the dialog box so you can see your image.

4 Click the Preview checkbox.

5 Choose Cyans from the Colors menu.

6 Make sure the Relative option is selected.

7 Drag the Cyan slider to the left until it reflects a 5 percent change.

The Relative option adjusts the existing CMYK values. For example, if one pixel is 100 percent cyan and one pixel is 50 percent cyan, a 10 percent decrease would change the first pixel to 90 percent cyan and the second pixel to 45 percent cyan (10 percent of 50 percent). The absolute option adjusts every cyan pixel by the percentage reflected in the sliders. See the *Adobe Photoshop User Guide* for more information on the Selective Color command.

8 Click OK. The changes are probably too subtle to see on your screen, but show when you print.

9 Choose Close from the File menu to close both files without saving changes.

And here's your final color-corrected image! Considering what you started with, you're probably amazed at the change in the image. You've covered a lot of territory in this lesson, and you should be proud of everything you've learned. With this knowledge, you are ready to tackle almost any color-correction challenge that you might encounter as you use Adobe Photoshop for your own work.

Lesson

8

Lesson 8: Scanning, Resolution, and Resizing

This lesson discusses choosing a scanning resolution and explains the relationship between resolution and resizing an image. When you first begin working with digitized images, the term *resolution* can be confusing. At various times, resolution is used to describe the amount of pixel information in an image, the number of bits of stored information in a single pixel, the output quality of a printer, or even the density of a halftone screen.

In this lesson, you'll be exploring resolution as it refers to the amount of stored information in a particular image. This type of resolution affects an image's file size, its size on the screen, and the final printed output. It should take you about an hour to complete this lesson.

In this lesson, you'll learn how to do the following:

- estimate the best scan resolution

- determine how file size affects image resolution

- resize an image with and without resampling

- crop an image proportionately

- combine images of different resolutions

At the end of this lesson, you'll have a composite portrait of the chef that takes her from a boring everyday work environment and puts her in a dramatic stage setting.

Source file (08Chef)

Source file (08Velvet)   *Ending image (08Final)*

ABOUT RESOLUTION

Several types of resolution are important regarding the properties of digitized images: bit resolution, device resolution, screen resolution (or screen frequency), and image resolution.

Bit resolution, or bit depth, measures the number of bits of stored information per pixel. This resolution determines how many colors can be displayed at one time on-screen (that is, 8-bit, 24-bit, or 32-bit color).

Device resolution, or output resolution, refers to the number of dots per inch (dpi) that the output device—such as a monitor, an imagesetter, or a laser printer—can produce. This resolution is measured in dpi. The device resolution for a monitor is typically 72 dpi. It cannot be changed through the Adobe Photoshop software.

Screen resolution, also known as *screen frequency*, refers to the number of dots per inch in the halftone screen used to print a grayscale image or color separation. Screen resolution is measured in lines per inch (lpi).

Image resolution refers to the amount of information stored for an image, typically measured in pixels per inch (ppi). The image resolution and the document's dimensions determine the overall file size of the document, as well as the quality of the output. The higher the image resolution, the more space on disk the image requires, and the more time it takes for printing and other operations.

SCANNING BASICS

The choices you make before scanning an image affect the quality and usefulness of the resulting digital file. Before scanning, be sure you do the following:

• define the area you want to scan

• decide what scan resolution you should use

• determine the optimal dynamic range (if your scanner lets you set black points and white points)

• check for color casts that you might want to eliminate during the scan

The following section discusses how to set the scan resolution. See the *Adobe Photoshop User Guide* for information about determining the optimal dynamic range and eliminating unwanted color casts.

Determining the correct scan resolution

The optimal scan resolution depends on how the image will be printed or displayed. If you're going to use the image as a screen display, its resolution need not be greater than the resolution of the target screen area—about 640 pixels by 480 pixels. The images in this lesson were scanned at low resolutions because they were meant to be displayed on-screen.

In many cases, however, you will be scanning images for later output on high-resolution devices. If you are producing a full-bleed magazine cover, for example, you will need considerably more data to work with—that is, the image will need to be scanned at a higher resolution.

If the image resolution is too low, Adobe Photoshop may use the color value of a single pixel to create several halftone dots. This results in *pixelization*, or very coarse-looking output. If the resolution is too high, the file contains more information than the printer needs. Image resolution that exceeds twice the screen frequency used to print the image can rob the image of subtle transitions in tone. This can result in a posterized or very flat image. When setting the scan resolution, your goal is to balance ideal resolution with a manageable file size.

Calculating the scan resolution

You calculate the correct scan resolution by using the screen frequency that will be used to print the final output, and the original and final image dimensions.

If you plan to separate a color image, a good rule of thumb is to capture pixels at twice the screen frequency to be used for printing. For example, if you are producing a magazine cover that will be printed using a 133-lpi screen, a good scanning resolution would be 266 ppi, or twice the screen frequency.

If the final image will be larger than the scanned original, you need additional data to produce a final image with the correct image resolution. If the final image will be smaller than the original, you need less data.

To calculate the scan resolution:

• Multiply the longest dimension of the final image size by the screen frequency; then multiply this value by the ratio of screen ruling (typically 2:1).

• For example, suppose you are scanning an image that is 2 inches wide by 3 inches high, and you want to produce a final image that is 4 inches wide by 5 inches high. You are using a screen frequency of 150.

• Multiply 5 (the longest output dimension) by 150 (the screen frequency) to get 750 pixels. Then multiply 750 by 2 (the ratio of the screen ruling). This equals a total of 1,500 pixels needed.

• Divide the total number of pixels needed by the longest dimension of the original image.

In this example, the longest dimension of the original image is 3 inches. Dividing 1,500 by 3 equals a scan resolution of 500 dpi.

Different color-separation procedures might require different pixel-to-line screen ratios. It's a good idea to check with your service bureau or print shop to finalize the resolution requirements before you scan the image.

BEGINNING THIS LESSON

In this lesson, you'll resize an image and change its resolution. Then you'll combine two images with different resolutions.

To begin this lesson:

1 Quit Adobe Photoshop, then throw away your *Adobe Photoshop 3.0 Prefs* file and empty the Trash.

2 Launch the Adobe Photoshop application.

3 Choose Open from the File menu, then open the *08Chef* file in the Lesson 8 folder. If the image doesn't appear at 1:1 view, double-click the zoom tool.

Note that this image contains only one layer—the Background layer.

4 Close or collapse all of the Adobe Photoshop palettes, except for the Layers palette group.

HOW RESOLUTION AFFECTS FILE SIZE AND DISPLAY

To work efficiently with scanned images, you determine the amount of image information you need, and then discard the rest. Doing this allows you to minimize the file size so that the image processes more quickly.

Image resolution affects file size in a proportional way. The size of a file is proportional to the square of its resolution. If you maintain the dimensions of an image but double its file size, the image resolution increases four times. For example, if you increase the resolution of a 72-ppi image to 144 ppi while keeping the same dimensions, the file size increases by four times.

Image resolution also affects how large the image appears on the screen. Since the resolution of your screen is always 72 dpi, a 144-ppi image is displayed at double its actual size. These relationships will become clearer as you work through this lesson.

CHANGING IMAGE SIZE AND RESOLUTION

Changing an image's resolution (or *resampling*) changes the amount of information contained in the image.

In general, it's not a good idea to decrease an image's resolution and later increase the resolution. For example, suppose you decreased an image's resolution because you were printing on a low-resolution device such as a 300-dpi laser printer. Decreasing the resolution deletes some of the original color information in the image. If you later increase the resolution, Adobe Photoshop calculates the color value of the missing pixels to add information. The resulting image is not as sharp as the original, higher-resolution image.

The Image Size command lets you resize an image while controlling the image resolution. You were introduced to this command in Lesson 5, when you used it to resize the brochure art. In this lesson, you'll use the Image Size command to change the size and resolution of the *08Chef* image. Before you begin making changes, however, you need to find out the current file size and dimensions of the image.

To change the image size and resolution:

1 Choose Show Rulers from the Window menu (or press Command-R).

2 Note the file size in the lower-left corner of the image, then hold down the Option key and press the mouse button to display the size preview box.

The file size is 841K, and the image is about 7 inches wide and about 7.9 inches high. The image resolution is 72 ppi.

3 Choose Image Size from the Image menu.

4 In the Image Size dialog box, make sure that inches appears in both pop-up menus.

5 Make sure that the Constrain Proportions option is selected.

This option changes the image dimensions without changing the height-to-width ratio. When you enter a new value for the height or width, the program automatically adjusts the other value to maintain the image proportions.

Resampling an image as you resize

When you *resample down* (decrease the resolution or decrease the dimensions and keep the same resolution), the program deletes information from the image. When you *resample up* (increase the resolution or increase the dimensions and keep the same resolution), Adobe Photoshop creates new pixel information based on the existing color values.

To resample the image:

1 Deselect the Constrain File Size option.

When you deselect this option, Adobe Photoshop either adds or deletes information from the file.

2 Enter **90** in the Resolution text box.

Increasing the resolution of this image (while keeping the same dimensions) increases the file size to 1.28 M (the *M* stands for megabytes), as shown at the top of the New Size box. This means Adobe Photoshop will add information to this file.

3 Click OK to resample up the image.

Because you increased the resolution beyond the monitor resolution of 72 dpi, the image appears larger on the screen. The actual size of the image (7inches by 7.9 inches) has not changed.

4 Click the lower-left corner of the document window to preview the page size and layout.

5 Choose Undo Image Size to return to the original image.

6 Choose Image Size from the Image menu and enter **3** in the Width box. The height changes to 3.387 inches. Leave the resolution at 72 ppi.

Decreasing the dimensions of the image (while keeping the same resolution) decreases the file size to 155K, indicating that the program will delete information from the file.

7 Click OK to resample down the image.

The smaller image reflects the new dimensions you have set while keeping the 72-ppi resolution.

8 Click the lower-left corner of the document window again to preview the page size and layout.

9 Choose Undo Image Size from the Edit menu to return to the original image.

Resizing without resampling

If you constrain a file size while you resize, Adobe Photoshop does not resample the image. The program automatically adjusts the other parameter so that no information is added to or deleted from the file.

To resize without resampling:

1 Choose Image Size from the Image menu and select the Constrain File Size option.

2 Enter **3** in the Width text box; again, the height changes to 3.387 inches to keep the same image proportions.

Decreasing the dimensions while constraining the file size increases the resolution to 168 ppi, but the current file size and new file size remain the same.

When you decrease the image dimensions without changing the file size, the same number of pixels must fill a smaller area so the resolution increases. (In the same way, if you increase the dimensions while constraining the file size, the resolution decreases because the same number of pixels must fill a larger area.)

3 Click OK.

The display of the image does not change even though you have reduced the image dimensions because the file still contains the same number of pixels.

4 Look at the rulers and note the change in size.

5 Display the size preview box to confirm the new dimensions and resolution.

6 Choose Save As from the File menu.

7 Type **08Work** for the file name, open the Projects folder and click Save.

Changing resolution as you crop an image

The cropping tool contains options that let you define the height-to-width ratio for the cropping marquee and the resolution of the cropped image. These options allow you to *crop proportionately*.

To specify the size of a cropped area:

1 Double-click the cropping tool in the toolbox. The Cropping Tool Options palette appears.

2 Click the Fixed Target Size checkbox in the Options palette, then enter **2** inches for the width and **2.5** inches for the height. Leave the Resolution text box blank.

When you specify a size but not a resolution, Adobe Photoshop determines the maximum resolution possible for the defined marquee size.

3 Zoom out so you can see the entire image.

4 Position the pointer in the middle of the second the yellow pasta cluster, then drag up and to the right to include the pasta machine and all of the pasta chef in the marquee.

The marquee is constrained proportionately by the dimensions you specified in the Cropping Tool Options palette. If the cropping border doesn't include all of the chef and the pasta machine, reposition the border by holding down the Command key as you drag a handle.

5 Click the scissors inside the marquee to crop the image.

6 Option-click in the size preview box to preview the image size (you may need to resize the window to see the file size).

The new file size is about 600K, and the new dimensions are 2 inches by 2.5 inches (the marquee size you specified). The new resolution is about 200 ppi (depending on the exact size of the marquee you drew). This is the maximum resolution possible, given the selected area. The resolution increased because you reduced the image size.

7 Use the cropping marquee to crop the image again, this time including just the pasta machine and part of the chef's hands.

8 Click with the scissors inside the marquee to crop the image.

9 Option-click in the size preview box to preview the image size (you may need to resize the window to see the file size).

The new file size is about 150K. The dimensions are still 2 inches by 2.5 inches, but this time the resolution has decreased to about 100 ppi.

The resolution has decreased because this is the maximum resolution possible, given the selected area and the amount of information the image needs to contain. Since the area you just cropped is an enlargement of the original image, the resolution decreased.

10 Choose Revert from the File menu and click the Revert button to return to the original *08Work* image.

Using Auto Resolution

Now you're ready to put the chef against her new background. Your first step is to return the *08Work* image to its original resolution of 72 ppi. One way to do this is to have Adobe Photoshop determine the resolution by using the Auto button in the Image Size dialog box.

To determine a suggested resolution for an image:

1 Choose Image Size from the Image menu, then click the Auto button in the Image Size dialog box. The Auto Resolution dialog box appears.

2 Use the default screen value of 133 lpi.

This screen value is used only to calculate the image resolution. (To specify the halftone screen frequency for printing, you must use the Halftone Screens dialog box. You'll learn more about this dialog box in Lesson 11.)

3 Click Draft for the Quality setting.

Draft produces a resolution that is the same as the monitor resolution (no higher than 72 pixels per inch). Because you will work with the image only on-screen, you do not need a resolution higher than 72 ppi.

4 Click OK to return to the Image Size dialog box.

The recommended resolution of 72 ppi is entered automatically in the Image Size dialog box, and the file size decreases to 155K.

5 Click OK to resize the image.

The image appears smaller on your screen since you have reduced the resolution.

6 Choose Save from the File menu.

COMBINING IMAGES WITH DIFFERENT RESOLUTIONS

When you combine two images, the results may be unexpected if the resolution of the images does not match. The background you are going to paste this image into has a different resolution from this file.

To compare the resolution of the files:

1 Choose Open from the File menu, then open the *08Velvet* file in the Lesson 8 folder.

2 Drag the image by its title bar so that it appears next to the *08Work* image. The *08Velvet* file appears much larger than the *08Work* image.

3 Option-click in the file-size box of each file to preview the size information for both images.

The *08Velvet* image is 3 inches by 3.7 inches—essentially the same size as the *08Work* image—but the resolution is 144 ppi, or double that of the *08Work* image. You will see how the different resolutions affect the combination of the two images when you paste the chef into the *08Velvet* image.

4 Double-click the magic wand tool, enter a tolerance of 50 in the Magic Wand Options palette, and make sure the Anti-aliased option is on.

5 Activate the *08Work* window and click the magic wand in the black background.

The entire background is selected.

6 Choose Inverse from the Select menu so that the chef and the table are selected.

7 Drag the chef into the *08Velvet* image.

The selection appears much too small for the velvet background. Pasting the *08Work* selection into the *08Velvet* image caused the 72-ppi resolution of the selection to double to 144 ppi, to match the resolution of the *08Velvet* image. Although the dimensions of the two original images almost match, the proportions appear distorted because the resolutions are different.

Reducing the resolution of a file

To make a composite of the two images, you need to reduce the resolution of the *08Velvet* image to match that of the *08Work* image.

To reduce the resolution:

1 Choose Undo Drag Selection from the Edit menu.

2 With the *08Velvet* window active, choose Image Size from the Image menu and make sure the Constrain File Size option is not selected.

3 Enter **72** in the Resolution text box.

The new file size is about 173K to reflect the decreased resolution.

4 Click OK.

The *08Velvet* image is resampled down to 72 ppi. The side-by-side images now appear to be about the same size. (If the sizes are not similar, make sure you're viewing both images at 1:1 view.)

5 Select the 08Work file and drag the Chef selection into the *08Velvet* file again.

The two images now appear correctly proportioned.

6 Drag the selection down if necessary, to make the table flush with the bottom of the window.

7 Create a new layer by double-clicking the Floating Selection thumbnail in the Layers palette.

8 Type **Chef** to name the new layer, then click OK.

9 Choose Save As from the File menu.

10 Type **08Comp** for the file name, open the Projects folder and click Save.

CHANGING THE SIZE OF THE CANVAS

To complete the lesson, you're going to put a border around the composite image. In Lesson 5, you learned how to create a border using the Stroke command. In this lesson, you'll use the Canvas Size command to create the border.

To use the Canvas Size command:

1 Set the background color to black by clicking the Switch Colors icon in the toolbox (all added canvas appears in the background color).

2 Choose Canvas Size from the Image menu.

3 Enter **3.25** inches in the Width text box and **4.08** inches in the Height text box, then make sure the center square in the placement box is selected.

This adds a border of one-eighth of an inch around the image.

4 Click OK to add the black canvas to the image.

Canvas is added to the Background layer of the image.

5 Click the eye icon to hide the Background layer. The Chef layer has one-eighth of an inch of transparent border.

6 Click the eye icon again to display the Background layer.

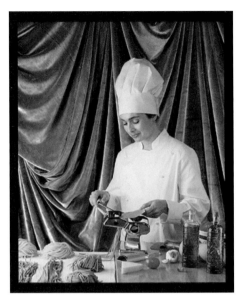

7 Choose Save from the File menu.

8 Choose Close from the File menu to close the files.

This lesson deals with several concepts that are central to working with digitized images, yet can sometimes be quite confusing. Understanding the relationship between image size and resolution, image display and resolution, resampling up, and resampling down can take some time. If you feel you need more review, try doing some of the tasks in this lesson again, or better yet, use the steps to experiment with your own favorite images.

Lesson

9

LESSON 9: ANNUAL REPORT COVER

In this lesson, you will have a chance to practice the techniques you learned in Lessons 7 and 8. Nothing new is introduced in this lesson.

The step-by-step instructions in this lesson provide all the information you need to complete the project. Because this is a review, detailed instructions aren't included. If you find that you can't remember how to do something, or need more precise instructions, refer back to Lessons 7 and 8. It should take you about 45 minutes to complete this lesson.

In Lesson 7, most of your efforts were directed toward *color-correcting* the *Portrait* image. In Lesson 8, you learned about resizing and cropping an image. In this lesson, you'll use many of the same techniques to combine three images to create the annual report cover for a Gourmet Visions Italian subsidiary called Casalingo Incorporated. You'll work with one familiar image and two new images in this lesson.

Source file (09Pepper)

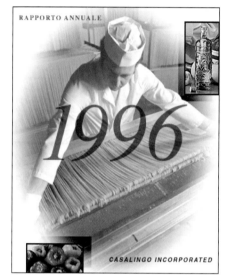

Ending image (09Final)

BEGINNING THIS LESSON

In this lesson, you'll modify your beginning image by adding cropped sections from two other images, and then add text to create the final composite image. All the files you'll work with in this lesson are in RGB mode.

To begin this lesson:

1 Quit Adobe Photoshop, locate the *Adobe Photoshop 3.0 Prefs* file in the Preferences folder in your System Folder and drag it to the Trash, then empty the Trash.

Source file (09Pasta)

Source file (09Oil)

2 Restart the Adobe Photoshop application.

3 Choose Open from the File menu, then open the *09Final* file in the Lesson 9 folder.

4 Click the Layers palette tab, then click the zoom box to resize the Layers palette.

This image has five layers: the Background layer, the White Overlay layer, the Insets layer, the Shadow layer, and the Text layer.

5 Zoom out to reduce the image, then drag the window to the upper-right corner of your screen.

6 Choose Open from the File menu, then open the *09Pasta* image in the Lesson 9 folder. If the image does not appear at 1:1 view, double-click the zoom tool.

7 Turn on the rulers in the *09Pasta* file.

8 Create a new group of palettes consisting of the Brushes palette, Layers palette, and Options palette.

9 Close the other palettes.

10 Choose Palettes from the Window menu, and Show Info from the submenu.

RESIZING A BACKGROUND

You'll begin making the composite image by resizing the *09Pasta* image so it can serve as the background for the annual report cover. After resizing the image, you'll remove some of the extra space at the bottom.

To resize the image:

1 Choose Image Size from the Image menu.

2 In the Image Size dialog box, deselect the Constrain File Size option. The Constrain Proportions option should remain selected.

You need to turn off the File Size option so you can resample as you resize. The current image is 4.25 inches wide by 6.34 inches high, with a resolution of 100 ppi. The file size is 790K.

3 Enter **4.5** inches for the width (the height automatically changes to 6.713 inches) and enter a resolution of 72 ppi.

Note that the new file size will be 459K. The file gets smaller because, even though you're making the dimensions larger, you're decreasing the image resolution.

4 Click OK to resize the image.

To crop the bottom of the image:

1 Choose Canvas Size from the Image menu.

2 In the Canvas Size dialog box, leave the width at 4.5, enter **5.75** inches for the height, and click the top-middle square in the placement box.

3 Click OK, then click Proceed at the warning.

The bottom part of the image is cropped. The remaining image has the correct proportions and resolution for the annual report cover.

4 Save the image as **09Work** in your Projects folder.

COLOR-CORRECTING AN IMAGE

In this part of the lesson, you will precisely correct the color in the *09Work* image by using the Levels dialog box.

Adjusting the overall contrast

As you learned in Lesson 7, when making color corrections, it's a good idea to correct overall contrast first by setting the black and white points, and then adjusting the midtones.

To adjust the overall contrast:

1 Choose Adjust from the Image menu and Levels from the submenu.

2 Move the Levels dialog box so you can see the man in the pasta image.

The histogram in the Levels dialog box shows the overall darkness of the image.

3 Click the black point eyedropper, then position the eyedropper on the left side of the chef's hair.

4 Move the eyedropper around the shadow area and watch the K values in the Info palette. Click the darkest point to set the black point (the value should be about 95 percent).

5 Hold down the Command key and the spacebar and click to zoom in on the baker's head.

6 Click the white point eyedropper in the Levels dialog box and position the eyedropper on the very top brim of the hat.

7 Move the eyedropper until the C, M, and Y values in the Info palette read about 1 percent or 2 percent, then click to set the white point.

8 Set the gamma value to 1.40 by dragging the Gamma slider to the left or entering the value in the Gamma text box.

9 Click OK to apply the color corrections to the image.

10 Zoom out to a 1:1 view.

11 Save the file.

ADJUSTING SATURATION IN SELECTED AREAS

In the final cover, you want to focus attention on the tray of spaghetti. To do this, you need to decrease the saturation of color in the other areas of the image to emphasize the color in the spaghetti tray.

To adjust the saturation:

1 Double-click the lasso tool.

2 Set the feather radius to 2 in the Lasso Options palette.

3 Press the Option key, then use the lasso tool to select the tray of spaghetti. (While you press the Option key, you can click with the lasso tool to select a straight-edged shape.)

You don't have to be precise, but try not to select the area on either side of the chef's hands.

4 Inverse the selection so that everything but the tray is selected.

5 Choose Adjust from the Image menu and Hue/Saturation from the submenu.

6 In the Hue/Saturation dialog box, be sure the Preview option is selected, then drag the Saturation slider left to –75.

This adjustment removes color from the background areas, creating the appearance of a partially colored photograph. Only a hint of color remains in the background areas, giving them the appearance of a grayscale and emphasizing the spaghetti in the foreground.

7 Drag the Lightness slider right to +25 to make the selection fade further.

8 Click OK to apply the changes.

9 Deselect the selection and save this image.

CREATING A SILHOUETTE

To complete the background, you will create a silhouette of the image.

To create a silhouette:

1 Double-click the marquee tool and choose the elliptical shape.

2 Enter **15** pixels in the Feather box.

3 Position the elliptical marquee tool on the center of the image at the 2¼-inch marker on the top ruler and at the 2⅞-inch marker on the left ruler.

4 Hold down the Option key and draw an oval selection from the center of the image that extends to about a quarter-inch to a one-half inch from the edges of the image.

The bottom of the Info palette should show a selection about 3.75 inches wide and 5 inches high.

5 Move the selection as needed to center it on the image.

6 Inverse the selection.

7 Click the Layers palette tab and create a new layer named **White Overlay**.

8 Choose Fill from the Edit menu, then select White from the Contents menu and click OK.

The selection is filled with white. The large feathering value creates a soft edge around the silhouette.

9 Deselect the selection and save the file.

With the background completed, you're ready to begin adding the inset images to the cover.

ADDING THE INSET IMAGES

Now you are ready to add the two inset images to the report cover. To add a little interest to these images, you're going to do some minor manipulations as you paste them into the final cover.

Adding emphasis through color and cropping

The first small image you'll add to the report is familiar to you from Lesson 7. The version of the *09Pepper* file in this lesson contains a saved selection of the center red pepper. Using the technique you just learned, you're going to make this pepper stand out by decreasing the saturation in the rest of the image. You'll crop the image, then give it a border.

To adjust the pepper:

1 Choose Open from the File menu, then open the *09Pepper* image in the Lesson 9 folder.

2 Double-click the cropping tool.

3 In the Cropping Tool Options palette, click the Fixed Target Size checkbox, then set the width to **1.25** inches and the height to **.625** inches.

4 Enter a resolution of **72** ppi to make the resolution of the *09Pepper* image match the resolution of the *09Work* image.

5 Position the cropping tool slightly above the far-left pepper and drag down and to the right, so that the red pepper is in the center of the cropping marquee.

Include a pepper on each side of the red pepper (the chef's hands and the bowl should not be inside the marquee). If necessary, hold down the Command key and drag one of the corner handles to reposition the marquee.

6 Click with the scissors icon to crop the image.

7 Zoom in to 2:1 and click the zoom box to resize the window.

8 Choose Load Selection from the Select menu, and make sure the Red Pepper channel is selected.

9 Click the Invert checkbox, then click OK.

This loads the Red Pepper selection stored in channel 4 and automatically inverses the selection.

Now everything but the pepper is selected.

10 Double-click the dodge tool, select Sponge from the Tool menu, make sure Desaturate is selected in the mode menu, then set the pressure to 100 percent.

11 Stroke through the selection until everything but the middle pepper is almost gray. (Use the final image for reference.)

The grayscale appearance of the other peppers serves to emphasize the red of the center pepper.

12 Deselect the selection.

Adding emphasis with a border

To complete the *09Pepper* crop, you need to outline the cropped image with a black border. In this instance, you'll add the border by using the Stroke command, as you did in Lesson 5.

To create the border and paste the inset image:

1 Set the foreground color to black.

2 Select all of the cropped *09Pepper* image.

3 Choose Stroke from the Edit menu, enter a pixel width of **2**, and select the Inside location option.

4 Make sure that the opacity is set to 100 percent and the mode to Normal, then click OK.

A thin border appears around the cropped image.

5 Click the move tool, then drag the image to the *09Work* file.

6 Drag the selection down, until the duplicated image is flush with the bottom of the window and is about a quarter-inch mark from the left ruler.

7 Click the Layers palette tab, then create a new layer and name it **Insets**.

8 Choose *09Pepper* from the Window menu, then choose Close from the File menu to close the file. Don't save changes.

Correcting imperfections through rotation and filtering

Again, in this section, you will make color adjustments as you add a second insert image to the report cover. In addition, you'll correct a slight angle and focus problem as you copy and paste the cropped image.

To rotate the selection as you crop:

1 Choose Open from the File menu, then open the *09Oil* image in the Lesson 9 folder.

You can see that the bottle is at a slight angle. As you crop the image, you will rotate it, to compensate for the angle.

2 Double-click the cropping tool.

3 In the Cropping Tool Options dialog box, make sure Fixed Target Size is still checked, then set the width to **.764** inches and the height to **1.5** inches.

4 Starting at about the middle of the chef's cuff, drag down and to the right to enclose the bottle and some of the garlic and bowl in the cropping marquee.

If necessary, hold down the Command key and drag a handle to center the bottle in the selection.

5 Using the angle information in the Info palette as a guide, hold down the Option key and drag the upper-right handle in a clockwise direction, until the vertical cropping border appears parallel to the side of the bottle. The angle should be about −3.5 degrees.

6 Click with the scissors icon to crop the image.

Making color corrections

Like the *09Pepper* image, the *09Oil* image has a selection stored in channel 4.

To adjust the saturation and color balance:

1 Load the background selection and hide its edges.

2 Double-click the sponge tool, and use it to desaturate the background of the image. Use the final file as a guide.

Now the focus of attention in this image is the bottle. The bottle still needs a few other color corrections.

3 Inverse the selection.

4 Choose Adjust from the Image menu and Color Balance from the submenu.

5 In the Color Balance dialog box, select the Midtones option and drag the Cyan/Red slider to –10 and the Magenta/Green slider to +10.

6 Click Shadows and drag the Magenta/Green slider to +10 again, then click OK.

This adjustment removes some of the red cast left from the reflection of the tomatoes in the glass. If this change isn't immediately apparent to you, use the Command-Z shortcut to undo and redo the color-balance change.

7 Deselect the image.

To sharpen the image with a filter:

1 Apply the Unsharp Mask filter at 50 percent to sharpen the image slightly.

2 With the foreground color set to black, select all of the *Oil* image.

3 Stroke the image using a width of 2 and starting from the inside of the selection. The opacity should be 100 percent and the mode should be Normal.

4 Click the move tool, then drag the selection to the *09Work* image.

5 Click the Layers palette tab.

The olive oil image will stay on the same layer as the pepper image.

6 Use the move tool to drag the floating selection up and to the right, until it is about three-eighths of an inch using the top ruler and flush with the right edge.

7 Deselect the selection and save the file.

8 Choose *09Oil* from the Window menu, then choose Close from the File menu to close the file. Don't save changes.

CREATING SHADOWS FOR THE INSETS

Next, you will create shadows for the inset photos in the *09Work* image.

To create the inset shadow for the first image:

1 Create a new layer and name it **Drop Shadow.**

2 Double-click the marquee tool, then create a fixed rectangular marquee with a width of 92 pixels and a height of 46 pixels.

3 Set the Feather option to 0.

4 Position the pointer about one-eighth of an inch above and from the left edge of the Pepper image, then click to make a selection slightly offset from the inset image.

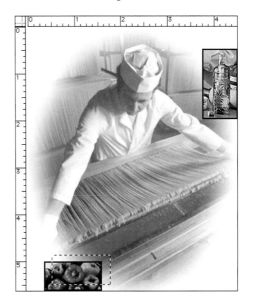

5 Return the marquee to the Normal setting.

6 Press the Command key, and starting at the upper-right corner of the pepper image, drag diagonally down to the lower-left corner of the image to subtract the image from the selection.

You are left with a one-eighth-inch-wide selection in the shape of a drop shadow, just above and to the right of the Pepper image.

7 Fill the selection with black.

8 Deselect the selection.

To create the inset shadow for the second image:

1 Create a fixed rectangular marquee with a width of 55 pixels and a height of 108 pixels.

2 Position the pointer about one-eighth of an inch below the top of the olive oil image and one-eighth of an inch from the left edge of the olive oil image, then click to make a selection slightly offset from the inset image.

3 Return the rectangular marquee to the Normal setting.

4 Hold down the Command key, and starting at the lower-left corner of the olive oil image, drag diagonally up to the right corner of the image to subtract the image from the selection.

You are left with an eighth-inch-wide selection in the shape of a drop shadow, just below and to the left of the olive oil image.

5 Fill the selection with black.

6 Deselect the selection.

7 Choose Overlay from the mode menu in the Layers palette.

8 Set the Opacity in the Layers palette to 75 percent.

9 Save the file.

ADDING THE TITLE TYPE

To complete the annual report cover, you will add type to the upper-left and lower-right corners.

To add the type:

1 Use the eyedropper to sample the red from the pepper to set a new foreground color.

2 Click the type tool and click in the upper-left corner of the image.

3 In the Type Tool dialog box, set the font to Times Bold, the size to 10 points, and the spacing to 1.5.

4 Enter **RAPPORTO ANNUALE** (in all caps) in the text box and click OK.

5 Double-click the Floating Selection thumbnail in the Layers palette and name the new layer **Text**.

6 Click the move tool, then use it to position the first letter of the type at the three-eighths-inch marker on the left ruler and the eighth-inch marker on the top ruler.

7 Click the default colors icon to set the foreground color to black.

8 With the type tool, click the lower-right corner of the image.

9 Set the font to Helvetica Bold Oblique, the size to 9 points, and the spacing to 1.5.

10 Enter **CASALINGO INCORPORATED** (in all caps) and click OK.

11 Position the type so that the first letter, *C*, is at the 2⅛-inch marker on the top ruler and at the 5¼-inch marker on the left ruler.

12 Deselect the type so it becomes part of the Text layer.

Creating transparent type

For the final element in the annual report cover, you're going to add the year in slightly transparent type.

To add transparent type:

1 Make sure that the Text layer is the target layer.

2 Using the type tool, click the center of the image.

3 Press Delete to clear out the previous text.

4 Set the font to Times Italic, the size to 120 points, the spacing to 0, then click the center alignment button.

5 Click in the text box and enter **1996**, then click OK.

6 Position the type so that the number 1 is over the chef's left arm (the type should be centered in the cover).

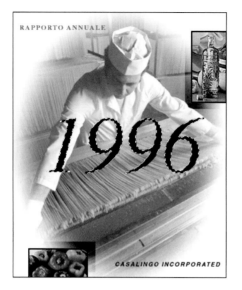

7 Drag the Opacity slider in the Layers palette to 60 percent.

8 Deselect the selection to see the final report cover.

KERNING THE TEXT

The number 1 needs to be moved closer to the number 9.

To kern the text:

1 Click the lasso tool, then drag to select the number 1 in 1996.

2 Press the right arrow key to move the numeral one about two pixels to the right.

3 Deselect the text.

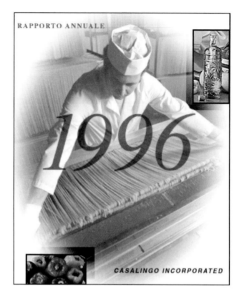

4 Save a copy of the file and name it **09WorkL**, then flatten the current file.

5 Save the flattened file.

6 Close the open files and don't save changes.

Good for you! You have completed a complex and compelling composite image suitable for the shareholders of Casalingo Incorporated. You've also had the chance to practice working with some common color-correction techniques that will help you achieve consistent and professional results with your own images.

LESSON 10: CONVERTING IMAGES

This lesson discusses color modes, image types, and converting images from one type of color mode to another. The lesson builds on the concept of channels, which you have been creating and using to store saved selections. The channels that Adobe Photoshop assigns to images (such as the red, green, and blue channels of an RGB image) are used as sources of color information. Using these color channels, you can make very specific adjustments to the individual color components of an image.

In this lesson, you'll use four RGB images, scanned from a photograph of an appetizer plate. After creating a different image type for each file, you'll combine the images into a composite file. This composite image will serve as the basis of a trade show poster, which you'll complete in Lesson 13. It should take you about an hour to complete this lesson.

In this lesson, you'll learn how to do the following:

• convert an RGB image to Lab mode, CMYK mode, indexed color mode, and grayscale mode

• convert an image to a multichannel image

• create a duotone and a tritone

• invert colors

• convert a grayscale image to bitmapped mode

The following images show the photographs you'll use and the final composition.

Source file (10Plate1)

Source file (10Plate2)

Source file (10Plate3)

Source file (10Plate4)

Ending image (10Final)

ABOUT MODES, IMAGE TYPES, AND CHANNELS

A *color mode* in Adobe Photoshop is the color model you use to display and print Adobe Photoshop documents. The most commonly used modes are Grayscale, for displaying black-and-white documents; RGB, for displaying color documents on-screen; and CMYK, for printing four-color separations. Adobe Photoshop also supports a variety of other image types, including bitmapped, duotone (including monotone, tritone, and quadtone), indexed color, and Lab color. You use the commands in the Mode menu to convert one type of image to another.

You should always save an image (with a unique name) before converting it. Since different color models comprise different colors, converting an image between modes may permanently change the color values in the image. Converting from one mode to another often requires you to flatten the file. By saving first, you'll always be able to recover your original image and all its layers.

BEGINNING THIS LESSON

In this lesson, you'll convert four parts of a larger image to separate modes, and then combine the images into a final file.

To begin this lesson:

1 Quit Adobe Photoshop, throw away your *Adobe Photoshop 3.0 Prefs* file, and empty the Trash.

2 Launch the Adobe Photoshop application.

3 Choose Open from the File menu, then open the *10Final* file in the Lesson 10 folder.

4 Zoom out to reduce the image, resize the window if necessary, then drag the window to the upper-right corner of your screen.

This file contains four layers.

5 Choose Open from the File menu, then open the *10Plate1* file and place it in the upper-left corner of your screen.

6 Hide the Text layer by clicking the eye icon in the Layers palette.

7 Create a palette group consisting of the Channels palette, the Layers palette, and the Options palette.

8 Close the remaining palettes.

9 Click the Channels palette tab to display the Channels palette, then click the zoom box to display all the channel information.

10 Choose Preferences from the File menu and General from the submenu. Select the Color Channels in Color option under Display, then click OK.

The channel thumbnails in the Channels palette appear in color. Viewing the channels in color will help you track the changes in individual channels as you convert from one mode to another.

CONVERTING AN IMAGE FOR COLOR SEPARATIONS

Probably the most frequent mode conversion you will make will be the one required to print a color image as color separations. To print a color separation from an RGB, indexed color, or Lab image, you convert an RGB image to CMYK. (If you're printing to a PostScript Level 2 color printer, you don't have to convert a Lab image to CMYK mode because the printer interprets and prints Lab images.)

For the first quarter of the image, you will work with the *10Plate1* file and create a Lab image, a CMYK image, and an indexed color image.

CONVERTING TO LAB MODE

You can convert RGB, CMYK, and indexed color images to Lab color. You were introduced to Lab color in Lesson 7. Because the Lab *gamut*, or range of colors, encompasses both RGB and CMYK gamuts, Lab is used internally by Adobe Photoshop when it converts images between RGB and CMYK modes. Lab color is also the recommended color mode for moving images between systems (since it is device-independent), and for printing to PostScript Level 2 printers.

When you convert an RGB image to Lab mode, the image still contains three channels. Instead of red, green, and blue, however, the color information is contained in a luminance (*L*) channel, and two color channels, *a* and *b*.

To convert an RGB image to Lab mode:

1 Make the *10Plate1* image active. Note that the RGB file size is about 100K.

2 In the Channels palette, click the Red thumbnail.

The red color information for the *10Plate1* file is displayed. If your Monitor control panel is set for 256 colors, you may see that the red channel for the final image appears also. When you are viewing 256 colors and select an individual channel in the Channels palette, all open files are displayed in that channel.

3 Click the Green and Blue channels to see their color information, then return to the RGB channel.

4 Choose Lab Color from the Mode menu.

You are prompted to choose whether or not you want to flatten layers in the image. Changing from one mode to another can change the way the layers composite or blend. You will go ahead and flatten this image.

5 Click Flatten. The image is converted to Lab mode. The title bar changes to indicate the current mode of the image. The Channels palette now shows the three Lab channels for the image.

6 Click the Lightness thumbnail in the Channels palette.

This channel appears in grayscale since it shows the lightness or luminance values (not color values) for the image.

7 Click on the *a* and *b* channel thumbnails.

The *a* component shows the color range from green to magenta; the *b* component shows the color range from blue to yellow.

8 Return to the composite Lab channel thumbnail.

The Lab mode is useful when you want to adjust the lightness or brightness of the image without changing its hue or saturation (for example, to create smoother blends). Once you have adjusted the image, you can convert it back to RGB or CMYK mode to perform other color corrections or to print it using process colors. Converting back and forth between Lab and other image types doesn't alter the original color values.

9 Choose Revert from the File menu and click Revert to return to the original RGB image.

CONVERTING TO CMYK

When you convert an RGB image to CMYK, the red, green, and blue values in the image undergo an intermediate conversion to Lab values, which are then converted to the cyan, magenta, yellow, and black values. The three-channel RGB image becomes a four-channel CMYK image.

Unlike Lab mode, converting back and forth between RGB and CMYK alters the original color values. When you plan to convert an RGB or indexed file to CMYK, be sure to save a copy of the RGB or indexed color image in case you want to reconvert the image. It's not a good idea to convert between RGB and CMYK mode multiple times, because each time the image is converted, the color values must be recalculated.

To convert an RGB image to CMYK:

1 Click the Layers palette tab.

2 Click the eye icon next to the Text layer to hide the text layer.

3 Choose CMYK Color from the Mode menu. Click Flatten to flatten the layers.

4 The file size is increased to 135K and the image contains four channels.

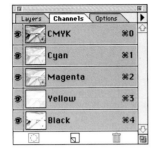

In the RGB to CMYK conversion process, Adobe Photoshop converts the RGB values to Lab values and builds a color table. It then uses these Lab values to determine the appropriate CMYK equivalents. Finally, the correct CMYK values for each Lab pixel are calculated by referencing the key values in the color table.

You can save individual color-separation tables and use them with other Adobe Photoshop documents. You might want to save different tables if you frequently print images using different printers, inks, or papers. For more information, see the *Adobe Photoshop User Guide*.

5 Click Cyan in the Channels palette to display the Cyan channel.

6 Click the Yellow and Black channel thumbnails.

7 Click the Magenta channel thumbnail.

In this channel, you can see that there is a concentration of color in the rosebud.

8 Double-click the marquee tool in the toolbox, then select the Elliptical option from the Shape pop-up menu.

9 Using the elliptical marquee tool, select the rosebud and delete it.

10 Choose None from the Select menu to deselect the rosebud.

You have now removed all of the magenta from this image in this specific location. Editing individual channels allows you to create special effects or make selective color corrections.

11 Click the Channels palette tab and return to the composite CMYK channel.

The remaining color information from the Cyan, Yellow, and Black channels shows through the selection. Without the magenta component, the color appears chartreuse.

CONVERTING TO MULTICHANNEL MODE

If you want to delete a channel from an RGB, CMYK, Lab, or Duotone image, you need to first convert the image to Multichannel mode.

1 Choose Multichannel from the Mode menu.

In Multichannel mode, the channels from composite images (with names such as *Red*, *Magenta*, *Lightness*, and so on) are assigned numbers. The individual channels are converted to grayscale information that reflects the color values of the pixels in each channel.

2 Click #2 (Magenta) in the Channels palette, then choose Delete Channel from the Channels palette pop-up menu (or drag the #2 thumbnail to the Trash icon at the bottom of the Channels palette).

3 Choose Revert from the File menu and click Revert to revert to the original RGB image.

CONVERTING TO INDEXED COLOR

You might want to convert an RGB image to an indexed color image to edit an image's color table, or to export an image to an application that supports only 8-bit color. Indexed color images are useful for creating a limited palette for export to multimedia applications, for example, or for animation and on-screen display.

While an RGB image contains millions of colors, an indexed color image is limited to 256 colors. This limited amount of information causes an indexed color image to appear pixelated, or coarse, when it's printed.

When converting an RGB image to an indexed color image, Adobe Photoshop builds a color table (or palette) for the indexed color image. The color table stores the colors used in the document and holds the maximum number of colors that can be displayed at once. Because an indexed color image can directly reference only 256 colors, the RGB color may not exist in the indexed color table. If the RGB color is not present, the program matches the requested color to the closest color in the color table or simulates the requested color using the available colors.

To convert an RGB image to indexed color:

1 Click the Layers palette tab.

2 Click the eye icon to hide the Text layer.

3 Choose Indexed Color from the Mode menu.

4 Click OK to flatten the visible layers and discard hidden layers.

The Indexed Color dialog box appears.

5 Click 8 bits per pixel for the resolution.

The resolution determines the number of colors that can be displayed at one time. For example, if you select 4 bits per pixel, 16 colors can be displayed at a time; if you select 8 bits per pixel, 256 colors can be displayed at a time.

6 Click Adaptive for the palette option. By default, the Adaptive palette uses the Diffusion Dither option to generate colors.

The Adaptive palette option creates a color table by sampling colors from the more commonly used areas of the color spectrum in the image. *Dithering* mixes the pixels of the available colors to simulate the missing colors. The Diffusion Dither option randomly adds pixels to simulate the colors not in the color table.

7 Click OK to convert the image to indexed color.

8 Click the Channels palette tab.

The image is displayed using 256 colors. The image size is reduced to 35K, and only one channel appears in the Channel palette.

9 Choose Color Table from the Mode menu. The Color Table dialog box appears.

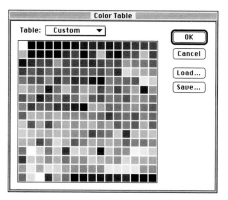

Because you chose the Adaptive palette option for the color table, the color table consists primarily of colors in the original image—browns and yellows.

10 Click OK to close the Color Table dialog box.

11 Choose Undo Mode Change from the Edit menu to undo the mode change.

12 Repeat steps 2 through 9, but for step 5 click 4 bits per pixel for resolution and note the results.

13 Choose Revert from the File menu.

Creating special effects using Indexed Color mode

You can also use the Indexed Color mode to create special effects. Working in Indexed Color mode is useful when a color image has a limited palette. For example, if you are working with an image that contains primarily yellows and greens, you might want to use an indexed color table consisting mainly of yellows and greens to give you the widest selection of tints within those hues.

You can convert an image to Indexed Color mode only from Grayscale or RGB mode. In this example, you'll convert the RGB image first to Grayscale and then to Indexed Color mode. Finally, you will create a custom color table for the image.

To convert to grayscale mode:

1 Click the Layers palette tab.

2 Click the eye icon to hide the Text layer.

3 Choose Grayscale from the Mode menu.

4 Click Flatten to flatten the visible layers and discard hidden layers.

5 Click OK again to discard the color information.

6 Click the Channels palette tab.

In Grayscale mode, the Channels palette shows only a single black channel.

7 Choose Adjust from the Image menu and Brightness/Contrast from the submenu.

8 Enter 45 for the contrast, then click OK.

To convert a grayscale image to indexed color:

1 Choose Indexed Color from the Mode menu to convert the image to indexed color.

The image still appears in grayscale since you have eliminated the color information. Now you're ready to add your own colors.

2 Choose Color Table from the Mode menu.

3 Make sure Custom is selected in the Table pop-up menu.

4 Starting in the upper-left corner, drag diagonally to the lower-right corner to select all the colors in the color table. The Color Picker dialog box appears.

5 Move to the CMYK text boxes in the lower-right corner and enter the following, then click OK.

```
C...................96 %
M..................87 %
Y.....................0 %
K.....................0 %
```

This defines the first color for the color table, a dark blue.

6 To select the last color for the table, enter the following values, then click OK.

```
C....................0 %
M...................0 %
Y..................90 %
K....................0 %
```

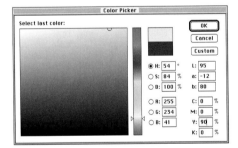

You return to the Color Table dialog box, which displays a color table ranging from blue to yellow.

7 Click OK to apply the table to the indexed color image. The result is a royal blue and yellow image.

8 Choose Save As from the File menu.

9 Type **10Work1** for the file name, open the Project folder and click Save.

You can compare this method of creating a two-color image to that of creating a duotone, which you'll do in the next section.

CREATING A DUOTONE

In this part of the lesson, you will create a duotone from the *10Plate2* file.

In Adobe Photoshop, the term *Duotone mode* applies generically to monotones, duotones, tritones, and quadtones. A monotone, duotone, tritone, or quadtone is a grayscale image printed with one, two, three, or four inks, respectively, to add tonal depth.

Creating a duotone involves three basic steps: you specify the type of duotone (monotone, duotone, and so on); specify the ink color to use; and adjust the duotone curve to determine how the ink is distributed across the image.

To create a duotone and load a duotone curve:

1 Choose Open from the File menu, then open the *10Plate2* file in the Lesson 10 folder.

2 Drag the *10Plate2* image to the right of the *10Work1* image, so that the borders are touching.

3 Choose Grayscale from the Mode menu and click OK to convert the *10Plate2* image to Grayscale mode.

To create a duotone from an RGB image, you must first convert the image to Grayscale mode. Adobe Photoshop treats duotones not as true color images, but as grayscale images in which the gray levels are enhanced by using an ink color (typi-

cally, in addition to black). In contrast, color images use different ink colors to reproduce a variety of colors.

4 Choose Duotone from the Mode menu. The Duotone Options dialog box appears.

If you are choosing Duotone mode for the first time, Monotone appears by default in the Type pop-up menu drop-down list. A duotone curve and color swatch appear in the Ink 1 field. The default duotone curve is a diagonal line extending from the lower-left corner to the upper-right corner—indicating an even distribution of ink across the range of gray in the image. The default color for Ink 1 is black.

5 Choose Duotone from the Type pop-up menu.

A duotone curve appears in the Ink 2 field. The ink color for Ink 2 is blank, since you must specify the ink color separately.

Typically, you specify the ink color and its distribution in two separate steps. You can also load a duotone curve that specifies an ink color and its distribution at the same time. The Adobe Photoshop program includes some duotone curves that you can apply to your own images.

Once you convert to Duotone, the Channels palette shows a single, duotone channel.

6 Click Load. A directory dialog box appears.

7 Select the *Magenta Bl 2* file from the Lesson 10 folder, and click Open.

The ink colors and curves appear in the Duotone Options dialog box. Notice that inks and curves for both Ink 1 and Ink 2 have been loaded. You can see that the curve for the black Ink 1 is no longer the default curve.

8 Click OK to apply the ink colors and distribution to the image. The image appears as a soft, almost rose tone.

9 Choose Save As from the File menu, name the file *10Work2,* open the Projects folder, then click Save.

CREATING A TRITONE AND ADJUSTING THE INK DISTRIBUTION

In this part of the lesson, you will work with the *10Plate3* file and add a third ink to the duotone you just created to make the color richer. Then you'll adjust the curves that control the ink distribution. To complete the tritone, you will invert the color in the image to create the effect of a negative.

The procedures for creating a tritone and a duotone are the same.

To create a tritone:

1 Choose Open from the File menu, then open the *10Plate3* image in the Lesson 10 folder.

2 Drag the *10Plate3* image down and to the right, to place it under the *10Work2* image. The borders should be touching.

3 Choose Grayscale from the Mode menu to convert the *10Plate3* image to Grayscale mode, then click OK.

4 Choose Duotone from the Mode menu.

The Duotone Options dialog box appears with the duotone curves and ink swatches you specified with the *Magenta Bl 2* file.

5 Choose Tritone from the Type pop-up menu. A distribution curve appears in the Ink 3 field.

To specify the third ink color:

1 Click the color swatch box for Ink 3. The Custom Colors dialog box appears.

2 Make sure that PANTONE Coated is selected in the Book pop-up menu.

3 Without clicking anywhere in the dialog box, type the number **107** quickly. PANTONE 107 CV, a bright yellow, appears selected. (You can also click a color to select it.)

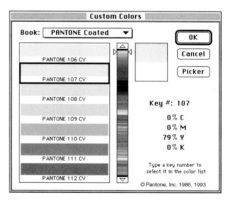

4 Click OK to add the third color to the Duotone Options dialog box.

When you are creating duotones, both the order in which the inks are printed and the screen angles you use dramatically affect your final output.

To produce fully saturated colors, darker inks should be printed before lighter inks. When entering colors in the duotone dialog boxes, make sure that the inks are specified in descending order—that is, the darkest ink should appear at the top and the lightest ink at the bottom. The order of inks affects how Adobe Photoshop applies screens when the duotone is printed.

To adjust the ink distribution:

1 Click the curve next to Ink 2 to display the Duotone Curve dialog box.

This duotone curve maps each grayscale value on the original image to the actual ink percentage that will be used when the image is printed. The horizontal axis shows the gray values in the original image; the vertical axis shows ink density values. The curve represents highlights in the lower-left corner, midtones in the center area, and shadows in the upper-right corner.

The default straight-line curve indicates that the current grayscale value of every pixel is being mapped to the same percentage value of the printing ink. At this setting, a 50-percent midtone pixel is printed with a 50-percent dot of the ink, a 100-percent shadow with a 100-percent dot of the ink, and so on.

To adjust the curve, you can drag points on the curve or enter values in the percentage text boxes.

2 Enter the following values for the different ink percentages:

• Leave 0 in the 0-percent text box.

• Delete the 2 from the 5-percent text box.

• Enter 20 in the 50-percent text box.

• Enter 17 in the 60-percent text box.

• Enter 61 in the 70-percent text box.

• Enter 100 in the 100-percent text box.

Leave all the other text boxes blank.

These values lighten the midtones in the image, and distribute more color in the highlights and shadows.

3 Click OK in the Duotone Curve dialog box. The adjusted curve appears next to Ink 2 in the Duotone Options dialog box.

4 Click OK to apply the color and ink distribution to the image. The magenta and yellow create a sepia-tone color.

5 Choose Save As from the File menu, type **10Work3** for the file name, make sure the Projects folder is open, then click Save.

CREATING ILLUSTRATIVE EFFECTS

Now you will create some special effects using the duotone and tritone you just created. As you learned in Lesson 4, you can create one type of illustrative effect by *posterizing* the colors. Inverting colors, to create a negative, produces another interesting effect.

To posterize the colors in an image:

1 Select the *10Work2* image.

2 Choose Map from the Image menu and Posterize from the submenu.

3 In the Posterize dialog box, enter a value of **7** for Levels and click OK.

This reduces the gray levels in the image from 256 to 7, giving the image a flat, painted look.

4 Choose Save from the File menu (or press Command-S).

You will use this file in the final composite image.

To invert colors:

1 Select the *10Work3* image.

2 Choose Map from the Image menu and Invert from the submenu (or press Command-I).

The tritone image is inverted, as if you created a negative of the image.

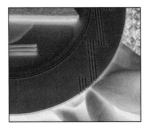

3 Choose Save from the File menu (or press Command-S).

You will also use this file in the final composite image.

CONVERTING A COLOR IMAGE TO A BITMAPPED IMAGE

To prepare the last part of the composite image, you will convert the *10Plate4* image to a bitmapped image, using a pattern. Before converting the file, you must store the pattern you want to use in the pattern buffer.

To convert a color image to a bitmap:

1 Choose Open from the File menu, then open the *Intricate Surface* file in the Lesson 10 folder. Accept the EPS Rasterizer default values and click OK to open the file.

2 Choose All from the Select menu, Define Pattern from the Edit menu, then close the file and don't save changes.

3 Choose Open from the File menu, then open the *10Plate4* file in the Lesson 10 folder.

4 Drag the file down and place it under the *10Work1* file and to the left of the *10Work3* file, with the borders touching.

5 Choose Grayscale from the Mode menu to convert the file to Grayscale mode, then click OK.

To convert a color image to a bitmapped image, you first must convert it to a grayscale image. This conversion removes the hue and saturation information from the pixels and leaves the brightness values. A bitmapped image treats the 256 levels of gray in a grayscale image as either black (0 to 127) or white (128 to 256).

6 Choose Bitmap from the Mode menu. The Bitmap dialog box appears.

You have a choice of five methods to use when converting a grayscale image to a bitmapped image. These options determine the quality of the new bitmapped image.

7 Leave the resolution at 72, click Custom Pattern, then click OK.

The image is converted to a bitmap using the pattern.

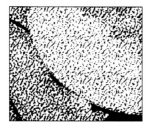

The file size decreases dramatically, to about 5K. Bitmapped images consist of 1 bit of color (black or white) per pixel, and require the least amount of memory.

8 The Channels palette indicates that bitmaps are one-channel images.

9 Choose Save As from the File menu.

10 Type **10Work4** for the file name, make sure your Projects folder is open, then click Save.

Note: You cannot use the magic wand to select colors in a bitmapped image, nor can you use filters to alter a bitmapped image.

COMBINING IMAGES INTO A COMPOSITE IMAGE

Now you are ready to combine the four separate images into a composite image. As you put each image into its own layer, you'll practice different methods for creating layers.

To add the first image:

1 Choose New from the File menu and type **10Comp** for the file name.

2 Enter **5.6** inches for the width and **4.8** inches for the height.

3 Make sure the resolution is 72 ppi, the mode is RGB Color and the contents are white, then click OK.

4 Click the Layers palette tab, then click the New Layer icon.

5 Type **Top-Left Plate** for the layer name, then click OK.

6 Choose *10Work1* from the Window menu.

7 Choose All from the Select menu, then click the move tool and drag the selection into the *10Comp* file. Position the plate image in the upper-left corner of the file.

8 Choose None from the Select menu (or press Command-D).

9 The floating selection becomes part of the Top-Left Plate layer.

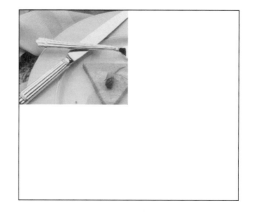

10 Choose Save As from the File menu, open the Projects folder, and click Save.

11 Select the *10Work1* image and choose Close from the File menu to close the file.

To add the second image:

1 Choose *10Work2* from the Window menu, choose All from the Select menu, then drag the selection to the upper-right corner of the *10Comp* file.

2 Double-click the Floating Selection layer thumbnail, then type **Top-Right Plate** for the layer name, and click OK.

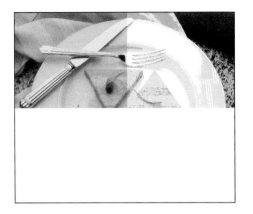

3 Select the *10Work2* file and choose Close from the File menu to close the file.

To add the third image:

1 Choose *10Work3* from the Window menu, choose All from the Select menu, then choose Copy from the Edit menu.

2 Choose Close from the File menu.

3 Make sure the *10Comp* window is selected, then choose Paste Layer from the Edit menu, name the new layer **Lower-Right Plate**, and click OK.

4 Drag the image into the lower-right corner of the image.

To add the fourth image:

1 Choose *10Work4* from the Window menu, and without making a selection, drag the image to the *10Comp* window.

A new layer named *Layer 1* appears in the Layers palette.

You can drag a layer from one file to another without making a selection.

2 Double-click the Layer 1 thumbnail in the Layers palette. The Layer Options dialog box appears.

3 Type **Lower-Left Plate** for the layer name, then click OK.

4 Drag the image into the lower-left corner to complete the composite image.

5 Select the *10Work4* window, then choose Close from the File menu to close the file.

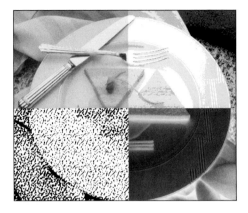

6 Choose Save from the File menu.

A similar image will be used when you create a poster in Lesson 13.

7 Choose Close from the File menu to close both files.

The information in this lesson has only touched on a few of the capabilities of Adobe Photoshop to convert images from one type to another. See the *Adobe Photoshop User Guide* for complete details on all the conversion options.

Lesson

11

LESSON 11: PRODUCING COLOR SEPARATIONS AND PRINTING

This lesson provides an overview of basic printing concepts and describes how to print using Adobe Photoshop. The lesson also discusses creating and printing color separations (a *separated image* is one that has been converted from RGB to CMYK mode). Specifically, this lesson explains how Adobe Photoshop converts RGB values to CMYK values.

Calibration ensures that what you see on-screen matches the printed output, and vice versa. For high-resolution printing, it's important to make sure that your system is calibrated correctly before you create or print separations. In Lesson 1, you began the calibration process by entering the default values in the Monitor Setup and Printing Inks Setup dialog boxes. This lesson provides more information on the settings in the Printing Inks Setup dialog box and discusses options in the Separation Setup dialog box. Before separating your own images, you should go through the entire system-calibration process, as detailed in the *Adobe Photoshop User Guide*.

Even if you don't have a printer connected to your computer, you might want to read through the sections on printing, so you understand the Adobe Photoshop printing options. You will then be able to set up your files correctly before sending them to an outside printer.

In this lesson, you'll separate an image (and use a pre-separated image) to learn about the process of color separation. You can then print one or both images. It should take you about an hour to complete this lesson.

In this lesson, you'll learn how to do the following:

• convert an RGB image to a CMYK image for printing

• view and convert out-of-gamut colors

• preview an image in CMYK

• adjust the color separation for dot gain, black generation, and trap

• print a color composite

• print a four-color separation

• print a selected area of an image

• print a halftone

This lesson uses two versions of the same image, *11RGB* and *11Trap*, and the chef image that you worked with in Lesson 7.

11RGB

11Trap

11Chef1

BEGINNING THIS LESSON

In this lesson, you will separate an image and open several images supplied in both RGB and CMYK mode, so you can compare changes made to the images. Because the settings in the Printing Inks Setup, Separation Setup, and Separation Tables dialog boxes are critical to creating correct color separations, you are going to start the lesson by once again throwing away your *Adobe Photoshop 3.0 Prefs* file. When you restart the program, Adobe Photoshop creates a new Prefs file using the program's default settings for the Printing Inks Setup, Separation Setup, and Separation Tables dialog boxes. This ensures that you will have the correct settings for the examples in this lesson.

To begin this lesson:

1 Quit Adobe Photoshop, throw away your *Adobe Photoshop 3.0 Prefs* file and empty the Trash.

2 Launch the Adobe Photoshop application.

Organizing palettes

You will collapse all the palettes.

To collapse the palettes:

1 Collapse the Brushes/Options palette group by clicking the zoom box in the upper-right corner of the palette group or double-clicking a palette tab.

2 Collapse the Picker/Swatches/Scratch group of palettes.

3 Collapse the Layers/Channels/Paths group of palettes.

PRINTING: AN OVERVIEW

The most common way to output images is to produce a positive or negative image on paper or film, and then transfer the image to a printing plate to be run on a press.

To print a continuous-tone image, the image must be broken down into a series of dots. These dots are created when you apply a *halftone screen* to the image. The dots in a halftone screen control how much ink is deposited at a specific location. Varying the size and density of the dots creates the optical illusion of variations of gray or continuous color in the image. In the case of a color printout, four halftone screens are used—cyan, magenta, yellow, and black—one for each ink used in the printing process.

In conventional graphics, a halftone is produced by placing a halftone screen between a piece of film and the image, and then exposing the film. In Adobe Photoshop, you specify the attributes for the halftone screen prior to producing the film or paper output. To achieve the best results, the output device you use, such as a PostScript imagesetter, should be set to the correct density limit, and the processor should be properly calibrated. If these factors are inconsistent, the results can be unpredictable.

To print color separations in Adobe Photoshop, you first convert the RGB image to CMYK, and then adjust how the various plates are generated (and, if necessary, correct for trap). After setting the other print options, you print the four images used for color separations (one image for each of the process colors).

Adobe Photoshop also lets you print an image as a grayscale halftone, as a composite image, or as individual channels.

PRODUCING A COLOR SEPARATION

Producing a color separation is the process of converting an RGB image to a CMYK image. The conversion splits the RGB colors into the four process colors: cyan, magenta, yellow, and black.

As you learned in Lesson 10, when Adobe Photoshop converts an RGB image to CMYK, it converts the RGB color values to Lab mode, builds a color table, and then references the table to complete the conversion to CMYK mode.

The information in the Monitor Setup dialog box is used for the first step of conversion (converting the RGB color values to Lab values). The information in the Printing Inks Setup and Separation Setup dialog boxes is used to build the color table. During the RGB–Lab–CMYK conversion, the program refers to the color table values to calculate the correct CMYK values for each Lab pixel. The program then converts the image to CMYK mode.

Once in CMYK mode, the program must reconvert the color values to RGB so that the image can be displayed on an RGB monitor. To do this, Adobe Photoshop converts the CMYK values back to Lab (using the same color table if no values in Printing Inks Setup and Separation Setup have been changed) and then back to RGB (again using the Monitor Setup information).

Separating an image

To see how separation works, you'll separate the *11RGB* image using the default separation options, and then compare the RGB color with its CMYK equivalents.

To separate the image:

1 Open the *11RGB* image in the Lesson 11 folder.

The images in this lesson each contain only one layer.

2 Choose CMYK Color from the Mode menu to convert the RGB image to CMYK mode.

The program builds color separation tables, using the information in the Printing Inks Setup and Separation Setup dialog boxes, and then converts the image.

3 Choose Save As from the File menu, and type **11CMYK** for the name. Make sure the Projects folder is open and click Save.

To compare how the color has been separated:

1 Reopen the *11RGB* image in the Lesson 11 folder.

2 Drag the *11RGB* image to the right until it is next to the *11CMYK* image.

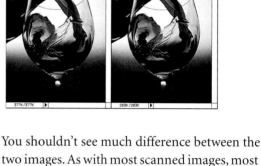

You shouldn't see much difference between the two images. As with most scanned images, most of the colors in the original RGB image were within the CMYK gamut, and didn't need to be changed. If the image had contained colors outside the CMYK gamut, the RGB colors would have been converted to their nearest CMYK equivalents. You'll see an example of this in a minute.

Displaying the individual channels

Each channel for the image displays the color information for one color component. It is the amount of each color of ink deposited at any point on the paper (and how much of the ink is absorbed) that determines the final printed color. To see how the channels will look when they are printed, you're going to display them individually.

To preview the printing of individual channels:

1 Double-click the Channels palette tab.

2 With the *11RGB* window active, click Red in the Channels palette.

The channel appears in grayscale. This is how the channel will print. Darker gray areas indicate where more color appears; lighter gray areas indicate less color.

3 Display the green and blue channels to see their color distribution, then return to the composite channel.

4 Select the *11CMYK* window.

The Channels palette now shows channels for the cyan, magenta, yellow, and black colors.

5 Click the zoom box in the upper-left corner to expand the palette to full-size.

6 Click each of the four process-color channel thumbnails.

You can see how each plate contributes to the overall color in the final image.

7 Choose Close from the File menu to close the *11CMYK* image.

WORKING WITH OUT-OF-GAMUT COLORS

Most scanned photographs contain RGB colors within the CMYK gamut, and all the colors are converted with no substitution when you change the image to CMYK mode. Images that were created or altered digitally, however, often contain RGB colors that are out of gamut. You were introduced to the idea of out-of-gamut colors in Lesson 7. As you may remember, out-of-gamut colors are indicated by an exclamation mark in the Picker palette, the Color Picker, and the Info palette.

When separating an RGB image, Adobe Photoshop converts colors that are out of the CMYK gamut to their closest CMYK equivalents. The conversion allows you to print the colors. To see how this works, you're going to add a gradient to the *11RGB* image that contains an out-of-gamut color.

To add an out-of-gamut color:

1 Choose Palettes from the Window menu and Show Info from the submenu.

2 Make the *11RGB* image active and be sure you are in the RGB composite channel.

3 Double-click the Swatches palette tab, then click the bright blue swatch in the first row of the palette (the fifth swatch from the left) to set the foreground color for the gradient.

The first six swatches in the Swatches palette are mixes of pure RGB colors and are out of gamut; they cannot be displayed or printed as CMYK equivalents. If you plan to separate an RGB image, it's a good idea to try not to use pure RGB colors.

4 Click the Picker palette tab.

An alert triangle appears under the color selection boxes in the Picker palette, indicating that this blue can't be reproduced as a CMYK color. The swatch next to the triangle shows the closest CMYK equivalent to the color.

5 Make sure the background color is set to white as the ending color for the gradient.

6 Double-click the gradient tool.

7 In the Gradient Tool Options palette, make sure the opacity is set to 100 percent.

8 Choose Darken from the Mode pop-up menu in the Gradient Tool Options palette.

9 Starting at the top of the image, drag the gradient tool down about 1½ inches. The blend appears.

CMYK Preview

When making color corrections in RGB mode or adjusting out-of-gamut colors, you can preview CMYK color values in an RGB image. This allows you to examine the difference in the two images before making the actual mode change.

1 Choose New Window from the Window menu.

By choosing the new window command you can see the original out-of-gamut color in one window and the CMYK preview in the other window.

2 Move the second window to the left of the first window.

3 Click the right window to make it active, then choose CMYK Preview from the Mode menu.

The color conversion of the blend with the out-of-gamut color occurs automatically. The royal blue in the RGB image appears as violet blue in the CMYK Preview image. The violet blue in the CMYK Preview image is the printable equivalent of the RGB royal blue.

If you plan on continuing to edit the RGB image, make sure to turn off the CMYK preview. Using this command displays a representation of the printable colors, not the colors as they appear in RGB mode.

4 Choose CMYK Preview from the Mode menu to turn the preview off.

IDENTIFYING OUT-OF-GAMUT COLORS

You can identify out-of-gamut colors by using the Info palette and the Gamut Warning command.

To display out-of-gamut colors:

1 Make sure the Info palette is in view.

2 Position your cursor in the bright blue at the top of the right window.

In the Info palette, the CMYK numbers display exclamation points that indicate the out-of-gamut colors.

3 Choose Gamut Warning from the Mode menu.

Adobe Photoshop builds a color conversion table and identifies the out-of-gamut colors by displaying a neutral gray color. The new gradient turns gray. You can change this warning color to make it stand out more from the image.

4 Choose Preferences from the File menu, then choose Gamut Warning from the submenu.

5 Click the medium-gray color swatch, then choose a bright green from the Color Picker and click OK.

6 Leave the opacity at 100 percent, then click OK.

All of the out-of-gamut areas turn bright green.

7 Choose Save As from the File menu, enter **11Work** for the file name, open the Projects folder and click Save.

CORRECTING OUT-OF-GAMUT COLORS

Once you have identified out-of-gamut colors, you can correct them using several different techniques. You have already seen how Adobe Photoshop can make the conversion automatically by converting to CMYK mode. If you need more control over the corrections, try these techniques.

If a small, contiguous area has been identified as being out of gamut, you can use the sponge tool to bring the color into gamut. You'll try that now.

To use the sponge tool to correct out-of-gamut colors:

1 Double-click the dodge tool in the toolbox, then choose Sponge from the Tool menu in the Toning Tools Options palette.

2 Make sure Desaturate is selected in the palette mode menu and change the pressure to 100 percent.

3 Click the Brushes palette tab, then choose a large, soft-edged brush.

4 In the window on the right, drag the sponge through the bright green color under the rim of the glass and to the right of the wine bottle.

Watch both windows. As the colors become less saturated, they come into the CMYK gamut and the bright green warning color disappears. In the second window, you can see the blue change from a bright blue to a less saturated color. Be careful not to desaturate too much or the color may become muddy or streaky.

Using the Color Range command to correct out-of-gamut colors

If the out-of-gamut colors make up a distinct area, such as a logo or painted area, you can use the Color Range command to select them.

To correct out-of-gamut colors:

1 Choose Revert from the File menu and click Revert.

The file reverts to the last-saved version.

2 Choose Color Range from the Select menu. The Color Range dialog box appears.

You tried the Color Range command in Lesson 4.

3 Choose Out Of Gamut from the Select pop-up menu in the Color Range dialog box.

You'll see the out-of-gamut areas in the preview box turn white.

4 Click OK to close the Color Range dialog box.

All the out-of-gamut pixels are selected.

5 Choose Adjust from the Image menu and Hue/Saturation from the submenu.

6 Drag the dialog box so that you can see the image.

7 Drag the Lightness slider to the left to –33.

8 Drag the Saturation slider to the left until the bright green gamut warning goes away (about –52). Click OK.

9 Choose None from the Select menu.

You have just made the changes required to bring the image into the range of printable colors.

10 Choose Close from the File menu to close both *11Work* images and save changes.

CUSTOMIZING SEPARATION OPTIONS

As you know, the separation of an image is controlled by the settings in the Monitor Setup, Printing Inks Setup, Separation Setup, and Separation Tables dialog boxes. An important concept to keep in mind is that these options do not affect RGB images. *They affect image data only when you convert the file from RGB to CMYK mode.* Therefore, if you convert an image to CMYK and then change the calibration settings, you must reconvert the image to CMYK for the changes to take effect. Because of this interaction between settings and conversions, you can use one of two strategies for creating color separations.

Working in RGB mode

One way to create color separations is to work in RGB mode, set the separation preferences to compensate for conditions on-press, and then convert the image to CMYK mode. During the conversion, Adobe Photoshop changes the image to compensate for the settings you have made. When converted to CMYK, the image appears the same on the screen as the original RGB image. The advantage to working in RGB is that it is faster than working in CMYK mode. The disadvantage is that you may need to track your colors more carefully to note out-of-gamut colors.

Working in CMYK mode

The second strategy for creating color separations is to print a color proof to show the needed corrections, then work in CMYK mode as you make color corrections until the screen display matches the desired output. The display will change and you will see the colors that will print. Working in CMYK mode is slower than working in RGB mode.

When you work in CMYK mode and set separation settings, such as dot gain, the CMYK display changes to *simulate* the settings and show how the image will appear when printed. For example, if you enter a dot gain of 30 percent while your image is in CMYK mode, the image will appear darker on the screen to approximate what the image would look like when printed on a press under those conditions. However, the actual image is not changed. (In contrast, the RGB image is altered when you convert it to CMYK mode.)

Adjusting the printing inks setup

In this part of the lesson, you'll experiment with different separation preferences to compare their effects. Two options that clearly illustrate the difference in separation settings are *dot gain* (in the Printing Inks Setup dialog box) and *black generation* (in the Separation Setup dialog box).

To adjust for printing inks and paper:

1 Choose Open from the File menu, then open the *11Chef1* file in the Lesson 11 folder.

You probably remember this image from Lesson 7. It's been resized for use in this lesson. The *11Chef1* image was separated using the default settings in the Monitor Setup, Printing Inks Setup, Separation Setup, and Separation Tables dialog boxes.

2 Choose Preferences from the File menu and Printing Inks Setup from the submenu.

3 Make sure SWOP (Coated) is selected in the Ink Colors pop-up menu in the Printing Inks Setup dialog box.

SWOP (standard web offset proofing) ink is the default ink color. Coated paper is also the default setting. This is the same setting used to separate the *11Chef1* image. By choosing the same ink, you'll be able to clearly see the difference caused by changing the dot gain.

When you're producing your own proofs, you typically obtain the ink type and dot-gain information from the print shop that will be printing your final job, or you choose your own printer from the Ink Colors list.

4 Enter a dot gain of **30** percent, then click OK.

Dot gain is a printing characteristic that causes dots to be printed larger than they should be, producing darker tones or color than expected. Different printers and papers have different dot gains. The default dot gain for SWOP is 20 percent, and this was the value used to separate the *11Chef1* image.

Adobe Photoshop builds a new color table using the dot gain setting you changed in the Printing Inks Setup dialog box. The CMYK image version now appears substantially darker, simulating what your image would look like if it were printed using a 30-percent dot gain. Remember that only the display has changed, *not* the actual CMYK image.

5 Choose Undo from the Edit menu to compare the effect of the default dot gain of 20 percent with that of the 30-percent dot gain you just applied.

In the Printing Inks Setup dialog box, try choosing other options from the Ink Colors pop-up menu and note how the default dot-gain settings for the inks or printers vary.

6 Choose Preferences from the File menu and Printing Inks Setup from the submenu.

7 Reset the options to the defaults of SWOP (Coated) ink color and 20-percent dot gain, then click OK.

Adjusting the black generation and undercolor removal

Because of impurities in all printing inks, a mix of the process colors yields a muddy brown instead of a pure black. To compensate for this deficiency, printers remove some cyan, magenta, and yellow in areas where the three colors overlap, and add black ink. There are two "styles" of removing or replacing color when converting RGB color to CMYK color: undercolor removal (UCR) or gray component replacement (GCR), also known as *black generation*. You will use the file you have open now, and an RGB version of the same image, to compare black-generation settings.

To adjust the black generation:

1 Choose Open from the File menu, then open the *11Chef2* image in the Lesson 11 folder and drag the image to the right so that it is side by side with the *11Chef1* image.

2 With the *11Chef2* image active, choose Preferences from the File menu and Separation Setup from the submenu. The Separation Setup dialog box appears.

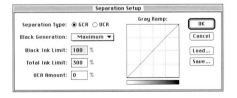

The dialog box displays a graph showing how the neutral colors in the image (that is, colors with equal parts of cyan, magenta, and yellow—sometimes called a "gray ramp") separate given the current Separation Setup parameters. The *x*-axis represents the neutral color value, from 0 percent (white) to 100 percent (black). The *y*-axis represents the amount of each ink that will be generated for the given value.

3 If necessary, click GCR.

This is the default option, used for coated stock. In GCR replacement, more black ink is used over a wider range of colors. GCR separations tend to reproduce dark, saturated colors and maintain gray balance better on-press than UCR separations. You would choose UCR if you were printing on uncoated stock or newsprint.

4 Choose Maximum from the Black Generation pop-up menu.

Notice that the ramp changes to show the new distribution of ink.

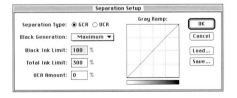

5 Click OK to close the dialog box.

6 Choose CMYK Color from the Mode menu to convert the *11Chef2* image to CMYK mode.

As with the Printing Inks Setup dialog box, Adobe Photoshop builds a new color table whenever you change a setting in the Separation Setup dialog box.

7 Compare the two images.

You probably can't see much of a difference even though the original CMYK image on the left was converted using the default Medium black-generation setting, and the image on the right used the Maximum setting. To better see the effect of black generation, you're going to compare the black channels in each image.

8 Click the Channels palette tab, then click the zoom box in the upper-right corner of the palette to see all the channels.

9 Click Black in the Channels palette tab to display the black channel for each image.

The separation on the left (the original CMYK image) appears lighter than the separation on the right (the converted image).

10 Watch the Info palette, while you use the eyedropper to sample the background along the left edge of each image. (Make sure that the window is active before trying to use the eyedropper.)

In the left image (converted using the Medium setting), the K values in the Info palette range from about 81 percent at the bottom of the image to 89 percent at the top. In the right image (converted using the Maximum setting), the K values range from about 91 percent at the bottom of the image to 96 percent at the top.

11 Choose Close from the File menu to close both chef files without saving any changes.

Creating trap

Trap is the overlap needed to ensure that a slight misalignment or movement of the plates during printing does not affect the final appearance of the printed image. Adobe Photoshop uses the trap setting to determine how far overlapping colors should be spread outward to compensate for misregistration on-press. Overprinting colors slightly to prevent tiny gaps from appearing in the printed image is known as *adding traps*.

Adobe Photoshop traps only by spreading; it does not choke colors. (A *spread trap* overlaps a lighter object onto a darker background. A *choke trap* does the opposite, overlapping a lighter background onto a darker object.) See the *Adobe Photoshop User Guide* for more information on the standard rules for trapping.

Most photos, unless they contain solid tints or letterforms, do not need to be trapped.

To add traps:

1 Choose Open from the File menu, then open the *11Trap* file.

In this image, distinctly different colors in the logo and surrounding areas touch and need to be trapped.

2 Click the zoom tool in the toolbox.

3 Position the zoom tool above the top left of the logo and drag a marquee down and to the right to surround the logo.

4 The image is magnified and fills your window. You can see how the color spreads.

Especially in the thinner stroke of the *V*, you can see how the yellow blends with the blue background. The blending is a result of the magenta and yellow in the letters spreading out underneath the dark blue. In Adobe Photoshop, lighter colors spread under darker colors. This means that yellow spreads under cyan, magenta, and black.

5 Choose Trap from the Image menu, enter a value of **4**, and click OK.

This causes the yellow to spread too much under the darker blue, as you can clearly see around the edges of the logo.

6 Choose Undo to return to the original image, choose Trap again, enter **1** in the dialog box, then click OK.

This amount of trap improves the letters and also causes a slight darkening in the high-contrast and shadow areas, especially near the top of the wine-glass stem. This subtle effect is hard to see in the composite view of the image, but shows up clearly if you look at the yellow channel.

7 Click Yellow in the Channels palette to display the yellow channel, then press Command-Z to undo and redo the trapping so you can see the effect.

Yellow channel before trap   *Yellow channel after trap*

8 Choose Save As from the File menu, type **11Work2** for the name, make sure your Projects folder is open, and click Save.

SELECTING PRINTING AND FILE OPTIONS

To select printing options, you first make choices from the File Info and Page Setup dialog boxes, then choose Options from the Print dialog box.

Entering file information

Adobe Photoshop supports the information standard developed by the Newspaper Association of America and the International Press Telecommunications Council to identify transmitted text and images.

To enter file information:

1 Choose Open from the File menu, then open the *11Chef2* file in the Lesson 11 folder.

2 Choose File Info from the File menu. The File Info dialog box appears.

3 Type **Portrait for Annual Report** in the Caption box.

4 Press Tab, then type **your name** in the Caption Writer box.

5 Press Tab twice, then type **Use Custom Line Screens** in the Special Instructions box.

Other areas of file information that you can use include *keywords* for use with image browser applications, *categories* for use with the Associated Press regional registry, *credits* for copyrighted images, and *origin* information.

6 Click the Section menu and choose Origin.

In the origin section you can enter information that you or others can refer to later, including an address, date, and other data.

7 Click the Today button to enter today's date in the date box, then click OK.

SPECIFYING SETTINGS FOR DIFFERENT IMAGE TYPES

The type of image you're printing, and the type of output you want, determine which selections you make in the Page Setup and Print dialog boxes.

The Page Setup dialog box lets you set up print labels, crop marks, calibration bars, registration marks, and negatives. You can also print emulsion-side down, and use interpolation (for PostScript Level 2 printers).

Printing a color composite

A color composite is a single print that superimposes the red, green, and blue channels of an RGB image (or the cyan, magenta, yellow, and black channels of a CMYK image). For your first printing task, you'll print an RGB file with the caption that you added in the File Info dialog box.

To print a color composite:

1 Choose Page Setup from the File menu.

2 Click the Caption, the Calibration Bars, the Registration Marks, and the Corner Crop Marks checkboxes, then click OK.

3 Display the page preview box by clicking in the lower-left corner of the window.

The crop marks, calibration and registration marks, and caption appear in the box. All of the settings you make in the Page Setup dialog box can be previewed before printing.

4 Choose Print from the File menu. The Print dialog box appears.

This will vary depending on the type of printer you have selected.

5 Select the Print Color/Grayscale option. (You may have to click an Options button to find this command.)

This option tells the printer to produce color output. If you do not use this option, the file prints as a black-and-white image. (This format varies depending on the type of printer you have selected.)

6 Click OK to print the file as a composite.

Printing a color-corrected version of an RGB or Lab image

You can print a color-corrected version of RGB, Lab, and indexed color images (if you're working with an indexed color image, convert the image to RGB before printing). This option allows Adobe Photoshop to make an on-the-fly conversion to CMYK colors for the RGB or Lab file, and usually produces better results than a print shop. The option works with color PostScript and Quick-Draw printers, but is not recommended for Post-Script Level 2 printers.

To print a color-corrected version of this image:

1 Choose Print from the File menu.

2 Click the Print in CMYK option in the Print dialog box, then click Print.

Adobe Photoshop prints the color-corrected image.

3 Choose Close from the File menu to close the file without saving changes.

Printing a separated image

By default, a single document is printed for CMYK images. You can choose to print the four separations for an image.

To print a separated image:

1 Choose Open from the File menu, then open the *11Chef1* image.

2 Choose Print from the File menu.

3 Make sure that the Print Color/Grayscale option is selected.

4 Select the Print Separations option to print the file as four separations, then click Print.

The image prints as four separate pieces of paper or film. If this option is not on, the CMYK image prints as a composite image.

5 Choose Close from the file menu to close the file without saving changes.

To print a selected area:

1 Select the *11Work2* image.

2 Click the CMYK composite channel.

3 Double-click the zoom tool to go to a 1:1 view.

4 Select the logo using the rectangular marquee tool. The rectangular marquee tool is the only selection tool you can use when choosing an area to be printed.

5 Choose Print from the File menu.

6 Click the Print Selected Area option.

7 If necessary, deselect the Print Separations option to print a composite, then click Print to print the logo.

Printing a halftone

To print an image with a halftone screen, you use the Halftone Screen option in the Page Setup dialog box. The results of using a halftone screen are apparent only in the printed copy; you don't see the halftone screen in the monitor display. Your computer must be connected to a printer before you can set up the halftone screen.

You use one halftone screen to print a grayscale image. You use four halftone screens (one for each color) to print color separations. In this example, you'll be adjusting the screen frequency and dot shape to produce a halftone screen for a grayscale image.

The *screen frequency* controls the density of dots on the screen. Since the dots are arranged in lines on the screen, the common measurement for screen frequency is lines per inch (lpi). The higher the screen frequency, the finer the image produced. Magazines, for example, tend to use fine screens of 133 lpi and higher because they are usually printed on coated paper stock on high-quality presses. Newspapers, which are usually printed on lower-quality paper stock, tend to use lower screen frequencies, such as 85-lpi screens.

The *screen angle* used to create halftones of grayscale images is generally 45 degrees. For color separations, you specify an angle for each of the color screens. Setting the screens at different angles ensures that the dots placed by the four screens blend to look like continuous color and do not produce moiré patterns.

Diamond-shaped dots are most commonly used in halftone screens. In Adobe Photoshop, however, you can also choose round, elliptical, linear, square, and cross-shaped dots.

To set up the halftone screen:

1 Choose Grayscale from the Mode menu to convert the *11Work2* image to Grayscale mode.

2 Choose Page Setup from the File menu.

3 Click the Screen button. The Halftone Screen dialog box appears.

4 Turn off the Use Printer's Default Screen checkbox to enter another number.

5 Enter **80** in the Frequency box and make sure that Lines/inch is chosen from the Measurement pop-up menu.

6 Leave the screen angle at the default setting of 45 degrees.

7 Choose Ellipse from the Shape pop-up menu.

8 Click OK twice to produce the screen.

To print the halftone:

1 If necessary, select a printer.

2 Choose Print from the File menu, then click OK to print the file.

3 Choose Close from the File menu to close the file. If you want to, you can save the grayscale version of this file.

This completes your introduction to producing color separations and printing using Adobe Photoshop. This is a very complex and rapidly changing area of digital technology, and you should be proud of what you've done in this lesson. For a more complete discussion of calibration, color separation, and all the printing options, see the *Adobe Photoshop User Guide*.

Lesson

12

Lesson 12: Importing and Exporting Files

This lesson explains how you open (or import) and save (or export) files that are not in the Adobe Photoshop format. So far, you've been working with Adobe Photoshop 3.0 files. Adobe Photoshop also allows you to open files in Photoshop versions 2.0 and above, Amiga IFF, BMP, EPS, FilmStrip, GIF, JPEG, MacPaint, PCX, PICT File, PICT Resource, PIXAR, PixelPaint, Raw, Scitex™ CT, Targa, and TIFF. In addition, Adobe Photoshop opens files scanned using the TWAIN interface, and opens and decompresses EPS files saved using EPS JPEG compression.

You can save Adobe Photoshop files in most of these same file formats, plus one additional format—Amiga HAM. Using export modules, you can also save EPS files using JPEG compression, export files for printing on a color ImageWriter®II printer, and export paths to Adobe Illustrator.

You can open Kodak PhotoCD files in Adobe Photoshop and manipulate the files just like any other digitized images. You must enter a resolution and file format when you open the files. If you open the file in Lab format, all the color information is preserved. You cannot save files in the PhotoCD format from Adobe Photoshop.

If these file types aren't familiar to you, don't worry. All you need to know is that Adobe Photoshop can open almost any file you might want to use in an image, and can save your files in the formats commonly used by other applications.

In most cases, opening and saving non-Adobe Photoshop files is as simple as using the standard Open and Save As dialog boxes. The different file formats appear in a pop-up menu in the dialog boxes, and you choose the format you want to open or save in. For a few file types, you import files using commands in the Acquire menu and export files using commands in the Export menu. Sometimes, opening and saving files requires an additional dialog box. These dialog boxes are described in detail in the *Adobe Photoshop User Guide*.

This lesson shows you how to use Adobe Photoshop and Adobe Illustrator in tandem. If you don't have Adobe Illustrator, you can skip the part of the lesson in which you create Adobe Illustrator artwork. The finished Adobe Illustrator file is included with the *Classroom in a Book* files. It should take you about 30 minutes to complete this lesson.

In this lesson, you'll learn how to do the following:

• open and save JPEG files

• save in EPS format

• export a path to Adobe Illustrator

• create type that follows a path in Adobe Illustrator

• place Adobe Illustrator art in an Adobe Photoshop file

At the end of this lesson you'll have a tempting advertisement that invites Gourmet Visions customers to sample the pleasure of fresh sushi.

Source file (12Sushi)

Source file (12Type.eps)

Source file (12Bar.eps)

Ending image (12Final)

BEGINNING THIS LESSON

In this lesson, you will open a beginning image and a reference file. Both of these files are in CMYK mode. You'll work directly in the CMYK mode for this lesson. In order to see some of the effects of saving on a file's size, you'll open the files in this lesson from the Lesson 12 folder.

To begin this lesson:

1 Quit Adobe Photoshop, then throw away your *Adobe Photoshop 3.0 Prefs* file and empty the Trash.

2 Open the Lesson 12 folder in the Finder. Drag the folder to a location on your screen where it will be visible after you've opened the two Adobe Photoshop files.

3 Choose By Name from the View menu (you must be in the Finder to change the window view).

Lesson 12			
Name	Size	Kind	La
🗋 12Bar.eps	65K	document	
🗋 12Final	925K	Adobe Photoshop™...	
🗋 12Sushi	473K	Adobe Photoshop™...	
🗋 12Type.eps	86K	document	

4 Double-click the *12Final* file in the Lesson 12 folder.

5 Click the zoom box in the upper-right corner of the Layers palette.

The *12Final* file contains three layers: the Background layer, which is a scan of sushi, the Type layer, and the Bar layer with the Japanese characters.

6 Zoom out to reduce the *12Final* image, resize the window if necessary, then drag the window to the upper-right corner of your screen.

7 Double-click the *12Sushi* file in the Lesson 12 folder in the Finder.

8 Close or collapse the Brushes/Options palette and the Picker/Swatches/Scratch palette. Make sure that the Layers/Channels/Paths group of palettes is open on your screen.

UNDERSTANDING COMPRESSION

Compressing a file can save large amounts of space on your storage disk, without noticeably affecting the quality of the image. When you're working with very large files, compression is especially important since graphic files can easily exceed 10 MB in size. (To understand how big these files are, think of how much information you store on your hard disk. If you have an 80-MB hard disk, you can store only eight 10-MB graphic files.)

There are several compression types. Adobe Photoshop allows you to save or compress files using the Joint Photographic Experts Group (JPEG) format. JPEG compression economizes on the way data is stored and also identifies and discards "extra" data—that is, information the human eye cannot see. Because data is discarded or lost, JPEG is referred to as "lossy" compression. With lossy compression, an image that is compressed and then decompressed is not identical to the original image. In most cases, the difference between the original and the compressed version of the image is indistinguishable.

SAVING A FILE IN JPEG FORMAT

Currently, the *12Sushi* file is in Adobe Photoshop 3.0 format. You are going to reduce the file size of this image by saving it in JPEG format.

To save a file in JPEG format:

1 Select the *12Sushi* file.

The size preview box indicates that the current file size is 578K.

2 Choose Finder from the Application menu in the upper-right corner of your screen.

3 Open your Projects folder and choose By Name from the View menu so you can see the file sizes.

4 Choose Adobe Photoshop 3.0 from the Application menu in the upper-right corner of your screen.

5 Choose Save As from the File menu.

6 Type **12Sushi.jpeg** for the file name and open your Projects folder.

7 Choose JPEG from the Format pop-up menu at the bottom of the dialog box and click Save. The JPEG Options dialog box appears.

JPEG lets you choose from four compression settings. In general, an image compressed using the Maximum option has a compression ratio of between 5:1 and 15:1. The higher the quality setting, the less the file is compressed and the less the file size is reduced.

8 Click the High setting and click OK.

9 Choose Close from the File menu to close the file.

10 In the Projects folder window make sure the view is *By Name*, then check the file size of the *12Sushi.jpeg* file.

You can see that using the high compression option reduced the file size from 578K to about 96K.

11 Double-click the *12Sushi.jpeg* file to reopen it.

Note that the size preview box in the lower-left corner of your window shows the original file size of 578K. This is because the file is decompressed as it is opened. This decompression is done automatically by Adobe Photoshop whenever you open a file saved in JPEG format.

12 Choose Close from the File menu to close the file once more. You will not be using the JPEG file again in this lesson.

IMPORTING ADOBE PHOTOSHOP FILES

In order to import Adobe Photoshop files into documents created in the most commonly used page-layout programs, you must save the files in a format other than the Adobe Photoshop 3.0 format. You cannot save an image that contains layers into another format; you must first flatten the image.

To view the file formats:

1 Click the *12Final* window to make it active.

This file contains three layers.

2 Choose Save As from the File menu, then click the Format menu.

All the formats except for Adobe Photoshop 3.0 are unavailable. Any file containing layers can only be saved in the Adobe Photoshop 3.0 format.

3 Click Cancel.

Now you'll flatten the image and convert it to the EPS format.

SAVING A FILE IN EPS FORMAT

The Encapsulated PostScript (EPS) language file format is supported by most illustration and page-layout programs. In order to use Adobe Photoshop images with these kinds of applications, you must save them as EPS files.

To save a file in EPS format:

1 Choose Flatten Image from the Layers palette pop-up menu.

2 Choose Save As from the File menu.

3 Type **12Final.eps** for the file name and open the Projects folder.

4 Choose EPS from the Format pop-up menu and click Save. The EPS Format dialog box appears.

There are several options available when you save a file in EPS format. The *Adobe Photoshop User Guide* explains these options. For this file, you're going to use the default values.

5 Make sure the Preview option is set to Macintosh (8 bits/pixel), the DCS (Desktop Color Separation) option is Off, and the Encoding option is set to Binary, then click OK.

The Binary option creates a file that is about half the size of a file saved with the ASCII option and takes half as long to transfer to the printer. However, some applications might not support binary EPS documents. When you're going to use these types of applications, use the ASCII encoding option.

Note: If you are saving a file to be used with another operating system, you may need to choose the TIFF (8 bits/pixel) preview option and make sure to add the .EPS extension to the file name.

6 Choose Close from the File menu.

EXPORTING A PATH TO ADOBE ILLUSTRATOR

For the final image, you're going to create a path in this EPS file, export the path to an Adobe Illustrator file, then use the path to determine the placement of the type. Just for practice, create and export the path even if you won't be working in Adobe Illustrator.

To export a path to Adobe Illustrator:

1 Choose Open from the File menu, then choose the *12Sushi* file in the Lesson 12 folder.

2 Click the Paths palette tab, then use the pen tool to draw a path around the plate. Place the first anchor point in the top center of the plate.

Drag the points to draw the curved outline. Be sure to close the path. Your path should look something like this.

3 Choose Save Path from the Paths palette pop-up menu and name the path **Plate**, then click OK.

4 Choose Export from the File menu and Paths to Illustrator from the submenu. A directory dialog box appears.

Adobe Photoshop automatically adds the extension *.ai* (for Adobe Illustrator) to the end of the file name.

5 Open your Projects folder and click Save to save the path file.

6 Choose Save As from the File menu, type **12Work**, make sure that the Projects folder is open, then click Save to save the path with the *12Work* file.

USING A PATH IN ADOBE ILLUSTRATOR

Now you're ready to use this path in an Adobe Illustrator file. If you don't have Adobe Illustrator, you can read through the following steps or skip to the *Placing Adobe Illustrator Files* section, later in this lesson.

The steps in this section assume you're using Adobe Illustrator 5.5. If you're working in an earlier version of Adobe Illustrator, follow your usual procedures to create type and view artwork.

The first thing you're going to do is display the path and the EPS file in Adobe Illustrator.

If you don't have Adobe Illustrator, skip to the next section.

To use the path in Adobe Illustrator:

1 Open the Adobe Illustrator application. A blank untitled window appears.

If you don't have enough memory to open both applications simultaneously, quit Adobe Photoshop for now.

2 Choose Open from the File menu (or press Command-O) and select the *12Sushi.ai* file from the Projects folder (this is your exported path file).

3 Choose Artwork from the View menu (or press Command-E).

You need to look at the file in Artwork view so that you can see the path. Because paths are exported from Adobe Photoshop with no fill and no strokes saved, you won't be able to see the path if you open it in the default Adobe Illustrator Preview view.

The path appears in the window. The crop marks indicate the size of the Adobe Photoshop image.

4 Click the selection tool in the toolbox, then click the edge of the path to select it.

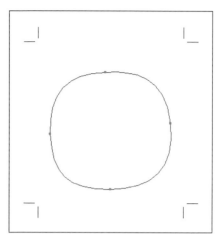

Adding type in Adobe Illustrator

Now you're ready to add the type. The top of the path is going to serve as the defining border of the type. In Adobe Illustrator this is called *path type* (as opposed to *area type*, which is like the type you can enter in Adobe Photoshop).

To create the type:

1 Select the path-type tool. The path-type tool is adjacent to the type tool in the toolbox.

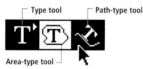

The path-type tool makes the type you enter follow the curve of the path. When you move into the image area, the insertion point appears with a curved line running through it.

2 Click the anchor point at the top center of the path to display the insertion point, then type **Kyoto Sushi**.

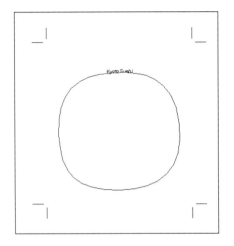

The type appears along the path. This type is in the default font of 12-point Helvetica. (If you don't see any type, you might need to install this font in your system.)

3 Choose Paragraph from the Type menu. The Paragraph palette appears.

4 Click the second alignment box from the left to center the type.

5 Close the Paragraph palette by clicking the close box in the top left of the palette title.

Setting the type attributes

Now you're ready to set the attributes for the type. In Adobe Illustrator, unlike in Adobe Photoshop, you can enter the type first and then set the type attributes.

To set the type attributes:

1 Choose Select All from the Edit menu.

2 Choose Character from the Type menu (or press Command-T). The Character palette appears.

3 Choose Helvetica from the Font pop-up menu and set the size to 48.

You can type in the font and size or choose them from the pop-up menus. As you change options in the Character palette, the type is automatically updated to reflect the new settings.

4 Choose Tracking from the Type menu (or press Command-Shift-K).

When you choose this command, the Character palette expands to show additional options. *Tracking* creates uniform spacing in type.

5 Enter **70** in the Tracking text box and press Return.

As a final adjustment, you're going to increase the tracking in the second word.

6 Click outside the type to deselect it, then double-click the word to select only *Sushi*.

7 Change the tracking to **100** in the Character palette and press Return.

8 Close the character palette by clicking the close box in the palette title.

9 Click the selection tool (the arrow pointer in the upper-left corner of the toolbox), and drag the top of the I-beam to center the type along the top of the path.

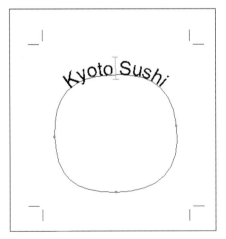

Changing the type color

Currently, the type appears in black around the top of the path. You want the type to be white in your final Adobe Photoshop image.

To change the type color:

1 Select the path-type tool and click anywhere in the type to display the insertion point.

2 Choose Select All from the Edit menu.

3 Choose Paint Style from the Object menu (or press Command-I). The Paint Style palette appears.

Click the white box in the top row of color selection options. The type becomes white.

4 Close the Paint Style palette by clicking the close box in the top-left corner of the palette.

5 Choose Save As from the File menu.

6 Type **12Type1.eps** for the name of the file, if you are working in Illustrator 5.0 or less set the Preview option to Color Macintosh, set the format to your version of Adobe Illustrator, then save the file in the Projects folder.

7 Quit the Adobe Illustrator application.

If you want to learn more about using Adobe Illustrator, see the *Classroom in a Book* available for Adobe Illustrator.

PLACING ADOBE ILLUSTRATOR FILES

To complete your advertisement, you're going to bring two Adobe Illustrator files into your Adobe Photoshop image. One file is a design element that includes the Japanese name for Kyoto Sushi. The other is the type file (either the one you just created or the file from the Lesson 12 folder).

When you want to use an Adobe Illustrator file as a new Adobe Photoshop document, you open the file using the Open command. In this case, you want to include the files in an existing Adobe Photoshop file, so you use the Place command.

To place the EPS files in the Adobe Photoshop image:

1 Choose Open from the File menu, then open the 12Work file in the Projects folder, then open the *12Final* file in the Lesson 12 folder.

If you quit Adobe Photoshop when you started Adobe Illustrator, double-click the file in the Lesson 12 folder to start the program.

2 Select the *12Work* file, then click the Layers palette tab.

3 Choose Place from the File menu.

4 Select the *12Bar.eps* file in the Lesson 12 folder, and click Open.

The red bar with Japanese type appears as a floating selection inside a rectangular box in the center of the image.

5 Click with the gavel to confirm the placement of the bar file.

6 Drag the bar to the lower-right corner, and position it as shown in the *12Final* file.

7 Double-click the Floating Selection thumbnail, then enter **Type Bar** for the name of the new layer, and click OK.

8 Choose Place from the File menu, select the *12Type.eps* file (or the *12Type1.eps* file if you created it in Adobe Illustrator), and click Open.

The placement of the type should be correct.

If you want to change the placement, drag a corner handle to resize the box. Hold down the Shift key as you drag to keep the same aspect ratio as the original Adobe Illustrator file.

9 Click with the gavel icon to confirm the placement. Then if necessary, use the arrow keys to reposition the type.

10 Double-click the Floating Selection thumbnail, enter **Type** for the name, and click OK.

CHANGING THE TYPE OPACITY

This imported type is now the same as any type you create in Adobe Photoshop and can be edited using the standard commands and tools. As a final touch to this image, you're going to change the opacity of the type.

To change the type opacity:

1 Make sure the Type layer is the target layer.

2 Type **8** to set the opacity in the Layers palette to 80 percent. You can see that the type is less distinct from the background.

3 Experiment with the Opacity slider in the Layers palette to see the effect of decreasing or increasing opacity.

4 Choose Save from the File menu.

Now you'll save a file in the TIFF format for use with other applications.

5 Choose Save a Copy from the File menu, and name the file **12Work2.tif,** then open the Projects folder.

6 Click the Flatten Image checkbox to flatten the layers in the image.

7 Choose TIFF from the Format pop-up menu.

Notice that the Flatten Image option is grayed out. When you save a copy of an image using any format other than Adobe Photoshop 3.0, the image is flattened automatically.

8 Click Save, then leave Macintosh selected and click OK.

9 Close all open files without saving changes.

And that's how easy it is to use other file types with Adobe Photoshop. This lesson showed you just one example of how you can use Adobe Photoshop with other file types and applications. You'll probably discover many other uses for the extensive file types you can import from and export to as you're using Adobe Photoshop in your own work.

Lesson

13

LESSON 13: TRADE SHOW POSTER

I n this lesson, you'll have a chance to review what's been covered in Lessons 10, 11, and 12. There are also a few tried-and-true procedures from earlier lessons that should be second-hand to you by now. Hopefully, as you complete this lesson in *Classroom in a Book*, you'll begin to see how you can put what you've learned to work in your own image creation and editing.

As in the earlier review projects, this lesson provides all the step-by-step instructions you need to complete the project. Detailed explanations, however, are not included. If you need to brush up on specifics, or can't remember how to do something, refer back to the earlier lessons. For a quick reference to the specific topics covered in each lesson, see the table of contents at the beginning of the book.

In Lesson 10, you learned how to convert images from one mode to another, and in Lesson 11, you prepared a color separation for printing. Lesson 12 explained how to open and save files in different formats and how to use Adobe Photoshop in conjunction with Adobe Illustrator. In this lesson, you'll use the composite plate you created in Lesson 10 as the main element in a trade show poster. You will then add type to the poster and prepare it for printing. If you have a color printer, you can print out the results. It should take you about half an hour to complete this lesson.

Source file (13Plate)   Source file (13Date.eps)

Ending image (13Final)

BEGINNING THIS LESSON

As you have done several times before, you will create a new file in this lesson and then copy components from other files into the new image.

To begin the lesson:

1 Quit the Adobe Photoshop application, throw away the *Adobe Photoshop 3.0 Prefs* file, and empty the Trash.

2 Open the *13Final* file in the Lesson 13 folder.

3 Click the zoom box in the Layers palette.

The final file contains four layers. The Background layer consists of four blocks of color. The other layers contain the plate image that you prepared in Lesson 10, the rectangular graphic element at the top of the poster, and the text.

4 In the *13Final* image, zoom out, resize the window if necessary, and move this reference file to the upper-right corner of your screen.

5 Create a new file named **13Work** that is 310 pixels wide and 400 pixels high with a resolution of 72. The mode should be RGB Color and the contents should be white. Click OK.

If necessary, use the pop-up menu in the New dialog box to set the units of measurement to pixels before creating the file.

6 Turn on the rulers in the document window.

7 Create a new palette group consisting of the Brushes, Options, Picker, Channels, Paths, and Layers palettes. (It can be open or collapsed).

8 Close the remaining palettes.

CREATING FIXED-SIZE RECTANGLES

To begin creating this poster, you need to draw and fill the blocks for the background.

To create the background:

1 Create a fixed rectangular marquee that is 155 pixels wide and 200 pixels high.

2 Click anywhere in the window to display the marquee and drag it to the upper-left corner. Use the arrow keys to place the marquee flush against the edges of the window.

3 Click the Picker palette tab, then choose CMYK Sliders from the palette pop-up menu.

4 Mix a foreground color in the Picker palette with the following values:

Cyan .... 95 %
Magenta ...... 85 %
Yellow .... 0 %
Black.............. 0 %

As an alternative, you can use the eyedropper to sample this color from the upper-left quadrant of the final image.

5 Use the paint bucket tool to fill the rectangle.

6 Set the foreground color to black.

7 Use the fixed marquee to create a selection in the lower-right corner of the window, then use the paint bucket to fill the rectangle with black.

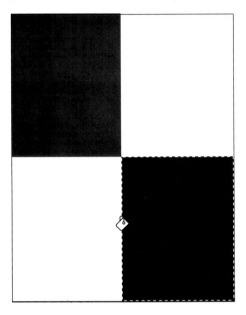

8 Deselect the rectangular selection.

9 Choose Save As from the File menu, then open the Projects folder and click Save.

COPYING A SELECTION FROM ANOTHER IMAGE

The first element you'll add to the poster is the composite plate you created in Lesson 10.

To copy the plate:

1 Open the *13Plate* file in the Lesson 13 folder.

The file in the Lesson 13 folder has a saved selection that is the outline of the plate.

2 Load the selection from channel #4.

3 Drag the *13Plate* window to the right so that you can see the *13Work* and the *13Plate* window.

4 Click the move tool and drag the plate selection to the *13Work* window.

5 Select the *13Plate* window, then choose Close from the File menu.

6 Drag the plate to the center of the window. Line up the four sections of the plate with the background quadrants to position the plate exactly in the center of the image.

7 Click the Layers palette tab, double-click the Floating Selection thumbnail, type **Plate** for the new layer name, then click OK.

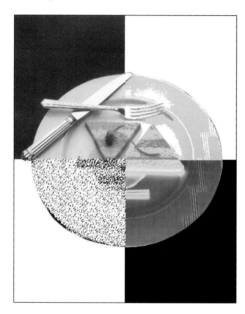

8 Save the file.

INVERTING A COLOR SELECTION

The two rectangles behind the *California Cuisine* type in this image are inverted versions of each other. You'll add these rectangles now and enter the type.

To create the type rectangles:

1 Double-click the marquee tool, then use a fixed marquee to create a rectangle that is 255 pixels wide and 40 pixels high.

2 Click to display the marquee and drag the upper-left corner of the rectangle to the one-quarter inch marker on the left ruler and at about the three-eighths-inch marker on the top ruler.

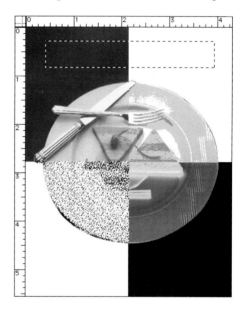

If you get a warning dialog box stating that the *selected area is empty,* you probably forgot to hold down the Command and Option keys. The rectangular marquee is currently floating on the transparent part of the Plate layer, so there are no pixels in the selection marquee.

3 Click the Layers palette tab.

4 To create an element using the colors in the underlying Background layer, click the Background layer thumbnail in the Layers palette to make it the target layer.

The selection marquee is now floating above the Background layer.

5 Choose Float from the Select menu.

Choosing Float puts a copy of the blue and white pixels in a floating selection above the background.

6 Choose Map from the Image menu and Invert from the submenu.

The left side of the rectangle becomes tan and the right side of the rectangle becomes black. When you invert a color selection, its complementary color (on the color wheel) is produced.

7 Double-click the Floating Selection thumbnail in the Layers palette, type **Color Bar** as the name of the new layer, then click OK.

Since you floated the selection, the background is unchanged.

Note that the Layers palette now contains three layers: the unchanged Background, the inverted color bar, and the plate.

ADDING THE TYPE

Now you're ready to add the *California Cuisine* type.

To add the type:

1 Click the type tool and click the insertion point in the tan half of the rectangle.

2 Set the font to Helvetica Bold, the size to 10 points, and the spacing to 4. Type **CALIFORNIA** (in all caps) in the text box and click OK.

3 Hide the edges of the selection and center the type in the tan box.

4 Double-click the Floating Selection thumbnail, type **Text** as the new layer name, then click OK.

5 Switch the foreground and background colors so the foreground is white.

6 Click the type tool, note that the Text layer is the target layer, and click the insertion point in the black half of the rectangle.

7 Set the font to Times Bold Italic, the size to 12, and the spacing to 10. Type **Cuisine** (upper- and lowercase) in the text box, and click OK.

8 Hide the edges of the selection and use the arrow keys to center the *Cuisine* type and align it with the *California* type.

9 Deselect the type so it becomes part of the target layer.

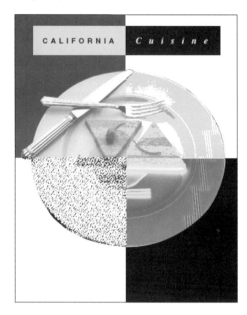

10 Save the file.

SAVING THE SELECTION AS A PATH

In earlier lessons, you saved a path as a selection so you could reuse the selection in other images. Adobe Photoshop also lets you go in the other direction—that is, you can save a selection as a path.

For the final image, you want to create type that will wrap around the bottom of the plate. You do this by saving the plate selection as a path and then exporting the path to Adobe Illustrator where you add the curved type.

To turn the selection into a path:

1 Click the Layers palette tab, then click the Plate layer thumbnail to make it the target layer.

2 Choose Load Selection from the Select menu.

3 Choose Plate Transparency from the Channel menu, then click OK.

When you have a specific layer selected as the target layer, a temporary channel is created that contains a selection of the opaque areas of the layer.

4 Click the Paths palette tab, then choose Make Path from the Paths palette pop-up menu.

You must convert the selection to a path in order to use it in Adobe Illustrator.

5 Make sure the tolerance is set to 2 and click OK to make the path.

It takes Adobe Photoshop a few seconds to convert the selection into a path.

6 Choose Save Path from the Paths palette pop-up menu, and name the new path **Plate Shape**.

7 Save the file.

8 Choose Export from the File menu and Paths to Illustrator from the submenu, name the file *13Date* (the *.ai* extension is automatically supplied), open the Projects folder and click Save.

ADDING THE TYPE IN ADOBE ILLUSTRATOR

As in Lesson 12, you can skip this section if you do not have Adobe Illustrator. The *13Date.eps* file in the Lesson 13 folder contains the type you need to complete this project. To continue creating the poster using the supplied file, turn to the *Placing the Type* section later in this lesson.

If you want more practice in creating type using paths, go ahead and complete this section. If you need help, refer to the detailed instructions for creating type in Adobe Illustrator in Lesson 12.

Entering the type in Adobe Illustrator

The first step toward creating the type is to display the path and enter the text.

To type the date:

1 If you don't have enough memory to run both Adobe Photoshop and Adobe Illustrator at the same time, quit the Adobe Photoshop application.

2 Launch the Adobe Illustrator application.

3 Choose Open from the File menu, then open the *13Date.ai* file in the Projects folder.

4 Go into Artwork view and select the path with the selection tool.

5 Click the path-type tool, then click the bottom center edge of the path to display the insertion point.

6 Type **1995** followed by five spaces, then type **2000**.

The type will follow the curve of the path but will be upside down. You'll fix the type in a second.

7 Choose Paragraph from the Type menu and click the center alignment box, then click the close box in the upper-left corner of the palette.

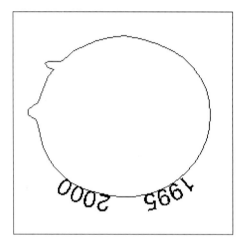

Changing the type style

Now you need to change the font, size, and position of the type.

To change the type style and position:

1 Select all the type.

2 Choose Character from the Type menu and set the font to Times Italic, and the size to 36 points.

3 Choose Tracking from the Type menu or click the key in the lower-right corner of the palette, and enter –35 in the Baseline Shift text box in the expanded Character palette and press Return.

4 Close the Character palette.

Entering a negative value for Baseline Shift makes the type appear under the path. In this case, the type jumps inside the path.

5 Click the selection tool and drag the upper end of the insertion point down, until the type flips beneath the plate.

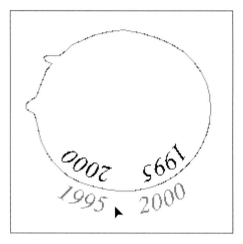

Filling the type

Right now the type is filled with black. In your Adobe Photoshop poster, the *2000* section of the type appears over a black background. Before bringing the type into the *13Work* file, you must fill the type with white so it will be visible.

To fill the type:

1 Use the type tool and drag to select the *2000* type.

2 Choose Paint Style from the Object menu and select the white swatch in the top row, then close the palette.

3 Choose Save As from the File menu, then type **13Date1.eps** for the file name, select any of the Adobe Illustrator or EPS file formats, open the Projects folder, then click Save.

4 Quit Adobe Illustrator and return to the *13Work* file in Adobe Photoshop.

PLACING THE TYPE

You're just about finished with the poster. Your final step is to place the EPS art from the Adobe Illustrator file into the Adobe Photoshop file.

To place the type:

1 With the *13Work* file active, choose Place from the File menu and open the *13Date.eps* file in the Lesson 13 folder (or the *13Date1.eps* file in the Projects folder if you created it).

2 Click with the gavel to confirm the placement.

It's okay if the date is not in its exact final position. You can always change the location using the Adobe Photoshop commands.

3 If necessary, use the arrow keys to slightly adjust the type position. The *2* in *2000* should be about 2½ inches from the left edge of the window.

The date should be about one-eighth-inch below the plate. Use the final image as a reference.

4 Click the Layers palette tab, then drag the Floating Selection thumbnail between the Plate layer thumbnail and the Text layer thumbnail.

5 Deselect the floating selection to add it to the Text layer.

6 Save the file.

CREATING A TWO-TONED DASH

Your poster is just about ready for the trade show. As a finishing touch, you're going to add a dash between the two years. You will create the dash in the same way that you created the two-toned bar.

To create the dash:

1 Double-click the marquee tool and using the Marquee Options palette, create a fixed rectangular marquee that is 20 pixels wide and 5 pixels high.

2 Center the marquee between the two dates (use the division between the black and white background rectangles as a guide, then press the Option key and click to center the marquee).

3 Click the Layers palette tab, then click to make the Background layer thumbnail the target layer.

4 Choose Float from the Select menu.

5 Choose Map from the Image menu and Invert from the submenu.

This turns the half of the selection in the white rectangle black, and the half of the selection in the black rectangle white.

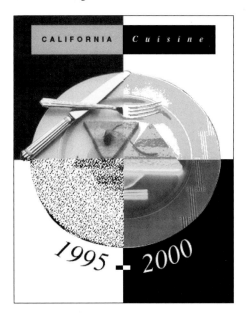

6 Drag the Floating Selection thumbnail in the Layers palette up above the Text layer thumbnail.

7 Deselect the type to add the dash to the Text layer.

8 Save the file.

CHANGING THE PRINTING INKS SETUP OPTIONS

As the last procedure in this lesson, you will prepare this image for color separation and print the image.

Before separating the image, you need to check the Printing Inks Setup options and note the dot-gain settings. This example assumes you are printing to a QMS ColorScript printer.

To check the Printing Inks Setup options:

1 Choose Palettes from the Window menu, and Show Info from the submenu.

2 Choose Preferences from the File menu and Printing Inks Setup from the submenu. Note that when the default SWOP ink is chosen, the dot gain is 20 percent. Click OK to close the dialog box.

3 Use the eyedropper to sample the blue rectangle in the image.

The Info palette shows the values for this color as about 95-percent cyan, 85-percent magenta, and 0-percent yellow and black.

4 Open the Printing Inks Setup dialog box again and choose QMS ColorScript® 100 Model 10 from the Ink Colors menu.

The default dot gain changes to 25 percent. Remember, dot gain is a method of compensating for different ink coverages. Changing the ink type may require more or less ink to ensure correct color in the final proof.

5 Click OK to close the dialog box.

6 Use the eyedropper to check the blue color values again.

Now the cyan value is 89 percent and the magenta value is 76 percent. This change in values subtracts from the percentage of each plate to compensate for heavier ink coverage on-press.

7 Choose Save a Copy from the File menu, type **13WorkL** for the file name, open the Projects folder and click Save. This file contains all the layers.

8 Choose CMYK Color from the Mode menu. If you convert between modes, you can choose to automatically flatten the image.

9 Click Flatten to flatten the layers and convert the image to CMYK.

10 Save the file.

PRINTING THE FILE

You can print this file in a number of ways, depending on what you want to see and the type of printer you have available. Although the effect is more dramatic on a color print, you can also try out this printing procedure on a black-and-white printer.

Because this image has white areas that would bleed into a white piece of paper, you're going to add a border as you print.

To print a composite of the CMYK image:

1 Choose Page Setup from the File menu and click Border.

2 Enter a value of **3** points in the Border dialog box and click OK.

3 Choose Print from the File menu and make sure that the Print Color/Grayscale option is selected and then click Print.

To print color separations of the image:

1 Deselect the Print Color/Grayscale option in the Print dialog box.

2 Select the Print Separations option and click Print.

The four color plates are printed.

3 Close all open files.

There you are! You have prepared and printed an attractive, four-color poster for a trade show. You've had a chance to work with exporting paths, importing EPS files, converting a file to CMYK, and printing color separations. In the next and final lesson, you'll explore some of the new, more advanced features of Adobe Photoshop 3.0.

Lesson

14

LESSON 14: LAYER MASKS AND GROUPS

This final lesson discusses advanced layer options including layer masks and clipping groups. You're already familiar with a variety of layer features, including creating new layers, showing/hiding layers, using layer options, and merging layers.

The more advanced layer features offer an infinite number of special effects and design options that take moments to achieve. These options give you creative flexibility and allow you to experiment before committing to an image or design idea. You can quickly composite multiple images and draw, edit, or use effects and filters on different layers. You can try different combinations without making multiple copies of the file or destroying image data.

In this lesson, you'll use a library of different images that are scanned from photographs or created in drawing programs. You'll combine the images to create a composite illustration that will be one of a series of photo-collages celebrating good food around the world. For your final lesson, you'll enjoy a sweet German dessert.

In this lesson, you will learn how to do the following:

• use and create a library of images

• use the Behind mode

• use a layer mask with a blend

• add and subtract from a layer mask

• create a clipping group

• drag-copy a path

The following images show the files you'll be working with in this lesson.

Source file (14Lib)   *Ending image (14Final)*

BEGINNING THIS LESSON

As you have done in previous lessons, you will create a new file and then copy elements from another file into the new image.

To begin the lesson:

1 Quit the Adobe Photoshop application, throw away the *Adobe Photoshop 3.0 Prefs* file, and empty the Trash.

2 Launch the Adobe Photoshop application.

3 Choose Open from the File menu, then open the *14Final* file in the Lesson 14 folder.

4 Click the zoom box in the Layers palette.

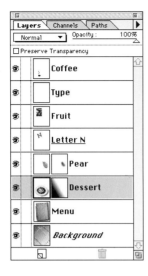

The final file contains eight layers: the Background texture, the Menu layer, the Dessert layer, the Pear layer, the three-dimensional Letter N layer, the Fruit layer, the Type layer, and the Coffee layer.

The double layer icons indicate layer masks that have been applied to the associated layer.

5 In the *14Final* image, zoom out to reduce the image, resize the window if necessary, and move this reference file to the upper-right corner of your screen.

6 Choose New from the File menu, type **14Work** for the name, type **4.8** inches for the width and **6** inches for the height. Make sure the mode is RGB Color, the resolution is 72 and the contents white, then click OK.

7 Turn on the rulers in the *14Work* file.

8 Choose Palette Options from the Layers palette pop-up menu, then select the next largest thumbnail option, and click OK.

9 Collapse all the palettes.

CREATING THE BACKGROUND

The first element that you will create is the textured background. This interesting, watery effect was created by combining a gradient with elements created with the paintbrush tool, then applying the ripple filter.

Before you create the background, you'll watch an Adobe Teach movie that shows how to create the background effect.

If you are able to run Adobe Teach movies on your system, play the movie named *Adobe Teach 3*. For information on how to play Adobe Teach movies, see the "Getting Started" chapter at the beginning of this book.

To create the background:

1 Click the gradient tool.

2 Click the foreground color selection box. Then in the color picker fill in as follows:

```
C...................89 %
M..................24 %
Y...................45 %
K...................32 %
```

3 Click OK, then make sure the background color is set to white.

4 Drag the gradient tool icon from the upper-left corner to the lower-right corner of the document window. A teal gradient appears.

5 Choose Save As from the File menu, open your Projects folder, then click Save.

6 Set the foreground color to white by clicking the switch colors icon in the toolbox.

7 Double-click the paintbrush tool in the toolbox.

8 Click the Brushes palette tab, then choose the first brush in the second row.

9 Draw a pattern of lines like a diagonal tic-tac-toe board (refer to the illustration below).

If you want to experiment, this is an opportunity for you to try different design effects. Feel free to try out different colors, brush shapes, and painting tools.

10 Set the foreground color to black, then repeat the diagonal tic-tac-toe design using the same tool and brush shape.

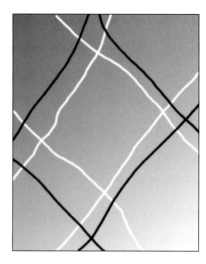

11 Choose Distort from the Filter menu and Ripple from the submenu.

12 Set the slider to 600, click the Large option, then click OK.

The combination of effects creates an interesting watery texture for the background.

13 Choose Save from the File menu (or press Command-S).

OPENING A LIBRARY

Instead of adding the rest of the images from individual source files, you will use an image library file that has been created in Adobe Photoshop 3.0.

1 Choose Open from the File menu, then open the *14Lib* file in the Lesson 14 folder.

2 Double-click the Layers palette tab, then expand the Layers palette to full size by clicking the zoom box in the upper-right corner.

The library contains six layers, each consisting of a separate image that will be used in the final photo collage. The images have been collected, cropped, resized, and named.

3 Experiment with hiding and showing the individual layers (hold down the Option key and click in the left column to display a single layer).

You can create your own library files that contain images you use frequently, or images that you have prepared for a specific project. Just create a new document, with separate layers for each image, then open the individual image files and copy the images into the library file.

Since a library contains multiple layers, a library file can become quite large. Note that this five-image library is over 1.5 MB in size.

DUPLICATING A LAYER

Now that you have your image library open, you will copy the menu image into the working file. You have already learned many different ways of copying images from file to file. In this exercise, you will duplicate a layer to the destination file.

To duplicate a layer:

1 Make sure the *14Lib* window is active and that the Layers palette is zoomed out to full size.

2 Click the Menu layer thumbnail in the Layers palette to make it the target layer, and choose Duplicate Layer from the Layers palette pop-up menu. The Duplicate Layer dialog box appears.

3 Choose *14Work* from the Document pop-up menu as the destination. The name of the layer automatically changes to *Menu*.

4 Click OK to duplicate the layer.

The *14Work* document becomes the active file and the menu image is centered in the document window. The Menu layer thumbnail has been duplicated into the working file above the previous target layer in the Layers palette, and the Menu layer becomes the target layer.

5 Choose Save from the File menu (or press Command-S).

You need to rotate the menu slightly to the left. You'll use the Info palette to measure the rotation.

6 Choose Palettes from the Window menu and Show Info from the submenu.

7 Choose Rotate from the Image menu and Free from the submenu.

8 Drag a corner handle to the left to rotate the image about 3.4 degrees counterclockwise. The Info palette should read about −3.4°.

9 Click the gavel icon to confirm the rotation.

Adding another layer

Now you'll add the dessert image to the working file. This time, instead of using the Duplicate Layer command, you will drag the layer thumbnail from the library file to the working file.

To drag-copy a layer thumbnail:

1 Choose 14Lib from the Window menu, then drag the window to the right so that you can see both the *14Work* and *14Lib* files.

2 Click and drag the Dessert layer thumbnail in the Layers palette from the *14Lib* file to the *14Work* file.

The *14Work* file becomes active and the Dessert layer thumbnail appears in the Layers palette. As you work with documents with multiple layers, you'll find that duplicating or dragging layers from file to file is a quick and easy way of inserting images into another file.

3 Click the move tool and position the dessert in the lower half of the book. The right edge of the bowl should be at the right edge of the wooden menu.

Before you create the special effect that causes the dessert bowl to fade away, you will hide the dessert image and create a drop shadow for the menu.

4 Click the eye icon for the Dessert layer to temporarily hide the layer.

ADDING DROP SHADOWS

The menu and the dessert bowl in the final file both contain a drop shadow. To create the drop shadows you will use the airbrush tool and the *Behind* mode in the Airbrush Options palette mode menu.

1 Click the Menu layer thumbnail to make it the target layer.

2 Double-click the airbrush tool, make sure the pressure is set to 50 percent, then choose Behind from the Airbrush Options palette mode menu.

The Behind mode only works in layers that contain transparency. The paint only affects the transparent pixels in the target layer. As you apply paint, it appears that you're painting behind the objects in the selected layer.

3 Click the Brushes palette tab, and choose the third brush from the left in the third row.

4 Make sure that the foreground color is set to black.

5 Click the airbrush at the upper-right corner of the menu and press the Shift key, then click at the bottom corner of the menu. A straight airbrushed line appears behind the menu.

Note: Make sure not to drag, but to click with the airbrush tool. If you drag, you will create a straight vertical line with the airbrush. If you click, you will create a straight line between clicks.

6 Position the airbrush at the lower-left corner of the menu, hold the Shift key, and click.

The shadow appears at the bottom of the menu.

If you want to experiment with this technique a little more, use the Erase to Saved option in the Eraser Options palette to remove the shadow, or choose Revert from the File menu and start over.

7 When you are finished experimenting, choose Save from the File menu (or press Command-S).

If you change your mind, you can use the Erase to Saved option in the Eraser Options palette.

Creating another drop shadow

Now you'll create a similar drop shadow for the dessert bowl.

To create another drop shadow:

1 Click the eye icon for the Dessert layer, then make the Dessert layer the target layer.

2 Click the Options palette tab.

3 Set the airbrush pressure to 30 percent in the Airbrush Options palette.

The brush shape remains the same and the Behind mode is still selected.

4 Collapse the Options palette.

5 To create the drop shadow, drag from the right-most edge of the bowl clockwise until you are slightly past the bottom of the bowl.

CREATING A LAYER MASK

Now you're ready to create the blend in the dessert artwork. To do this you will use a *layer mask*. A layer mask is an option that lets you experiment with seeing different parts of a layer in your composite image.

A layer mask temporarily makes a layer transparent, as if you had erased it. As you add to the mask, you temporarily delete sections of the layer. This lets you see the effect of erasing part of a layer without actually changing any of the pixel information in the layer.

To create a layer mask:

1 Make sure that the Dessert layer is the target layer.

2 Choose Add Layer Mask from the Layers palette pop-up menu.

A blank page icon appears to the right of the Dessert layer icon in the Layers palette. A dark outline surrounds the mask icon, indicating that it is selected.

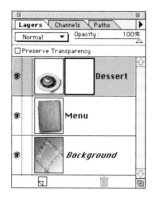

When working with a layer mask, you will use black and white paint to add to or subtract from the mask. The layer mask is actually an 8-bit grayscale channel, so the foreground color converts to grayscale values when you have the layer mask icon selected.

3 Make sure that the Info palette is visible.

4 Click the gradient tool in the toolbox, then position the cursor at the intersection of the white bowl and the fruit sauce (refer to the illustration below).

5 Drag up and to the right. As you drag, watch the Info palette. You want to drag about 2 inches at about a 38 percent angle.

Don't worry if your numbers aren't exactly the same. You're looking to create the same basic effect.

Adding a gradient to a mask creates a blend effect in the selected layer. The dessert image fades from left to right. Now examine the layer mask icon in the Layers palette. The black area of the mask makes the matching area of the layer transparent, the gray area of the blend makes the Dessert layer translucent, and the white area of the mask layer makes the underlying Dessert layer opaque.

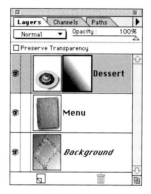

6 To make the changes permanent, choose Remove Layer Mask from the Layers palette pop-up menu, then click Apply.

The mask icon disappears from the Layers palette and the changes are reflected in the Dessert layer thumbnail. The mask and the Dessert layer are merged.

7 If you notice any of the plate image hanging over the left edge of the menu, use the Eraser tool to clean up the Dessert layer.

8 Choose Save from the File menu.

ADDING AND SUBTRACTING FROM A MASK

The next element that you will add to the image is the pear. You will create another layer mask, then use the painting tools to add and subtract from the mask.

To subtract from a layer mask:

1 Select the *14Lib* file.

2 Click the Pear layer to make it the target layer, then drag the Pear layer thumbnail to the *14Work* window.

3 Click the move tool, then position the pear near the upper-right rim of the dessert bowl.

4 Double-click the paintbrush tool, click the Brushes palette tab, then select the third brush from the left in the second row.

5 Collapse the Brushes palette.

6 Make sure that the Pear layer is the target layer, then choose Add Layer Mask from the Layers palette pop-up menu.

7 Begin dragging the paintbrush through the inside of the pear.

Because black is the foreground color, when you paint the layer mask you are hiding the pear image without affecting the Pear layer. Examine the layer mask thumbnail to see the black-on-white effect.

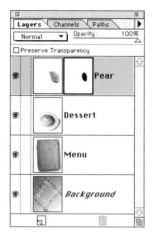

Don't worry about being too accurate at this point. You are not deleting the pixels in the pear image, but in the layer mask. Using a layer mask allows you to experiment with a variety of different effects before you commit to any one design.

8 Continue dragging through the inside of the pear until you can see most of the dessert through the pear.

Now you'll add some of the mask back to the pear image.

To add to the layer mask:

1 Double-click the airbrush tool and set the pressure to 25 percent.

2 Click the switch colors icon to set the foreground color to white.

3 Start painting the inside of the pear. As you spray the mask with white, you add back the mask, so you start seeing the pear reappear.

4 Experiment with using white and black and several different painting tools to add and subtract from the layer mask until you achieve the effect that you want (use the final file as a guide).

5 When you are finished experimenting, remove the mask by choosing Remove Layer Mask from the Layers palette pop-up menu, and clicking Apply.

6 Choose Save from the File menu (or press Command-S).

This is just a small taste of what you can do with layer masks. For more information, see the *Adobe Photoshop User Guide*.

GROUPING LAYERS

The next element you will add to the dessert menu image is the fruity letter *N*. You will create the image by grouping two layers, or creating a *clipping group*. The letter *N* and the fruit image are two separate layers in the library file. Start by examining the two images you will use to create the fruity *N* effect.

To add layers for a clipping group:

1 Select the *14Lib* file, press the Option key, and click the eye icon for the Letter N layer.

This three-dimensional letter was created using Adobe Dimensions software.

2 Press the Option key, then click in the far-left column next to the Fruit layer.

This fruit image will provide the pattern for the three-dimensional letter *N*.

3 Drag the Letter N layer thumbnail to the *14Work* file.

4 With the move tool, position the letter *N* in the upper-middle of the menu (you'll reposition it in a minute).

5 Select the 14Lib file, then drag the Fruit layer to the *14Work* file.

6 With the move tool, position the fruit image on top of the *N* so that it completely obscures the letter underneath.

Now you will clip the Fruit layer to the Letter N layer.

To create a clipping group:

1 Make sure that the Fruit layer is the target layer, then choose Layer Options from the Layers palette pop-up menu.

2 Make sure that the Preview box is checked, then move the dialog box so that you can see the fruit image in the document window.

3 Click the Group With Previous Layer checkbox.

Look in your image and note that the top layer groups or *clips* to the opaque areas of the bottom or *base* layer.

4 Click OK to view the clipping group.

In the Layers palette, the two layers are now grouped together. The Letter N layer is underlined, indicating that it is the base or lowest layer. A dotted line separates the base layer from the clipped layer.

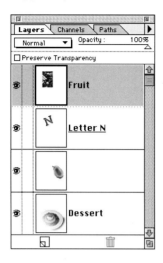

Use clipping groups to work with a group of layers as a single unit. For example, you might want to have a shape in one layer, a texture in another layer, and a lighting effect in a third layer, yet you might want to see the effects only as they apply to the bottom shape.

In a clipping group the bottom or base layer controls the mode and transparency for all the other layers in the group.

You can turn off a clipping group by using Layer Options, or you can use a shortcut.

To use the clipping group shortcut:

1 Position your cursor over the dotted line between the Fruit and Letter N layers, then press the Option key. The Grouping/Ungrouping cursor appears.

2 Click the dotted line to turn off the layer group. The letter *N* disappears behind the fruit image.

3 Press the Option key again and click with the Grouping cursor to group the layers together again.

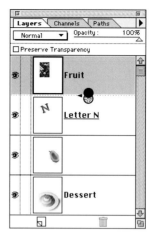

4 Click the move tool, then make sure that the Fruit layer is the target layer.

5 Drag on the fruity *N* in the document window. Because you have the Fruit layer selected, just the fruit part of the letter *N* is moving. You can reposition the layer so that the middle part of the *N* contains the red grapes.

To move just the letter *N* part of the group you would make the Letter N layer the target layer. To move both elements together, you need to link the two layers.

Moving a group of layers

To move a group of layers you need to first link the layers.

To move the clipping group:

1 Click in the column to the right of the eye icon in the Letter N layer in the Layers palette. The move icon appears next to the Letter N layer and the Fruit layer.

2 In the document window, drag the *N* to the upper-left corner of the menu.

3 Click the move icon in the Layers palette to unlink the layers.

4 Click the zoom tool, and marquee zoom around the letter *N* to zoom in on that part of the image.

5 Make sure the Fruit layer is the target layer, then choose Overlay from the Mode menu in the Layers palette.

The Overlay mode allows you to see the highlights and shadows of the underlying layer, while using the colors of the top layer. It looks like the fruit pattern has wrapped around the three-dimensional letter *N*.

6 Examine the overlay effect by pressing Command-Z to undo the effect, then redo the effect.

7 Double-click the zoom tool to return to a 1:1 view.

8 Hide the Background layer, the Menu layer, the Dessert layer, and the Pear layer by dragging through the eye icons in the left column. Only the Letter N and Fruit layers should be visible.

9 Choose Merge Layers from the Layers palette pop-up menu.

10 Double-click the new layer and type **Fruity N** for the name and click OK.

11 Press the Option key, then click the eye icon for the Fruity N layer to view all the layers.

12 Choose Save from the File menu.

ADDING MORE TYPE

Now you'll add the final piece of text to the image. If you have Adobe Garamond Semibold installed in your system, then you will use the type tool. If you do not, then you'll use a file in the Lesson 14 folder.

To add type:

1 Click the New Layer icon and name the new layer **Type.**

2 Set the foreground color to white.

3 If you installed the Adobe Garamond Semibold font then go to the next step. If you don't have that font installed, then skip to step 7.

4 Click the type tool, then click at the top of the image.

5 In the Type Tool dialog box, choose Garamond Semibold, enter **30** points for the size, click in the text entry box and type **ACHTISCH** (all caps). (*Nachtisch* is German for *Dessert.*)

6 Click OK, then skip to step 10 to rotate the text.

7 If you do not have Adobe Garamond Semibold installed in your system then open the *14Type* file in the Lesson 14 folder.

8 Choose All from the Select menu, then choose Copy from the Edit menu and close the file.

9 Select the *14Work* file and choose Paste from the Edit menu.

10 Choose Rotate from the Image menu and Arbitrary from the submenu, then enter 28 CCW for the angle and click OK.

11 Click the move tool, then position the text near the lower leg of the fruity letter *N* then deselect the text.

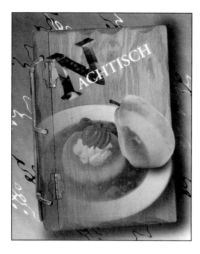

USING THE LINE TOOL

To add the line under the text you will use the line tool.

To draw a line:

1 Make sure the Info palette is visible then click the line tool in the toolbox.

2 Position the cross hair cursor below the left part of the letter *A* and drag up and to the right until you're under the letter *H*.

3 Watch the Info palette to match the rotation to the 28 degrees of the text.

If you want a slightly thicker line, double-click the line tool to access the Line Tool Options.

DRAGGING A PATH

Just as you can drag-copy layers from one file to another, you can drag-copy paths from one file to another. The final element that you will add to the menu is the coffee cup in the lower-left corner of the final image. This file was created in Adobe Illustrator, then exported as a path into Adobe Photoshop. The path is stored in the library along with the other images that you've been working with.

To drag-copy the Coffee Cup path:

1 Create a new layer named **Coffee**.

2 Select the *14Lib* file.

3 Click the Paths palette tab. The Coffee Cup path thumbnail appears.

4 Drag the Coffee Cup path thumbnail from the *14Lib* file to the *14Work* file.

The *14Work* file becomes the active file and the Coffee Cup path appears in the Paths palette and in the document layout.

5 Click the arrow tool in the Paths palette and position the path in the lower-left corner of the menu (use the final file as a reference).

Once you have created or selected a target layer, you can fill the Coffee Cup path with color.

6 Set the foreground color to black.

7 Click the Fill Paths button located at the left of the row of buttons in the Paths palette. The Coffee Cup path fills with black.

8 Click the Layers palette tab.

9 To achieve the translucent look of the final file, choose Overlay from the mode menu in the Layers palette.

If you need to adjust the position of the coffee cup, click the move tool and fine-tune the positioning of the image.

10 Choose Save a Copy from the File menu.

11 Type **14WorkL** for the name, open your Projects folder, and click Save.

12 Choose Flatten Image from the Layers palette pop-up menu.

13 Choose Save from the File menu to save the flattened file, then print the file if you want to.

14 Choose Quit from the File menu to close all the files. Don't save changes.

Congratulations! This ends the *Classroom in a Book* lessons. You've accomplished quite a bit since you began using the painting tools and making simple selections. As you continue to work with Adobe Photoshop, you might want to refer to specific lessons in this book to remind yourself of particular procedures, or remember how to create an individual effect.

As you work on your own projects you'll probably find the *Adobe Photoshop User Guide* a helpful and comprehensive reference to all of Adobe Photoshop's features and capabilities. As your knowledge and experience expand, look for the *Adobe Photoshop Advanced Classroom in a Book*. It's filled with advanced projects that utilize the latest and greatest features of Adobe Photoshop 3.0. Have fun and be creative, as you explore the ever-increasing world of digital imaging.

INDEX

COLOPHON

DOCUMENTATION

Writing: Kate O'Day, Judith Walthers von Alten

Revised by: Patrice Anderson

Art Direction: Sharon Anderson

Editing: Bob Rumsby

Illustrations: Jonathon Caponi, Laura Dower, Andrew Faulkner, Heather Hermstad, Kim Isola

Photographs: Robert Cardellino (Chef, Velvet Curtain), Matthew Farruggio (Crawdads, Wine Glass), Michael LaMotte (Asparagus, Assorted Vegetables, California Cuisine), Scott Peterson (Crab), Charles West (Pasta Factory)

Photographs from Lesson 14 (Menu, Fruit, Dessert, Pear) are courtesy of PhotoDisc ©1994 PhotoDisc, Inc. 1-800-528-3472

Book Production: John Doughty

Production Consultant: Jeffrey Schaaf

Book Production Management: Kisa Harris

Publication Management: Kisa Harris

Adobe Teach Movies: Andrew Faulkner, Patrice Anderson

Cover Design: Sharon Anderson

Film Production: Cheryl Elder, Karen Winguth

Legal Advisor: Paul Klein

Adobe Press: Patrick Ames

Training Manager: Kisa Harris

Special thanks to: Adobe Technical Support Staff, Carita Klevickis, Mary Anne Petrillo, Nora Sandoval, Glen Pierre, Frank Gomez, Tom Harmon

Beta Test-Teach Participants:

Matt Brown, Adobe Technical Support
Chuck Desmares, Adobe Technical Support
Bud Martz, Adobe Technical Support
Bob Bullock, Graphic Designer
Kisa Harris, Adobe Training Manager
Patrice Anderson, Instructional Designer

PRODUCTION NOTES

This book was created electronically using FrameMaker on the Macintosh Quadra 700 and 800. Art was produced using Adobe Illustrator, Adobe Photoshop, and SnapJot on the Macintosh Quadra 800. Working film was produced with the PostScript language on an Agfa 5000 Imagesetter. The Frutiger and Minion families of typefaces are used throughout this book.

Adobe Training Resources

The Classroom in a Book™ series, a set of intermediate and advanced workbooks, guides you through many step -by-step lessons to help you learn to master the powerful features of Adobe's products. The series is available for Adobe Illustrator™, Adobe Photoshop™ and Adobe Premiere™.

If finding time to focus is difficult, or if you think an instructor-led training program will augment your learning curve, investigate some of the many profes- sional training businesses or educational institutions using this very same Classroom in a Book. Instructors can provide feedback and guidance that go beyond the contents of this book in a classroom setting.

For training referral suggestions in North America, call: **Adobe's Customer Services at 1-800-833-6687.** In Europe and the Pacific Rim, call your local distributor.